Battleground Europe

GALLIPOLI: SUVLA
AUGUST OFFENSIVE

CW00821157

Battleground series:

Stamford Bridge & Hastings *by* Peter Marren
Wars of the Roses - **Wakefield / Towton** *by* Philip A. Haigh
Wars of the Roses - **Barnet** *by* David Clark
Wars of the Roses - **Tewkesbury** *by* Steven Goodchild
Wars of the Roses - **The Battles of St Albans** *by*
Peter Burley, Michael Elliott & Harvey Wilson
English Civil War - **Naseby** *by* Martin Marix Evans, Peter Burton
and Michael Westaway
English Civil War - **Marston Moor** *by* David Clark
War of the Spanish Succession - **Blenheim 1704** *by* James Falkner
War of the Spanish Succession - **Ramillies 1706** *by* James Falkner
Napoleonic - **Hougoumont** *by* Julian Paget and Derek Saunders
Napoleonic - **Waterloo** *by* Andrew Uffindell and Michael Corum
Zulu War - **Isandlwana** *by* Ian Knight and Ian Castle
Zulu War - **Rorkes Drift** *by* Ian Knight and Ian Castle
Boer War - **The Relief of Ladysmith** *by* Lewis Childs
Boer War - **The Siege of Ladysmith** *by* Lewis Childs
Boer War - **Kimberley** *by* Lewis Childs

Mons *by* Jack Horsfall and Nigel Cave
Néry *by* Patrick Tackle
Le Cateau *by* Nigel Cave and Jack Shelden
Walking the Salient *by* Paul Reed
Ypres - **Sanctuary Wood and Hooge** *by* Nigel Cave
Ypres - **Hill 60** *by* Nigel Cave
Ypres - **Messines Ridge** *by* Peter Oldham
Ypres - **Polygon Wood** *by* Nigel Cave
Ypres - **Passchendaele** *by* Nigel Cave
Ypres - **Airfields and Airmen** *by* Mike O'Connor
Ypres - **St Julien** *by* Graham Keech
Ypres - **Boesinghe** *by* Stephen McGreal
Walking the Somme *by* Paul Reed
Somme - **Gommecourt** *by* Nigel Cave
Somme - **Serre** *by* Jack Horsfall & Nigel Cave
Somme - **Beaumont Hamel** *by* Nigel Cave
Somme - **Thiepval** *by* Michael Stedman
Somme - **La Boisselle** *by* Michael Stedman
Somme - **Fricourt** *by* Michael Stedman
Somme - **Carnoy-Montauban** *by* Graham Maddocks
Somme - **Pozières** *by* Graham Keech
Somme - **Courcelette** *by* Paul Reed
Somme - **Boom Ravine** *by* Trevor Pidgeon
Somme - **Mametz Wood** *by* Michael Renshaw
Somme - **Delville Wood** *by* Nigel Cave
Somme - **Advance to Victory (North) 1918** *by* Michael Stedman
Somme - **Flers** *by* Trevor Pidgeon
Somme - **Bazentin Ridge** *by* Edward Hancock
Somme - **Combles** *by* Paul Reed
Somme - **Beaucourt** *by* Michael Renshaw
Somme - **Redan Ridge** *by* Michael Renshaw
Somme - **Hamel** *by* Peter Pedersen
Somme - **Villers-Bretonneux** *by* Peter Pedersen
Somme - **Airfields and Airmen** *by* Mike O'Connor
Airfields and Airmen of the Channel Coast *by* Mike O'Connor
In the Footsteps of the Red Baron *by* Mike O'Connor
Arras - **Airfields and Airmen** *by* Mike O'Connor
Arras - **The Battle for Vimy Ridge** *by* Jack Sheldon & Nigel Cave
Arras - **Vimy Ridge** *by* Nigel Cave
Arras - **Gavrelle** *by* Trevor Tasker and Kyle Tallett
Arras - **Oppy Wood** *by* David Bilton
Arras - **Bullecourt** *by* Graham Keech
Arras - **Monchy le Preux** *by* Colin Fox
Walking Arras *by* Paul Reed
Hindenburg Line *by* Peter Oldham
Hindenburg Line - **Epehy** *by* Bill Mitchinson
Hindenburg Line - **Riqueval** *by* Bill Mitchinson
Hindenburg Line - **Villers-Plouich** *by* Bill Mitchinson
Hindenburg Line - **Cambrai Right Hook** *by* Jack Horsfall & Nigel Cave
Hindenburg Line - **Cambrai Flesquières** *by* Jack Horsfall & Nigel Cave
Hindenburg Line - **Saint Quentin** *by* Helen McPhail and Philip Guest

Hindenburg Line - **Bourlon Wood** *by* Jack Horsfall & Nigel Ca
Cambrai - **Airfields and Airmen** *by* Mike O'Connor
Aubers Ridge *by* Edward Hancock
La Bassée - **Neuve Chapelle** *by* Geoffrey Bridger
Loos - **Hohenzollern Redoubt** *by* Andrew Rawson
Loos - **Hill 70** *by* Andrew Rawson
Fromelles *by* Peter Pedersen
The Battle of the Lys 1918 *by* Phil Tomaselli
Accrington Pals Trail *by* William Turner
Poets at War: Wilfred Owen *by* Helen McPhail and Philip Gu
Poets at War: Edmund Blunden *by* Helen McPhail and Philip G
Poets at War: Graves & Sassoon *by* Helen McPhail and Philip
Gallipoli *by* Nigel Steel
Gallipoli - **Gully Ravine** *by* Stephen Chambers
Gallipoli - **Anzac Landing** *by* Stephen Chambers
Gallipoli - **Suvla August Offensive** *by* Stephen Chambers
Gallipoli - **Landings at Helles** *by* Huw & Jill Rodge
Walking the Italian Front *by* Francis Mackay
Italy - **Asiago** *by* Francis Mackay
Verdun: Fort Douaumont *by* Christina Holstein
Walking Verdun *by* Christina Holstein
Zeebrugge & Ostend Raids 1918 *by* Stephen McGreal

Germans at Beaumont Hamel *by* Jack Sheldon
Germans at Thiepval *by* Jack Sheldon

SECOND WORLD WAR

Dunkirk *by* Patrick Wilson
Calais *by* Jon Cooksey
Boulogne *by* Jon Cooksey
Saint-Nazaire *by* James Dorrian
Normandy - **Pegasus Bridge** *by* Carl Shilleto
Normandy - **Merville Battery** *by* Carl Shilleto
Normandy - **Utah Beach** *by* Carl Shilleto
Normandy - **Omaha Beach** *by* Tim Kilvert-Jones
Normandy - **Gold Beach** *by* Christopher Dunphie & Garry Johns
Normandy - **Gold Beach Jig** *by* Tim Saunders
Normandy - **Juno Beach** *by* Tim Saunders
Normandy - **Sword Beach** *by* Tim Kilvert-Jones
Normandy - **Operation Bluecoat** *by* Ian Daglish
Normandy - **Operation Goodwood** *by* Ian Daglish
Normandy - **Epsom** *by* Tim Saunders
Normandy - **Hill 112** *by* Tim Saunders
Normandy - **Mont Pinçon** *by* Eric Hunt
Normandy - **Cherbourg** *by* Andrew Rawson
Normandy - **Commandos & Rangers on D-Day** *by* Tim Saun
Das Reich – **Drive to Normandy** *by* Philip Vickers
Oradour *by* Philip Beck
Market Garden - **Nijmegen** *by* Tim Saunders
Market Garden - **Hell's Highway** *by* Tim Saunders
Market Garden - **Arnhem, Oosterbeek** *by* Frank Steer
Market Garden - **Arnhem, The Bridge** *by* Frank Steer
Market Garden - **The Island** *by* Tim Saunders
Rhine Crossing – **US 9th Army & 17th US Airborne** *by* Andrew
British Rhine Crossing – **Operation Varsity** *by* Tim Saund
British Rhine Crossing – **Operation Plunder** *by* Tim Saund
Battle of the Bulge – **St Vith** *by* Michael Tolhurst
Battle of the Bulge – **Bastogne** *by* Michael Tolhurst
Channel Islands *by* George Forty
Walcheren *by* Andrew Rawson
Remagen Bridge *by* Andrew Rawson
Cassino *by* Ian Blackwell
Anzio *by* Ian Blackwell
Dieppe *by* Tim Saunders
Fort Eben Emael *by* Tim Saunders
Crete – **The Airborne Invasion** *by* Tim Saunders
Malta *by* Paul Williams

Battleground Europe

GALLIPOLI: SUVLA AUGUST OFFENSIVE

Stephen Chambers

Series Editor
Nigel Cave

Pen & Sword
MILITARY

First published in Great Britain in 2011
Pen & Sword Books Ltd
47 Church Street
Barnsley
South Yorkshire
S70 2AS

Copyright © Stephen Chambers 2011

ISBN 9781848845435

Pen & Sword Books Ltd incorporates the Imprints of Pen & Sword Aviation, Pen & Sword Maritime, Pen & Sword Military, Wharncliffe Local History, Pen and Sword Select, Pen and Sword Military Classics, Leo Cooper, Remember When, Seaforth Publishing and Frontline Publishing.

For a complete list of Pen & Sword titles please contact
PEN & SWORD BOOKS LIMITED
47 Church Street, Barnsley, South Yorkshire, S70 2AS, England
E-mail: enquiries@pen-and-sword.co.uk
Website: www.pen-and-sword.co.uk

CONTENTS

Rum Jars – Fragments still litter the battlefield today.

İngiliz Rom testileri
British Rum jars

SERIES EDITOR'S INTRODUCTION

SUVLA BAY is a beautiful place to visit; more or less unspoilt by any form of development and 'progress' (which does, admittedly have some downsides, like poor roads and minimal possibilities for refreshments) since the summer days of 1915.

Suvla Bay has a terrible resonance in British military history – lost opportunity after lost opportunity; chaos and confusion; a textbook case of the difficulties of sea borne landings. The operation was rushed, information and intelligence were not passed down the chain of command (in fact it hardly moved at all from the top), maps were lacking or useless: it really makes for depressing reading. It reveals the wholly inadequate (and quaint) system of allocating command positions, highlights petty jealousies and illustrates the vital part that sound logistics play in any successful operation. Communication systems – the weakness of which were a major characteristic of the Great War – were abysmal, even by the low standards that epitomised the Gallipoli campaign in its entirety.

What is also quite apparent is how resentful the men who were asked to do the fighting were about the whole assault, expressed in letters and diaries of the time and in bitter commentaries afterwards. Troops at all levels could see clearly, even at the time, how much of a botched job the operation was. New divisions, composed of men who had almost no fighting experience amongst them and command staffs who were not much better off, were called upon to carry out utterly vague tasks. These new formations were often split up, further confusing matters;

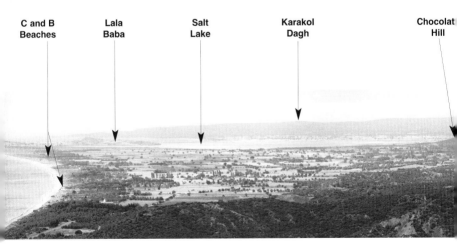

C and B
Beaches

Lala
Baba

Salt
Lake

Karakol
Dagh

Chocolat
Hill

whilst often much of the artillery and other vital elements of the divisions were not even with them when they fought the campaign.

So, for the British (notably for the Irish and the Welsh – both these parts of the United Kingdom had divisions that took part in the fighting) there is hardly anything at all that is positive that can be taken from the August fighting in and around Suvla Bay. It was an attack that had potential; but the intrinsic difficulties of such an operation, fraught with pitfalls, were made fatal by operational incompetence on a grand scale.

The soldiers fought as well as they could under these trying conditions, to which were added chronic shortages of water and the risk of horrible death because of fire, in addition to the weaponry aimed at them by a resolute foe. The particular circumstances at Gallipoli meant that many of those who died were never buried, their bones scattered on the battlefield, which adds to the poignancy of the place.

Touring Suvla Bay in the footsteps of these men is a haunting experience; but the grandeur and the beauty of the place, largely unaltered by the passing of the decades, makes a visit there truly worthwhile. Its relative inaccessibility and limited facilities, along with the rugged terrain, takes it off the increasingly well beaten 'Gallipoli trail'; hopefully Steve Chambers' book will bring many more here to pay their respects to the fighting men of Britain, Ireland, Anzac, Newfoundland and Turkey.

Nigel Cave
Collegio Rosmini, Stresa

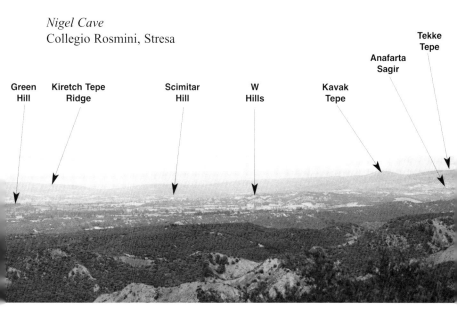

Green Hill   Kiretch Tepe Ridge   Scimitar Hill   W Hills   Kavak Tepe   Anafarta Sagir   Tekke Tepe

INTRODUCTION

The Allied objective in the Gallipoli Campaign was, by capturing Constantinople (now Istanbul), to force German's ally, Turkey and its Ottoman Empire, out of the war. This would also open an ice-free sea supply route from the Aegean through the Dardanelles and into the Black Sea to aid Russia. It was also hoped that pressure on Turkey would influence the then neutral states of Bulgaria, Romania and Greece to enter the war on the allied side.

After the failure of the naval actions that culminated on 18 March 1915, when British and French battleships attempted to force a path through the Dardanelles, a land campaign was planned. The purpose was to aid the Navy's attack by the capture of the Dardanelles forts which dominated the straits minefields.

The amphibious landings on 25 April 1915 were the beginning of Sir Ian Hamilton's Mediterranean Expeditionary Forces invasion on the Gallipoli Peninsula. Ashore, but with many casualties and little more than a beachhead to show for their losses, the following months would prove to be disastrous for the allies. In the north, the Australian and New Zealand Army Corps (Anzac) were hemmed in and attempts at an offensive failed in May; equally, attempts by the Turks to force the Anzacs into the sea also failed. Further south, at Helles, the British and French had repeatedly failed to capture Krithia and Achi Baba and make any real progress towards Kilid Bahr, which led Hamilton to look for a solution elsewhere to break the deadlock.

Born out of the earlier failures was the August Offensive, as will be described in the following pages. Unfortunately this, as with the earlier plans to bring the campaign to a head, failed and the last few days of summer, through to autumn and winter continued the bitter struggle. The opposing armies suffered crippling casualties and had endured great hardships throughout the eight month period on Gallipoli that ended in defeat for the allies and was thus a great victory for the Turks. This is the story of Suvla during August 1915.

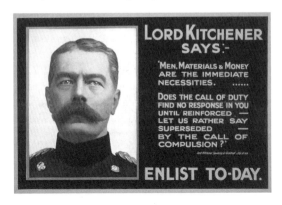

ACKNOWLEDGEMENTS

Without the help of many individuals and organisations this book would not have been possible. Special thanks in the UK are due, in no particular order, to Peter Hart, IWM Oral Historian and military author *extraordinaire*, who has been tremendously helpful throughout the journey of this book. John Shephard, in providing so much help and information on the Dorset Yeomanry and the Scimitar Hill area, and also to Andrew French on helping with information on the Berkshire Yeomanry and Lieutenant Niven. Thanks is also due to David Empson for bringing to my attention a wealth of untapped local newspaper information about the Norfolk battalions, a resource that is rich with personal accounts and, of course Dick Rayner, whose excellent article '*The Sandringhams at Suvla Bay*' helped de-myth some of the legend. Both Michael Robson and Michael Pegum have also been of enormous help. The Gallipoli campaign can only truly be understood by treading the very ground that the men, from both sides of the trenches, had fought on, bled and died; a huge thanks therefore goes to both Guy Marner and Jon Saunders who have, on several occasions, accompanied me on battlefield trips to Gallipoli, keeping me sane, protected from the marauding dogs and suitably supplied with the local amber nectar. In Turkey thanks must go to the experts who live and breathe Gallipoli. Firstly two historians and authors: Haluk Oral, who has helped me see Gallipoli through Turkish eyes; and, Sahin Aldogan, who has been studying the campaign and walking the ground since 1965, and whose knowledge of the battlefield is second to none. Also in Turkey thanks need to go to Bill Sellars, local historian, journalist and Australian, for sacrificing his time to take me to some of the most inhospitable parts of the battlefield and to share not only his knowledge on the campaign but the odd beer as well. Also out in Gallipoli is Eric Goossens, who with Özlem Gündüz, run a perfect little hotel, tucked away in Kocadere; a perfect base for me whilst researching. And of course, by no means least, Nigel Cave, Series Editor, whose guidance along the way has kept me on the straight and narrow as always.

From individuals to organisations, museums, libraries, websites and the like, the list is almost endless but, to start, thanks need to go to the staff at the National Archives, Imperial War Museum, National Army Museum, Berkshire Yeomanry Museum and The Keep Military Museum. The tireless work performed by the Commonwealth War Graves Commission cannot go without mention in their caring for the British and Commonwealth war dead in Gallipoli, and all around the world. Also worth a mention is the Gallipoli Association, which since 1969 has been helping keep the memory alive, an association worth joining; a website worth visiting and a journal worth reading. The contribution from veterans, their descendants, and many professional and enthusiastic amateur military historians over the years has been enormous; a source of information I have well tapped over the years.

Sadly, the veterans have long since faded away, but they are are not forgotten; their stories continue to be told, and used here to give the human aspect of war. Contemporary material in the form of war diaries, divisional, regimental and the battalion histories have also been referenced. For example, the published diary of Sir Ian Hamilton and also Cecil Aspinall-Oglander's Official History are both a 'must' read. I have also used many personal accounts in the form of letters and diaries as well as a large assortment of maps and photographs, many never published before. The originators of these must all be thanked, because without this material there would be no story to tell. With historical documents it is always difficult to trace all the copyright holders, so for any who have not been contacted, please accept my sincere apologies, and feel free to contact me if you feel it necessary. To all these people and any I have mistakenly forgotten to mention, please accept my sincere apologies and thanks.

Last, and by no means least, thanks to my long suffering wife Joanne, along with Lewis and Jess, who have sacrificed so much in allowing me space to pursue my passion for Gallipoli.

Stephen Chambers
West Sussex and Suvla, 2010

Author standing at the Boot with the Turkish positions in the background.

ADVICE TO TRAVELLERS

GETTING THERE: Turkey is very much on the tourist map and today Gallipoli and the nearby ancient city of Troy, are firmly part of that industry. Most people fly to Turkey as they would be coming great distances; the major airports are in Istanbul and Izmir, although a local airport in Çanakkale has recently opened. Because of the vastness of the Gallipoli battlefields, car or motorcycle hire is a must, which can be arranged at the airports or locally in Çanakkale. To do this on a budget there are regular coaches that travel to the region, and once in the area bicycle hire is also possible. For the latest details see http://www.tourismturkey.org/ or, once in Çanakkale, visit the Tourism Information Office that is located near the ferry jetty square, where you can get detailed information, maps and brochures of the area.

EQUIPMENT: When visiting the battlefields, preferably with at least one other person, always take a good supply of bottled water, a walking stick (also useful to fend off any shepherd's dogs), sun cream, wide-brimmed hat, long trousers for any bush walking, camera/binoculars, pen/notepad, penknife and a pair of sturdy boots with ankle support. If you are unfamiliar with the area and going off the beaten track, a map and compass is recommended. Put this all together in a small rucksack with this book, and you should have a good recipe for an excellent tour. A mobile phone can also be useful in emergencies (with the number of hotel and, if applicable, the car-hire or tour company). It is also a good idea to tell someone else where you are planning to go for the day and what time you are planning to return. Most importantly, bring a camera with a good supply of film, or digital storage, and plenty of batteries. It is also worth noting that Suvla, although a beautiful area to visit, is still very inhospitable and as remote as you can get on the Gallipoli peninsula. It has a lack of toilets and refreshments for the modern visitor, indeed the lack of almost anything useful for sustenance and comfort, so travel prepared. Most hotels can provide pack lunches and the towns of course have shops to stock up on food and drink before you depart for the day. If you are planning to visit a Commonwealth grave, please check the CWGC website for cemetery/memorial plans and references before you head over, as none of the battlefield cemeteries or memorials contain a register.

ACCOMODATION: Most of the hotels are not expensive and usually include breakfast and an evening meal. There are also numerous camping sites in the area for those on a lower budget. Eceabat and Çanakkale have a good selection of restaurants and cafes and all very reasonably priced. For the easiest access to Suvla it is best to stay in Eceabat, although Çanakkale offers pretty much everything. From Çanakkale, you will need to take the ferry every morning to cross the Narrows, and the drive will cut the time you could spend at Gallipoli by about an hour. Do not expect the luxuries that you may be accustomed to at other European hotels. Rooms are often basic, although many do have air conditioning.

WARNING: Be aware that the whole of the Gallipoli Peninsula is a national historical "Peace Park", dedicated to the memory of those who died on both sides. Please respect this. A lot of the area is still farmland and private property. When walking please be aware of the crops and respect the privacy of the people who live here. If you do find a wartime relic, such as a shell, grenade or bullet, please leave it alone. Photograph it by all means, but please do not touch it as these things are usually in a highly dangerous condition, and can still cause death and injury. It is also strictly forbidden by the Turkish authorities to remove any artefact from the battlefield. Lastly the area has many goatherds and small farm settlements that, of course, keep dogs. These can be quite ferocious if you happen to go too close, so keep at a distance, keep together and always carry a stick.

Çanakkale Hotels

Hotel Akol
Tel: + 90 (286) 217 9456
Website: www.hotelakol.com

Hotel Anzac
Tel: +90 (286) 217 7777
Website: www.anzachotel.com

Hotel Anafartalar
Tel: +90 (286) 217 4454
Website: www.hotelanafartalar.com

Hotel Truva
Tel: + 90 (286) 217 1024
Website: http://www.truvaotel.com

Eceabat Hotels

Hotel Kum
Tel: +90 (286) 814 1455
Website: www.hotelkum.com

TJ's Hotel Eceabat
Tel: +90 (286) 814 2458
Website: www.anzacgallipolitours.com

The Gallipoli Houses, Kocadere
Tel: + 90 (286) 814 2650
Website: www.gallipoli.com.tr

Seddülbahir Hotels
Pansiyon Helles Panorama
Tel: + 90 (286) 862 0035

Other Useful Addresses:
Çanakkale Tourist Information Office
Iskele Meydani, 67
Çanakkale
Tel: + 90 (286) 217 1187

Commonwealth War Graves Commission (CWGC)
2 Marlow Road,
Maidenhead,
Berkshire, SL6 7DX
Tel: +44 (0) 1628 634 221
Website: www.cwgc.org

CWGC (Çanakkale Office)
Cimenlik Sohak,
Bagkur Ishani No.9,
Buro No.10
17001 Çanakkale.
Tel +90 (286) 217 1010

Turkish Gallipoli Casualty Database
Website: www.binibirkanal.com/canakkale–sehitleri.aspx

The Gallipoli Association
PO Box 26907,
London, SE21 8WB
Website: www.gallipoli-association.org

The Gallipoli Association's key objectives are to keep alive the memory of the Gallipoli Campaign of 1915/16, in order to ensure that the men who fought and died in the campaign are not forgotten, and to encourage and facilitate the study of the campaign so that lasting benefit can be gained from its valuable lessons. As well as an excellent website, a journal called *The Gallipolian* is produced three times a year for members, containing many articles and useful information. The association also runs tours to the Gallipoli battlefield.

GULF OF
SAROS

Kireteh Tepe Sirt

Suvla Pt.

GhaziBaba

SUVLA
BAY

Lala Baba

Nibrunesi Pt.

Asmak Dere

SALT
LAKE

BEACH "A"

BEACH "C"
BEACH "B"

OCEAN BEACH

BRIGHTON BEACH

Kavak Tepe

Tekke Tepe

Kuchuk Anafarta
Ova

Anafarta Sagir

Scimitar Hill

Yilghin Burnu

Chocolate Hill

Ismail Oglu Tepe

Anafarta Biyuk

Hill
60

Kabak
Kuyu
Damakjelik Bair

Aghil Dere

Koja Chemen Tepe

Bauchop's Hill   Hill Q

Chailak Dere

Table
Top

Fishermen's Huts

Rhododendron
Spur

The Farm

Chunuk Bair

SARI BAIR

Sazli Beit Dere

Quinns

Ari Birnu

ANZAC COVE

MAP OF THE
ANZAC-SUVLA
AREA
—
Scale of Miles.

0   ¼   ½   ¾   1   2

Lone Pine

Koja Dere

Gabe Tepe

14

Chapter One

PRIOR PLANNING AND PREPARATION

A major operation that might change the whole course of the war in twenty-four hours.

Captain William Wedgwood Benn, 1/1 County of London Yeomanry, wrote of Suvla Bay being:

... a bay of exquisite beauty. Think of the most lovely part of the west coast of Scotland; make the sea perfectly calm, perfectly transparent and deep blue; imagine an ideal August day; add an invigorating breeze; and you can picture our impression of the coast of Gallipoli.[1]

Suvla, just north of Anzac, is a beautiful crescent shaped bay almost two miles long, with two rocky promontories forming the horns of the bay: Suvla Point to the north, Nibrunesi Point to the south. Towards the southern end, nearly touching the sea, is a large salt lake; in summer 1915 it was practically dry, with the exception of a few small pools. Between the Salt Lake and sea is a narrow causeway of sand, the same pure white sand that covers the beaches of this eclipse shaped shore. The country inland is generally flat, a semi cultivated valley but covered with low sand hills and under features, with patches of scrub, broken by ravines and gullies, drainage ditches and farms. This plain is encircled by hills, covered with thick, thorny, dwarf oak scrub, almost resembling woodland in places. Suvla was to become a name that brought sorrow into many households, a name associated with lost hope and failure.

The Dardanelles Committee met in London on 7 June 1915. As the Third Battle of Krithia, on the Helles front, had been fought to an unsuccessful closure, Lord Kitchener, the Secretary of State for War, decided it was now time to reinforce General Sir Ian Hamilton's Mediterranean Expeditionary Force. He planned to dispatch two Territorial Army divisions, the 'Saturday Night Soldiers' as they were known – men with some weekend military training, summer camp attendance but not professional soldiers; and also three New Army divisions. Hopefully this reinforcement, which could all be got ready by the end of July, would allow Hamilton to break through on this front and end the campaign once and for all. The situation at Gallipoli at this stage was one of stalemate, with heavy casualties and with little progress having been made since the initial landings. Anzac remained little more than a beachhead, an area smaller than three-quarters of a square mile, and all efforts to break out of the main Helles front were equally disastrous. On the Western Front the situation was no better, the allied Artois Offensive in the spring had failed and all there was to show was a large butcher's bill and a dwindling store of shells. Gallipoli was once again back on the War Office agenda and, with knowledge of reinforcements, a plan penciled back in May by Lieutenant General William Birdwood, the Anzac commander, was quickly adopted.

The original plan had the hopes of a *coup de main* assault, which would capture the Sari Bair ridge, push back the Turkish right wing, and drive south towards Kilid Bahr, thus securing a position across the narrow part of the Peninsula, to Maidos. As planning progressed a problem arose: how to accommodate five new divisions, and then manoeuvre them in battle when the Anzac area was already congested. A landing at Suvla, which was only going to be a limited affair in support of the main Sari Bair assault, was now expanded. Originally a small force would be landed at Suvla to destroy a Turkish artillery battery on Ismail Oglu Tepe, which could enfilade the

Lieutenant General Sir William Birdwood, GOC Anzac Corps

Sari Bair attack; but as Suvla also offered space to support an operation of this size, its involvement was expanded. However, the operation would no longer be a *coup de main*; the primary objective was changed, in order to guarantee success, to capturing the Sari Bair heights only, whilst the Suvla landing was limited to securing a support base for the

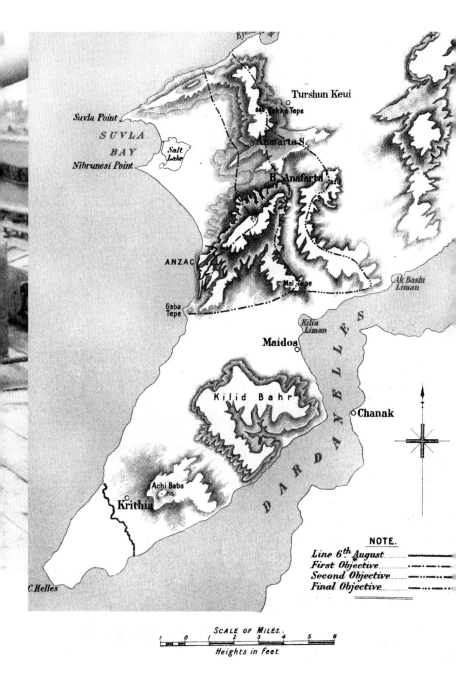

Objectives for August Offensive.

offensive. Any advance across the Peninsula to the Narrows would be secondary to this operation.

The offensive was planned to begin during the morning of 6 August 1915 with several diversionary actions designed to confuse the Turks. These ranged from a British naval squadron, which bombarded Sigacik Koyu near Smyrna (Izmir), to a detachment of about 300 Greek volunteers, commanded by Lieutenant Gruparis, which landed near Enez, north of the Gulf of Saros. The main diversions on 6 August were local, which consisted of a feint attack at Helles, the plan being to draw Turkish attention and reserves to the south. During the same afternoon a similar attack would take place against Lone Pine, at Anzac, where the Australians hoped to attract Turkish attention there. This would allow a night breakout and surprise rush of the Turkish outposts to the north of Fisherman's Hut. Four columns would then follow through to open up the northern perimeter, allowing the capture of the highest parts of the Sari Bair ridge, namely Koja Chemen Tepe, Chunuk Bair and Hill Q. As this area was a maze of treacherous scrub covered spurs and ravines, it was only lightly held by the Turks, so if the Anzacs could find their way through the hinterland there was a great opportunity that they could outflank the main Turkish defences by capturing these heights.

Whilst this was in progress, the newly formed IX Corps would land at Suvla Bay. As the British were coming ashore here, it was hoped that the Anzac assaulting columns would be closing on the Sari Bair heights, to capture them by moonrise on 7 August. This Anzac movement would be critical, for without the seizing of Sari Bair the whole success of the operation would be in jeopardy. The primary objective of IX Corps was the capture of Suvla Bay and establishment of a supply port for the Anzac breakout. In order to achieve this it was expected that the Corps would also need to secure Yilghin Burnu as well as Ismail Oglu Tepe before daylight, as it was here that Turkish artillery was positioned. Once these objectives were secured, the ring of hills that surrounded the Suvla plain were to be captured, from a village called Anafarta Sagir in the south to Ejelmer Bay in the north. Only after this would Suvla Bay be truly secure. The weakness of the plan, however, was its over complexity and reliance on the completion of each step, each critical to the success of the overall offensive. Any delay posed a threat, and as the whole idea relied upon a rapid advance and use of initiative, things that had been lacking so often in the execution of the campaign so far, it did not bode well for success.

According to intelligence collected in late July, it was estimated that the Turks had approximately 30,000 men north of Kilid Bahr, of which

General Sir Ian Hamilton Commander in Chief, MEF.

12,000 were in the trenches opposing the Anzacs. The majority of the remaining 18,000 were known to be in reserve about Boghali, Koja Dere and Eski Keui. Closer to Suvla were estimated to be five battalions, three in the area around the villages of Anafarta, one at Ismail Oglu Tepe and another at Yilghin Burnu, with outposts at Lala Baba and Ghazi Baba. It was also known that the hills around Suvla were garrisoned by Gendarmerie[2], and a Turkish artillery battery was positioned at Ismail Oglu Tepe and Yilghin Burnu, protected by trenches and a little barbed wire, but nothing that was thought to prove a significant obstacle. It would be a race to land as many British troops as possible and capture the objectives before the Turks could bring forward their reserves from Bulair. It was estimated, soon to prove accurate, that the road march from Bulair to Suvla would take approximately thirty hours, which meant Turkish reinforcements would arrive sometime on the 8 August. It was thus vital to be in possession of the high ground by that time.

To achieve the Suvla objectives the plan was to land simultaneously the three infantry brigades of 11th (Northern) Division, a total disembarkation of 13,700 men and twelve guns. The landing was scheduled for the night of 6/7 August when it was known to be pitch black, thus helping mask the initial landing and, with moonlight at 2.00 am, this would assist the men with the advance from the shore. In the morning a further 7,000 infantry from the 10th (Irish) Division would land, followed by forty-four additional guns, not forgetting all associated horses, mules, ammunition, vehicles and stores of an army corps. It was hoped that the first ten thousand men would be landed in about an hour from purpose-built motorised armoured lighters, each capable of holding 500 soldiers. Nicknamed 'beetles', because of their black paint and prominent antennae like prows that held the landing ramp, they would allow the quick disembarkation of the troops, hopefully putting ashore a division in little more than an hour. Their official name was 'X' Lighters, and were part of an original order by the Admiralty in February 1915 for a proposed landing in the Baltic. The shallow draft craft, powered by heavy oil engines with hull constructions similar to the London barges, were designed with a spoon-shaped bow and a drop down ramp to allow easy access to and from the shore. The beetles, the forerunner of the modern landing craft, soon became the workhorse of the Royal Navy at Gallipoli and were used to carry troops, horses, field guns and stores; some were even converted to carry and pump water. They were used for the remainder of the campaign, including helping in the final evacuation. What Hamilton did not want was a repeat of the April landings when, due to these craft not being ready in time, he was forced to use open rowing boats and tows with a consequent high cost in casualties and delays in getting troops ashore.

Commanding the landing flotilla was Commander Edward Unwin, Captain of SS *River Clyde*, who was awarded the Victoria Cross for supporting the landings at V Beach on 25 April 1915. During the night of 6 August Unwin would be using three landing beaches, code named A, B and C. Both B and C beaches were to the south of Nibrunesi Point, whilst A Beach was inside Suvla Bay. When it got light the plan was to perform a full reconnaissance of Suvla Bay in order to find the best beach in which to land the main force. This force would then be disembarked on barrel and trestle piers that were to be constructed on the main landing beach within the bay. The success of this scheme would be dependent on the bay being secured before daylight, namely stringing out an anti-submarine net to safeguard the fleet and for the covering force successfully to drive back the enemy from the area.

The newly formed British IX Corps initially comprised two brigades of the 10th (Irish) Division and the entire 11th (Northern) Division. The 13th Division and 29 Brigade (10th Division) were to reinforce Birdwood at Anzac. Command of IX Corps was given to Lieutenant General Sir Frederick Stopford. Stopford was chosen not because of his experience or his energy and enthusiasm but because of his position on the list of seniority. Hamilton wanted Lieutenant General Sir Julian Byng or Lieutenant General Sir Henry Rawlinson, both of whom were experienced Western Front corps commanders. However this would not be possible, even if Kitchener could prise either of these men from General Sir John French, the BEF commander in chief, as both officers were junior to Lieutenant General Sir Bryan Mahon. Mahon, commander of the 10th (Irish) Division, was favoured by Kitchener for promotion to corps commander; however Hamilton thought he had reached his peak as a divisional commander and so rejected him. As time would tell, this was probably a costly mistake. If it was not to be Mahon, Kitchener stipulated that whoever commanded IX Corps must be senior to him. The British Army at the time still used this much outdated practice of seniority, whereby the system placed its faith on date of the commission listing as opposed to evident talent. So, this left only two generals, Lieutenant General Sir John Ewart and Lieutenant General Sir Frederick Stopford. Hamilton ruled out Ewart due to *his constitutional habit*, stating that he would not *last out here for one fortnight*. Hamilton went on to write in his diary:

> *With regard to Ewart. I greatly admire his character, but he positively could not have made his way along the fire trenches I inspected yesterday. He has never approached troops for fifteen years, although I have often implored him, as a friend, to do so.*[3]

So, by a process of elimination, this left only Stopford.

The elderly Stopford was 61 years old at the time of his selection as IX Corps commander. Stopford was a career soldier but by 1915 had been retired for six years due to ill health and was in the position of Lieutenant of the Tower of London. From a predominantly staff background, with little active service experience, his new posting as a corps commander of raw troops on what was one of the most demanding battlefields of the war was to be a stark

Lieutenant General Sir Frederick Stopford, GOC IX Corps.

contrast to his ceremonial London posting. However there was no alternative at that time, and this recipe for disaster was to result in Stopford, who lasted only a week on the battlefield, becoming a scapegoat for the failure of the August offensive. His incompetent generalship, it is only fair to point out, could be shared with many of the Gallipoli generals. Interestingly, in Stopford's *Who's Who* entry for 1920 there was no mention of his time as corps commander; this taint was wiped from what he probably thought were the annals of history. But Suvla was not wiped from these annals, and it came to represent the greatest 'if only' of Gallipoli, and thus one of the greatest tragedies of a blighted campaign. Known to the Turks today as the Anafartalar battles, Suvla was a great Turkish victory against overwhelming odds. The dynamic leadership of Liman von Sanders and Mustafa Kemal, such a contrast to the British generals, and the counter attacks that began on 9 and 21 August 1915 defeated Britain's last hopes for a successful outcome to the campaign.

The plan was first shown to Stopford on 22 July, who acknowledged that, *it is a good plan. I am sure it will succeed and I congratulate*

Brigadier General Hamilton Lyster Reed VC.

whoever has been responsible for framing it. But not all were as supportive, including Stopford's Chief of Staff, Brigadier General Hamilton Reed VC. Reed[4], who gained his Victoria Cross during the Boer War for helping to save the guns at Colenso, succeeded in swaying Stopford, as he believed no frontal assault on entrenched positions could be made without artillery support. The influential Reed did not state this without experience. He had served with the Royal Field Artillery and was very much an artillery man, and everything from his Boer War to recent Western Front experience confirmed this belief and only went to underline his view. Added to this, the earlier fighting at Anzac and Helles had gone to prove that artillery support was necessary to give the best chance of success. At Suvla, however, the irony was that there were only the equivalent of three Turkish battalions not five, their defences being either illusory or, when entrenched, lacked barbed wire and machine guns. It was surprise and speed that was needed at Suvla to overrun the Turkish positions. Kitchener had already warned of this, and he did not want the operation to be another lost opportunity:

> *The only way to real success for an attack is by surprise. Also, that when the surprise ceases to be operative, in so far that the advance is checked and the enemy begins to collect from all sides to oppose the attackers, then perseverance becomes merely a useless waste of life. In every attack there seems to be a moment when success is in the assailant's grasp. Both the French and ourselves at Arras and Neuve Chapelle lost the opportunity.*[5]

During a GHQ dinner, on the night of 5 August, Lieutenant Edward Compton Mackenzie, a Staff Officer, wrote:

> *The one next to me was Sir Frederick Stopford, a man of great kindliness and personal charm, whose conversation at lunch left me at the end of the meal completely without hope of victory at Suvla. The reason for this apprehension was his inability to squash the new General opposite* [not named, but probably Reed], *who was one of the Brigadiers in his Army Corps. This Brigadier was holding forth almost truculently about the folly of the plan of operations drawn up by the General Staff, while Sir Frederick Stopford appeared to be trying to reassure him in a*

fatherly way. I looked along the table to where Aspinall and Dawnay were sitting near General Braithwaite; but they were out of earshot, and the dogmatic Brigadier continued unchallenged to enumerate the various military axioms which were being ignored by the Suvla plan of operations. For one thing, he vowed, most certainly he was not going to advance a single yard until all the Divisional Artillery was ashore. I longed for Sir Frederick to rebuke his disagreeable and discouraging junior; but he was deprecating, courteous, fatherly, anything except the Commander of an Army Corps which had been entrusted with a major operation that might change the whole course of the war in twenty-four hours.[6]

Any real fortifications were further south at Anzac, however, whilst at Suvla there was very little that should have worried Reed, especially if he was basing his theory on the reconnaissance reports that had revealed few prepared fortifications. Lieutenant Colonel Cecil Aspinall showed Reed the aerial photographs of the area that confirmed the limited defences of the Turks. Suvla was partly entrenched at the Karakol Dagh, Hill 10 and Yilghin Burnu, with an outpost on Lala Baba. Apart from these unconnected positions, Suvla lay virtually undefended, and it was these fundamental facts that Stopford and Reed did not seem to grasp. The result of waiting for guns before making any serious movement forward against these 'fortifications' limited the objectives of the landing from the very beginning.

The final issued orders, after a little dilution by GHQ, failed to mention the importance of speed in securing the surrounding hills before the Turkish reinforcements arrived. This put the overall strategic reason for Suvla, firmly securing a safe port to aid the subsequent exploitation of the Anzac breakout, in danger of failing. Compton Mackenzie went on to write of this dogmatic Brigadier:

Well, General Dash is not going to advance a single yard until the Divisional Artillery is ashore. He doesn't seem to grasp the elementary principles of this push as we've had it explained to us.

The final orders issued by Stopford and Hammersley showed little dash, instructing that the high ground shall only be taken if possible, a polite term that was to become typical of all the Suvla orders. The orders for the 11th (Northern) Division, which would act as the spearhead, were only issued during the evening of 5 August, leaving little time to prepare. Stopford also wanted 34 Brigade to be landed within Suvla Bay itself, despite the advice of the navy. Landing inside

Major General Hammersley and his 11th Division staff.

the bay would give the advantage of reducing the distance to the objectives of Hill 10, Karakol Dagh and Yilghin Burnu, so a risk he wanted to take. What could not be confirmed was whether the Salt Lake, which was visibly dry, would support the weight of troops crossing it, so using the lake as a short cut was ruled out. Landing and securing the immediate beach area was of course a priority, but it was then expected that a rapid advance into the hills would follow whilst the element of surprise was with the British. With vague and changing orders, the objective of the Suvla operation had become so blurred at this stage, that Major General Frederick Hammersley, 11th (Northern) Division commander, believed that one of the main reasons for the Anzac operation was in fact to distract attention away from the Suvla landings! GHQ then went on to make the matter worse by watering down the part to be played at Suvla. It was actually to Stopford's credit that he enforced the need to capture Yilghin Burnu and Ismail Oglu Tepe, which had been removed by Hamilton in an earlier draft. Without these the Suvla 'base' would not be truly secure. Likewise the Anafarta ridge would also be key to the attack and security of the base, so this was put back into the final orders drawn up for IX Corps by Stopford.

One glowing omission was the plans for the 10th (Irish) Division. They were not given any task in the orders with the exception of 29 Brigade being mentioned as support for the Anzac Corps. During an earlier dinner on 3 August aboard SS *Andania*, with Brigadier General Felix Hill, 31 Brigade, 10th Division, Compton Mackenzie observed:

> *Every officer present believed that the Brigade was going to land*

somewhere in Asia Minor. I would not be sure that even General Hill himself knew the real objective. The group of officers seated near me were anxious not to ask awkward questions; at the same time they hungered for information.

Amazing to say, Hill did not find out the plan for his brigade until he had been landed at Suvla!

The commander of the Ottoman *Fifth Army*, General Otto Liman von Sanders, was well aware that a new landing was imminent, as he had been receiving reports of troop build-ups in the Greek islands; however he was unsure of where the landing would be made. He thought that Hamilton might attack south of Anzac at Gaba Tepe, or make a new landing either at the Gulf of Saros or maybe

General Otto Liman von Sanders.

on the Asia coast. To protect the shores, von Sanders was forced to locate three divisions on the Asiatic coast whilst a further three were positioned about thirty miles north of Suvla, at Bulair. Suvla was not thought a likely place that Hamilton would attack and was defended by three battalions of the *Anafarta Detachment*, under the command of a Bavarian cavalry officer, Major Wilhelm Willmer. These comprised the *Bursa Gendarmerie* and *Gelibolu Gendarmerie* battalions and the regular Turkish *31 Regiment*, a total of approximately 3,000 men. His task was to delay any enemy advance until reinforcements arrived, but to do this he had no machine guns, hardly any wire and few field artillery pieces. Making the most of what resources he had available, Willmer constructed three defensive strongpoints along the coastal hills; one at the Karakol Dagh to the north, one on Hill 10 in the centre and one on Yilghin Burnu, near the southeastern end of the Salt Lake. Smaller pickets were also positioned elsewhere, including on Lala Baba, a small hill between the beach and the Salt Lake. Here they waited, keeping a careful eye on any activity out to sea.

1 Wedgwood-Benn, W., *In the Side Shows* (London: Hodder & Stoughton, 1919).
2 The Turkish Gendarmerie was organized by the French in the 1870s along the lines of their system, and served in rural areas where there were no police. Due to the shortage of soldiers in the war, they became part of the Ottoman Army. The Constantinople Fire Brigade were another such paramilitary unit that also fought alongside the regular army at Gallipoli.
3 Hamilton, Sir I., *Gallipoli Diary*, Vol.I., (London: Edward Arnold, 1920), p.307.
4 Reed had experience of the Ottoman Army having been Military Attaché with Turkish Forces during the Balkan War 1912-13. After Gallipoli he went onto command 15th (Scottish) Division 1917-19. He died in 1931.
5 Hamilton, Sir I., *Gallipoli Diary*, Vol.II., (London: Edward Arnold, 1920), p.1.
6 Mackenzie, C., *Gallipoli Memories* (London: Cassell & Co., 1929), p.353.

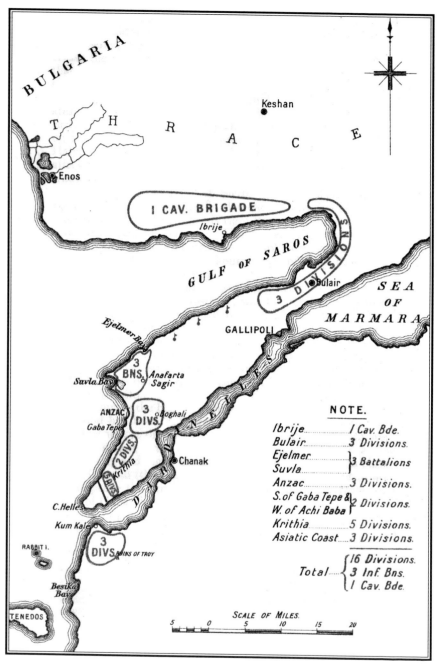

Turkish Dispositions on 6th August.

Chapter Two

THE LANDING – 6/7 AUGUST

Our first sight of rifle fire, our first glimpse of war

Hammersley was to initiate the night landing at 10.00 pm on 6 August, on A, B and C Beaches and then to secure Suvla Bay for the disembarkation of the rest of IX Corps. The most important and difficult task was given to Brigadier General William Sitwell's 34 Brigade, which would land within Suvla Bay. They were to capture Hill 10, which overlooked the beach, a task allotted to 9/Lancashire Fusiliers, whilst 11/Manchesters, after clearing the enemy post at Ghazi Baba, would climb the Kiretch Tepe ridge, clear another post at Karakol Dagh and advance along the ridge for two miles before digging in. When the remaining two battalions of the brigade landed (8/Northumberland Fusiliers and 5/Dorsets) they were to join the Lancashire Fusiliers on Hill 10 and advance together, no later than 1.30 am on 7 August, to seize Yilghin Burnu by first light. Support, if needed, was to be offered by Brigadier General Henry Haggard's Brigade.

The plan for Haggard's 32 Brigade was to land 6/Yorks and 9/West Yorks on the northern end of B Beach, capture Lala Baba and advance via the Cut to meet 34 Brigade on Hill 10. As soon as the rest of the brigade (8/West Ridings and 6/York & Lancs) reached Hill 10, they were to come under the orders of Sitwell to support his attack on Yilghin Burnu. As with all the battalions landing during the night, the men would go into action with their rifles unloaded. Brigade Headquarters had ordered that:

> [It] *Wishes especially that men are warned that water will have to last until tomorrow night. Iron rations may have to last four days. Magazines shall not be charged until daylight. No firing until then. Bayonets only to be used. Men to be informed that if firing is heard it is the Australians attacking.*[1]

Brigadier General Robert Maxwell's 33 Brigade was to land on the southern side of B Beach. The first two battalions (9/Sherwood Foresters and 7/South Staffords) were to protect the right flank by entrenching from the beach to the southeast corner of the Salt Lake. The remaining two battalions (6/Lincolns and 6/Borders) and the divisional pioneers (6/East Yorks) were to position themselves 500 yards east of Hill 10, forming the divisional reserve.

Just before sunset, on a crowded Imbros pier, Lieutenant Edmund Priestman, 6/York & Lancs, described the scene in a letter home:

> Lying by the temporary landing-stage were half a dozen steam-driven 'lighters', long black barges capable of carrying two hundred or more men and, in the open blue water beyond, more of these lighters were plying backwards and forwards between the shore and the small fleet of torpedo destroyers lying half a mile away. As soon as one of the lighters was packed with khaki from the thick masses of men on the shore, it steamed away and its place was taken by a new one, on to which fresh lines of troops filed till it too was packed to its full capacity. Then out it would puff, carrying a dense freight of singing Tommies, whose legs swung hazardously over the bulwarks and whose heels kicked time to their favorite song, 'Are we downhearted? No, not while Britannia rules the waves (not likely!!)'.
>
> With the night came an army of clouds like a legion of angels to guard us from the eyes of our enemies. Then, as silently as their

Troops embarking at Imbros for Suvla, 6 August.

protecting wings were slowly spread over the deepening blue, so silently we began to move out of the harbour into the unknown. Over the packed decks there hung a tense atmosphere of suppressed excitement, too full for spoken or musical comment, officers and men alike rearranging their respective outlooks upon life to suit the new conditions and the great adventures looming among the shadows ahead.[2]

It was not until the early morning of 6 August that the units of 11th Division were first informed of the landing. Men quickly got busy preparing and were instructed to sew on white bands to each arm and a white patch on the back, and in some battalions these were supplemented by pieces of shaped tin or even a polished mess tin. The aim was to provide identification in the dark and later for artillery to distinguish friend from foe when it got light. Unfortunately the Turks also found these markings just as useful! All packs, blankets and valises were to remain at Imbros. Lieutenant Colonel Harry Welstead, the Lancashire Fusiliers commanding officer, remarked that *it would all be over in three days* and with this confidence promised the men that all their packs and blankets would be with them soon. Unfortunately he and many of his men were never going to see these items again. There

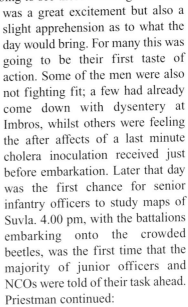

was a great excitement but also a slight apprehension as to what the day would bring. For many this was going to be their first taste of action. Some of the men were also not fighting fit; a few had already come down with dysentery at Imbros, whilst others were feeling the after affects of a last minute cholera inoculation received just before embarkation. Later that day was the first chance for senior infantry officers to study maps of Suvla. 4.00 pm, with the battalions embarking onto the crowded beetles, was the first time that the majority of junior officers and NCOs were told of their task ahead. Priestman continued:

And now came a thrill. The sealed orders containing our programme for the coming

Embarking the Beetles.

Beetle K5 packed with men.

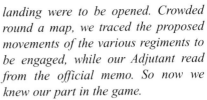

landing were to be opened. Crowded round a map, we traced the proposed movements of the various regiments to be engaged, while our Adjutant read from the official memo. So now we knew our part in the game.

At the time the Aegean was crawling with Turkish spies, so an effort went into distributing thousand of maps of the Asiatic Coast to officers and NCOs in order to deceive them as to the actual landing place. The extra security, almost verging on paranoia, had the disadvantage of leaving many officers, some senior, unaware of where they were landing until they actually were standing on the Suvla beaches; and even then were ignorant as to the task demanded of them. The map situation did not improve, and throughout the whole campaign they were, on the whole, scarce and inaccurate, many hand drawn. Private John Hargrave, who served in the 32 Field Ambulance, wrote:

A map! Why this is better than a gallon of fresh water! But when I spread it out and looked at it, the gleam of excitement faded. It shows the whole of the Gallipoli Peninsula, the whole of the Dardanelles, and most of the Sea of Marmara! In other words it would be – and was – utterly useless wherever we might land, why bother to issue it? I stuffed the wretched thing into my haversack with a disgusted grunt.[3]

In late August the Yeomanry also received a long awaited batch of new maps of the area, but upon opening them they actually found them to be maps of Norfolk, England!

Waiting until it got dark, at 7.45 pm, the

flotilla, a rag tag band of destroyers, motor-lighters, picket-boats, North Sea trawlers, sloops and many small boats, left Imbros and began their night journey towards Suvla Bay. Hot tea and rum was issued, and many of the men were in high spirits, singing merrily, until an order was issued for silence about two miles from Suvla. Captain Marmion Ferrers-Guy, 9/Lancashire Fusiliers recounted:

> *All lights were out and no noise allowed when once we started; but there was a sight and a noise which all that saw and heard will not easily forget, and that was the battle being fought at Cape Helles and Anzac. The battleships and cruisers were firing at the Turkish positions, as were also our batteries on land. There was a terrific rifle fire and one could see the flashes from the rifles all along the trenches; truly a magnificent sight and one imagined and hoped that every Turk would be drawn towards that quarter.[4]*

Whilst the British at Helles were in the throes of their diversionary attacks and the Australians were capturing Lone Pine, ten thousand men of Kitchener's New Army (10th and 11th Divisions), the first to be taken to the field in war, were nearing their baptism of fire. Initially an all-volunteer army, the New Army was formed in the United Kingdom following the outbreak of hostilities in World War I. Eventually totaling thirty fighting divisions, these New Army men went on to prove their worth, not only on the battlefields of Gallipoli, Salonika, Palestine, Mesopotamia and Italy but also in France and Flanders, testing their mettle during the battles of the Somme and Passchendaele.

> *At last, straining our eyes, we thought we could see right ahead a mass which we hoped was Lala Baba. If it were, we were in the right position. We kept on slowly, and suddenly came on a destroyer; she told us that she hoped she was opposite C Beach. We replied with great fervour that we also hoped she was.[5]*

With the destroyers 500 yards from the shore,

> *... anchors were eased down; and, with every man's pulse beating a wild tattoo, the lighters made for the beach. Not a sound came from the land. Fleecy clouds hid the stars. A slight breeze ruffled the quiet sea.*[6]

Shortly before 10.00 pm, in perfect conditions, 32 and 33 Brigade approached the undefended shores of B Beach, just south of Nibrunesi Point.

> *The night was utterly still; if there was firing at Anzac I did not hear it any longer, our attention was so concentrated. After a few minutes, I thought I could hear a very low and gentle pebbly sound, and almost at the same time a faint thin line of white appeared ahead of us. It was what we had all been waiting for, the sand.*[7]

The first wave of armoured beetles grounded at the water's edge and lowered their ramps. Private John Hargrave, 32 Field Ambulance, wrote:

The Landing – painting by Norman Wilkinson.

*The engine shut off as we ran in. We felt the soft sand-
cushioned bump and the sliding scrape as the heavy, flat-
bottomed lighter dredged to a standstill: heard the rattle-
and-creak of running tackle and rusty chains as the iron-
plated ramp at the bow lowered like a drawbridge.*

Four battalions were safely landed without a casualty,
leaving the beetles to return for the next load.

Serving alongside Commander Unwin VC was Midshipman
George Drewry, who was also decorated with the Victoria
Cross during the V Beach Landing in April. Suvla was such
a contrast to the Helles landings, Drewry wrote:

*It was uncanny, the troops got ashore in record time and
then came batteries and mules and munitions. I could not
understand it, I stood on the beach and saw guns being
landed and horses, and behind us a few yards away was
the dark bush, containing what? There was little firing,
now and then a sharp rattle quite close and then silence. I
thought of Helles and then wondered if we had landed by mistake
at Lemnos.*

As planned, 9/Sherwood Foresters and 7/South Staffords of 33 Brigade
landed on the right and they immediately began to entrench a line from
the beach to the edge of the Salt Lake in order to protect the right flank.
The only resistance reported was from two Turks who fired their rifles
from about half a mile inland before making a hasty retreat into the
night.

Captain Francis Loyd, who was the Sherwood's adjutant, wrote:

*On the 7th ... it seemed to be a very half-hearted sort of affair as
far as the 10th and 11th Divisions were concerned. There was no
really serious attack being made as far as we, on the right of the
11th Division, could see, and we received orders to remain where
we were and entrench. This was disheartening, as we all expected
to move rapidly at daybreak, and all ranks were feeling so
'bucked' that I feel sure if the order for a general advance had
been given we would have gone across to Maidos with little
difficulty. In addition there was at that time no considerable force
of Turks in front of us, and our landing had been a complete
surprise. This is evident, or we should not have been allowed to
carry it out so easily. Our 9th Battalion actually had no
casualties when landing.[8]*

C and B Beaches, 2010.

To the left, 6/Yorks and 9/West Yorks of 32 Brigade also came ashore virtually unmolested, with the exception of some rifle fire from further up the beach. Private John Hargrave, 32 Field Ambulance, wrote:

> *Suddenly, a running sparkle broke out of the gloom ahead in sporadic fusillades of flickering red and orange glitter-dust, sweeping back and forth like swarms of angry fireflies. Our first sight of rifle fire, our first glimpse of war.*

One company of 6/Yorks was dispatched to set up a piquet line on the southern end of the Salt Lake whilst another, under the command of Major William Shannon, was sent to clear the Turks from the small knolls near Nibrunesi Point. The two remaining companies, under Major Archibald Roberts, prepared themselves to assault Lala Baba, supported by 9/West Yorks. Their first action was about to begin.

The Landing at Suvla Bay

You may talk of Balaclava,
      And of Trafalgar Bay,
But what of the Eleventh Division
      Who landed at Suvla Bay?

They're part of Kitchener's Army,
      Who had left mothers, children, and wives,
But they fought for England's freedom,
      Fought for their very lives

It was on the 6th of August,
        They made their terrible dash,
As the Turks upon the hillside
        They were trying our boats to smash.

The order came "Fix Bayonets!"
        As out of the boats we got,
Yet every man was a hero
        Who faced the Turkish shot.

Ships' sides and funnels were shattered,
        And the sea in some parts red,
But the lads fought the way to the shore,
        To the beach that was covered with dead.

Then creeping at length up the hillside,
        While shot and shells fell around,
They made their last desperate effort,
        And charged the Turkish ground.

The Turks began to tremble
        When they saw the bayonets play,
Then they turned their backs on the British
        And returned from Suvla Bay!

There were Lincolns, Dorsets and Staffords,
        The Border Regiment too,
The good old Sherwood Foresters,
        And the R.A.M.C. true.

Then came the gallant Manchesters,
        With the Fusiliers by their side,
Those trusty lads from Lancashire
        Who filled our hearts with pride.

The Yorks, East Yorks and West Yorks,
        And Yorks and Lancs, as well,
All fought for the honour of Britain
        And with the bravest fell.

The Fighting Fifth were at it,
        Northumberland lads, you know,
While the Duke of Wellington's did their best
        Driving back the foe.

Far away up the hillside,
        Buried 'neath the Turkish clay,
Lie sons of Britain's heroes

Who landed at Suvla Bay.

So remember the Eleventh Division,
　　　Who are all volunteers, you know,
They fought and died like Britons
　　　While fighting their deadly foe.[9]

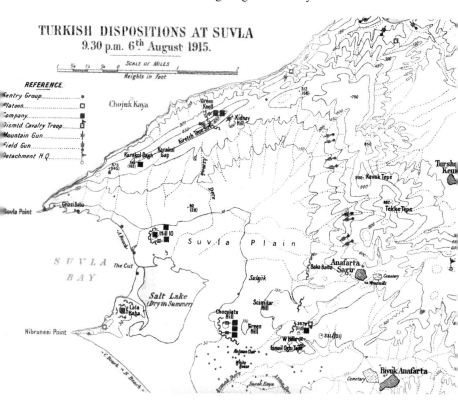

Lala Baba

In the first action fought by any unit of the New Army, the two companies from 6/Yorks attacked the small hillock of Lala Baba, believed to be defended by a Turkish company. As the round topped hill, just visible against the northern sky, was neared, a flare was suddenly fired; the element of surprise was gone. The rifle fire that had been sporadic until now soon increased and casualties quickly began to mount. As it was still dark the Yorkshires were ordered to attack with the bayonet only, but this discipline did not last long. Major Shannon, on his return from clearing two Turkish posts near Nibrunesi Point, joined the attack, ordering C Company to charge the hill:

> *On arriving at the base of Lala Baba I ordered a charge and we ran up the hill. About three-quarters of the way up we came upon a Turkish trench, very narrow and flush with the ground. We ran over this and the enemy fired into our rear, firing going on at this time from several directions. I shouted out that the Yorkshire Regiment was coming, in order to avoid running into our own people. We ran on and about twelve paces further on, as far as I can judge, came to another trench; this we also crossed and again were fired into from the rear. I ordered the company to jump back into the second trench, and we got into this, which was so narrow that it was quite impossible for one man to pass another, or even to walk up it unless he moved sideways; another difficulty was that if there were any wounded or dead men in the bottom of the trench it was impossible to avoid treading on them in passing. There was a little communication trench running from right to left behind me, and whenever I shouted an order a Turk, who appeared to be in the trench, fired at me from a distance of apparently five or ten yards. I had some difficulty in getting anybody to fire down the communication trench in order to quiet the enterprising Turk, who was endeavouring to pot me with great regularity, but I eventually got him shot.[10]*

Shannon took his men over the hill and met up with the survivors from A and B companies that were on the reverse slope. Gathering these men he swept the hill of any further resistance, clearing the slopes all the way down to the Cut, the narrow wedge of muddy sand that separated the Salt Lake from the sea.

> *A little way down the reverse slope we came to some groups of men, several of whom were lying about apparently awaiting orders, and one group on the left was 'scrapping' with some Turks in a trench a few yards distant from them. In response to shouting*

> *I got an answer from two directions and picked up Lieutenant Whitworth and Second Lieutenant Simpson. These were all the officers then present. I formed such of the Battalion as could be collected into a line facing north and we charged down to the base of the hill facing the further beach – afterwards known as A Beach.*

Lala Baba, looking from Nibrunesi Point, 2010.

Although Lala Baba was taken, as a result of inexperience the casualties were heavy, especially amongst the officers. Out of the three companies, all but three of the Yorkshires' officers became casualties, as did one third of the men. The battalion also lost Lieutenant Colonel Edward Chapman, the commanding officer, and Major Roberts, who later died of his wounds. Chapman's cousin, Captain Wilfrid Chapman, was also killed in this action.

Second Lieutenant Priestman, whose battalion had just come ashore, wrote of the carnage on Lala Baba in one of his letters home:

As we push on, through sweet, sickly-smelling scrub now, the darkness in front takes the form of a peaked hill and we meet the first slopes of its flank. And then, to our straining ears, there comes a voice from the blackness on our right. Almost inaudible at first, it swells up into a shrill, wordless whine, quavers for a moment, and then dies again into silence. Then again, 'Ah-h-h-h-h ...' This time it halts and inflects as though trying to frame some word, then, almost as though it would sing a few quivering notes, it sinks down the scale into the night and the shadows again ...our front line has met something exciting now, and – 'spit, spit, whissss!' a swarm of bullets rushes over our heads into the night. We scramble on among the rough stones of the hillside and find ourselves on the edge of a long, deep trench, where are lying discarded rifles and their owners. The desultory rifle fire has ceased, but as we reach the hilltop a shell, our first, flutters over and bursts behind us, followed by another and another. But we are safe in a dip of the hill now, and there we stay until dawn brings with it more shells.[11]

Both 32 and 33 Brigade were ashore successfully, being followed by 6/East Yorks, the divisional signal company, three engineer field companies and the mountain artillery brigade and a battery of 18 pounders. Lala Baba was captured and piquets were in position as prescribed. One could not have asked for a better start; however, this is where misfortune struck, and any advantages gained during the landing were close to being lost.

Following Lala Baba's capture, 6/Yorks and 9/West Yorks should have advanced via the Cut to meet 34 Brigade on Hill 10, and then act as support for Sitwell's attack on the Yilghin Burnu. This did not happen. It was still pitch black and out in front of the two Yorkshire battalions, now under the command of Lieutenant Colonel John Minogue, was a crackle of rifle fire. Minogue decided not to advance immediately on Hill 10, but to first send out an officer's patrol to get in touch with Sitwell. Unfortunately the officer was shot and the patrol fell back. For the following two hours no further effort was made to contact Sitwell, and likewise Sitwell made no effort to contact 32 Brigade. Sitwell was a promising general who had experience from campaigns in Afghanistan, Bechuanaland, Ashanti, the Nile Expedition, Omdurman and South Africa. During the Boer War he commanded a mobile column and later, in India, an infantry brigade. At Suvla he was not to shine.

As the Yorks were beginning their attack on Lala Baba, 34 Brigade had already entered Suvla Bay, where their lighters were set free to continue the last mile to the beach under their own steam. The first two battalions would approach the shore in three armoured beetles, *K1*, *K2* and *K3*. Once the Lancashire Fusiliers and Manchesters were ashore the lighters would return to pick up the Dorsets, Northumberland Fusiliers and brigade headquarters. Captain Ferrers-Guy, 9/Lancashire Fusiliers, wrote:

> *The only sound was the puffing of the lighters, K2 in the centre, K1 in the left, K3 on the right. Certainly anyone on the hills or the beach could hear, and even see, that something was approaching. The night was pitch dark, favourable for the landing, but unfavourable when once the beach was gained.*[12]

But this was not going to be the first problem experienced. Initially the destroyers (HMS *Grampus* and *Bulldog*) conveying the brigade anchored a thousand yards too far south and on the wrong side of the channel, the Cut, that drained the Salt Lake into the bay. This was the very area where shallow water had been reported, which caused the

beetles from *Grampus* and *Bulldog* to ground upon a shoal about 50 yards out. Ferrers-Guy, noted:

> *K2 came to an abrupt stop and the sailor down by the gangway told us to get off. The Adjutants of the 9th Lancashire Fusiliers and the 11th Manchester Regiment went down the gangway and reported that there was at least 4ft. 6 ins. of water. The sailor disputed this, saying it was only 2ft. 3 ins., but being ordered to get the pole to sound it, found it was 4ft. 7 ins. The O.C. Manchester Regiment, who was senior officer on the lighter, asked the sailor at the wheel to work the lighter nearer the shore,*

41

but he said it was stuck and he could not move. At that moment the Turks opened a frontal fire on us from the beach and right flank fire from Hill 40 at Lala Baba, wounding three in the lighter. All dropped down and the Officer Commanding 11th Manchesters gave the order to get off and go ashore.

A rope was fixed to the shore that aided the men to the beach. Fortunately casualties were light; however the main problem from this 'wet' landing would occur later, when the men came to use their weapons. Apart from the Manchesters dropping their machine gun, which was later recovered, many of their rifles were later found to be unserviceable, caused by the mixture of salt water and sand, causing the bolts to jam and barrels to block. One unit found the only way to open them was to urinate onto the bolt!

K1 also had a similar problem, running into a shoal about 40 yards from the shore, but with only four feet of water the journey to the beach, although wet, was quicker. K3 came into shallow water with fewer problems.

As well as anchoring too far south, another problem became apparent when the men reached the shore; they found themselves on the wrong part of the beach. Perhaps owing to the darkness or lack of co-ordination, the *Grampus* and *Bulldog* had positioned themselves in the wrong order. The *Grampus*, with three companies of the 9/Lancashire Fusiliers, should have positioned itself to the south of the *Bulldog*, with three companies of the 11/Manchesters to the north. However, they had somehow become swapped. This meant that the Manchesters, who were

An artist's impression of the landing.

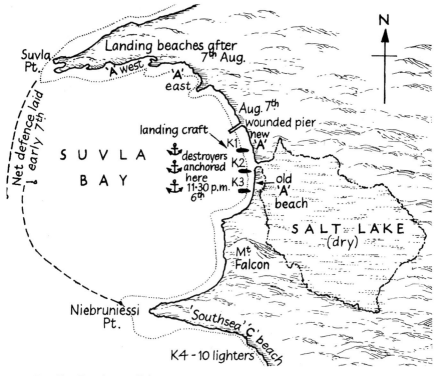

Landing Beaches on 7 August.

to clear Suvla Point and Kiretch Tepe ridge to the north, came ashore near the Cut, on the right, whilst the Lancashire Fusiliers came ashore where the Manchesters should have landed.

This was not necessarily a major problem but, with the beetles grounding, it caused initial confusion and delays in gaining their objectives, and also delays in bringing ashore the remainder of the brigade. Turkish rifle fire during the night was minimal, but what there was was accurately directed at the officers and NCOs of the two leading battalions. It was also a surprise for the 6/Yorks, who were attacking Lala Baba at the time, and bayonet charged the Manchesters by mistake. The Manchesters had been landed too far south, on the wrong side of A Beach, but luckily this little exchange was quickly resolved as both units realised each other was not the enemy.

The Manchesters then departed company with the Lancashire Fusiliers and followed the beach to the north around the bay, to continue their original mission. At bayonet point they successfully cleared the isolated Turkish outpost at Ghazi Baba and then ascended onto Kiretch Tepe ridge. Here they advanced through sporadic rifle fire until they reached the 400 foot Karakol Dagh, where they came under deadly fire and shelling from the Turks, who had positioned themselves on the other side of the Karakol Gap. At 10.00 am the Manchesters, with rifles and machine gun now cleared of blockages, attacked. Under the cover of machine gun fire the men of the Manchesters suddenly rose and went forward, surprising the Turks, who almost immediately retreated. The Karakol was now in the hands of the British; another objective had been taken. The Manchesters advanced on, but dogged by a consistent Turkish rearguard action, they soon came to a halt just short of a high point of the Kiretch Tepe ridge, later to become known as Jephson's Post. This battalion, faced with difficult circumstances, had done everything asked of it. It was now midday. The Manchesters were alone with no support, no water, a quickly diminishing ammunition supply and a growing number of wounded. It was one of the hottest summers on record, and with the heat and the salt water many of the men had inadvertently swallowed during the landing, the suffering from thirst was becoming agonising. An old stone flagged Turkish well was eventually found upon the heights, but there was disappointment as it was found to be poisoned, carcasses of mules and dead Turks were lying in the water, putrefying in the heat of the sun. Isolated and continuingly sniped at, the high spirits, dogged determination underpinned by effective leadership allowed the Manchesters to advance a full three miles that day. The New Army were proving themselves worthy on the battlefield, but this initial success was not to last.

Hill 10

With the exception of the Manchesters success, there were no other movements inland. The plan was for a rapid advance but, due to the bedlam within Suvla Bay, this did not happen. By 3.00 am the moon had risen, but below there was confusion caused by the night landing, with intermixed units and officers unable to locate their position or their objectives in the dark. Many of them chose to sit still until light. John Hargrave, 32 Field Ambulance, recalled this moment:

When the protective cloak of darkness was snatched away, the ghastly lunar radiance not only lit up a sepulchral landscape of corpse-pale beaches, silver-livid salt pan, carbon black scrub, and the glimmering catafalque of scar faced hills, but at once revealed the wan shadows and shapes of transports and battleships in the bay, the stranded lighters, and the mass of wading, straggling, lost, and already wearied troops, some huddled for cover behind sand dunes, some drifting in scattered groups along the sea wet lip of the shore.

After four hours, 34 Brigade had only landed two battalions, whilst 8/Northumberland Fusiliers and 5/Dorsets were still at sea. A beetle managed to get back to the *Grampus* and returned with three companies of the Northumberland Fusiliers, but struck a shoal a long way out from the beach, so had to wait until cutters could be sent to take the men ashore. Even after *Bulldog's* beetle was refloated it was not until 2.30 am that it started its second journey ashore, and again it struck a shoal. Like a sitting duck, attracting Turkish fire, it did not manage to disembark all its men until 4.30 am, when it was light.

Ashore 9/Lancashire Fusiliers were faring badly. Its companies were in two disconnected groups just north of the Cut and, now illuminated by the moon, their white armbands were proving good targets for the Turks. The Battalion had yet to find, let alone capture, Hill 10. Their commanding officer, Lieutenant Colonel Harry Welstead, who was already wounded and had become separated from the main body of his Battalion, was waiting for reinforcements to arrive. Unbeknown to him, the rest of the Brigade (Northumberland Fusiliers and Dorsets) were still stuck on their lighters; however close-by there were six battalions from 32 and 33 Brigade sitting idle a little further down the beach. This was also unknown to brigade command, who were also still stuck out at sea.

There were also problems getting the specially converted steamer *Prah* into position, along with four water lighters that needed to get their vital supplies to the shore. These were meant to provide the initial supply of water to the troops before the army moved inland to make full use of the ground wells. The *Prah*, which carried water pumps, hose, tanks, troughs, entrenching tools and all other tools needed to develop wells and springs, arrived at Suvla early on 7 August, but it left for some unknown reason and did not return until 9 August. By 7 August only two lighters had made it to Suvla, and both had become grounded out in the bay. It was too far away to run a pipe so it was not until 8 August that they were eventually dislodged from the shoal for water to be finally got ashore. About the same time the second two lighters that had become adrift also finally made it to where this precious liquid was needed. Once the lighters had been anchored by the shore the water had to be pumped through canvas fire hoses into large beach based water troughs. The whole water affair was mismanaged from the very start, with a lack of any sense of urgency to get this water ashore. Men went into action with a single pint and a half of water in their bottles, which was filled during embarkation at Lemnos on 6 August. By the morning of 7 August many had run dry, let alone having anything like enough to last until the morning of 8 August, when the water lighters were eventually freed by the navy. This was not the end of the problem, as there appeared to be no plan, let alone containers, to get the water to the front line, where men would go crazy with thirst. Even though portable receptacles for 100,000 gallons in the shape of petrol tins, milk cans, camel tanks and water bags had been requisitioned, they,

along with the mules needed to take the water inland, were not available during the first couple of days when it was most needed.

Sitwell's 34 Brigade, eventually made it ashore about 3.30 am and discovered, after communication with Welstead, that Hill 10 had not been captured. Very soon after this, Welstead was killed. It was getting light and soon the transports with more troops would be approaching the shore, so it was critical that this hill was taken. Without waiting for reinforcements, Sitwell ordered 9/Lancashire Fusiliers, now under the command of Major Cyril Ibbetson, to attack the hillock they understood to be Hill 10. This in fact turned out to be a large sand dune

Filling water bottles from a makeshift trough.

Taking a water tank inland.

about 400 yards to the south of the real Hill 10. Upon reaching the top of this undefended hillock, Ibbetson was confronted with Turkish fire from the actual Hill 10 and a trench about 200 yards in front. He charged and captured this trench, but in the process was wounded. Reinforcements from 32 Brigade arrived, including a mixed body of men under Major William Shannon, 6/Yorks, but there was confusion as to what they were expected to do, so the attacks soon petered out.

It was now 5.00 am. John Hargrave, 32 Field Ambulance, recalled that the Suvla sunrise:

> *... sprang out of the first streak of dawn like a slow motion flight of flamingoes flooding up and up in a boundless oriflamme of surprise pink. No English daybreak ever burst in such a paroxysm of Greek Fire and Turkish Delight. Death himself was taken by surprise.*

Daylight had come and instead of the 11th Division having secured Suvla Bay and the surrounding hills, all it had secured were the two horns of the bay. Out of twelve battalions only three had directly engaged the Turks (6/Yorks, 9/Lancashire Fusiliers and 11/Manchesters); the others were sitting virtually idle, awaiting orders. Hammersley's Divisional Headquarters and the Corps Commander knew nothing of what was happening at this stage, so no direction, when it was most needed, was forthcoming.

About the same time Colonel Hans Kannengiesser, commanding the Turkish 9th Division, had been informed that enemy troops had landed north of Ari Burnu. From the heights he could observe the situation, recalling:

> *Suvla Bay lay full of ships. We counted ten transports, six warships, and seven hospital ships. On land we saw a confused mass of troops, like a disturbed ant-heap, and across the blinding white surface of the dried salt sea we saw a battery marching in a southerly direction. With glasses I was able to pick up bit by bit Willmer's companies north of the Asmak Dere on the east border of the flat country, and I saw English troops on Lala Baba and, on the flat, in certain places, entrenching. Nowhere was there fighting in progress. During the reconnaissance we found a Turkish battery whose battery commander I had to awaken, as he had no idea of the altered battle front. He opened fire on the troops crossing the dried salt sea, but could only reach with high explosive.*[13]

Hammersley and his staff soon landed at B Beach and began to establish their headquarters near Lala Baba. Hammersley, who was already feeling under the weather, sent out runners to get in contact with his brigades. These runners became lost and no news was received until well after daybreak. Soon Hammersley got to hear that Sitwell was

Landing stores at West Beach harbour.

held up and had not taken Hill 10, so he ordered Brigadier General Henry Haggard's 32 Brigade to give immediate support. At about 5.30 am on 7 August, Haggard advanced from Lala Baba with two battalions (9/Yorkshire and 6/York & Lancs), but upon reaching the Cut found a mixed crowd of men from all battalions. At this time Hill 10 was held by only a company, approximately a hundred men of the *Bursa Gendarmerie* under Major Tahsin Bey. The remainder of the defenders, a further 500 men, had already pulled back in the direction of Anafarta Sagir. Advancing on the hill with the equivalent of two and a half battalions was enough to encourage the outnumbered Turks to abandon their position. The Turks had done what was requested of them, holding back the British advance until the last moment, during which time valuable intelligence was regularly sent back to Major Willmer. By 7.00 am Hill 10 was finally in British hands.

The time table was getting behind; Hill 10 should have been captured by 1.00 am but was not taken until six hours later. Actually by 1.30 am Yilghin Burnu should have been seized, so where were the battalions that were to take this objective? The 8/Northumberland Fusiliers, 5/Dorsets and 9/Lancashire Fusiliers were scattered around Hill 10, whilst on the southern side of the Cut, by Lala Baba, were most of Haggard's supporting 32 Brigade in the process of digging in.

Sitwell ordered 5/Dorsets to move in a northeasterly direction towards the Karakol Dagh to join up with 11/Manchesters. As the Dorsets advanced they spotted an opportunity.

Just before we reached the limit of our advance, there occurred an incident that nearly resulted in the capture of two field guns. These guns were in a ravine in well concealed emplacements and were very much troubling our left and the Manchesters' right; during our advance the naval guns had tried to 'get' these guns but had failed to do so. We were about 300 yards away when a party was sent forward under Lieutenant Bowler to try and reach the guns; at the same time a party was despatched from the extreme right, to cut off the guns on the flank at the opening of the

49

ravine in the valley; the guns now limbered up and made off, the flank party got within 150 yards of them, and opened fire but they got away.[14]

Almost a captured battery!

The 9/West Yorks were then sent in support of the Dorsets and by midday were in and around Hill 28, the rise of a small spur about 1600 yards from the beach, northeast of Hill 10. There was now little resistance, with the exception of sniping, and no orders thus far were given for the next attack, the capture of Yilghin Burnu, better known as the Chocolate Hills.

Chocolate Hills

After the attack on Hill 10, 8/Northumberland were withdrawn to the beach as Divisional Reserve whilst 9/Lancashire Fusiliers remained on Hill 10 until the following day, when they were also sent forward in support of 5/Dorsets. Just ashore on C Beach was a confused 31 Brigade, who, with Brigadier General Hill, were expecting to be landed on A Beach. The Royal Navy, with all the earlier problems with the rock and sand shoals during the night, now considered A Beach to be unsafe. Actually the navy as early as 17 July knew of these uncharted shoals but the landing here nevertheless had gone ahead. The decision was now made to redirect the Irish to the southwest of the Salt Lake, two miles away from their intended landing place. When Hill arrived he had no idea where he was and what he was suppose to do. Hill had received no orders, and although he knew he was part of a major landing, it was stated that:

> *It might have been at Walvis Bay or Botany Bay for all the information he had been given. He had no map of Suvla, had never seen a map of Suvla, did not know where Suvla was, and had no instructions what to do now that he was there!*[15]

Sitwell should have taken the Chocolate Hills by first light, but had most of his men strewn literary just a few yards from the beach. Both 32 and 34 Brigades were badly intermixed, only 33 Brigade was in any order, and they were holding the line from the Salt Lake to the edge of B Beach. 31 Brigade, who were just landing, only added to the congestion. Sitwell would not budge, despite the demands of Hammersley, who sent a staff officer to explain the situation and utmost importance of capturing the Chocolate and W Hills immediately. Patrols from 34 Brigade had returned from Küçük Anafarta Ova and reported that very few Turks were in the neighbourhood, Sitwell,

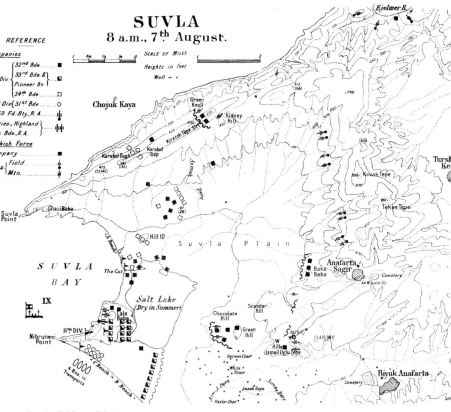

Suvla 8.00am 7th August.

however, appeared more focused at that moment on consolidating Hill
10 and the beach area than mounting another attack. With the plan in
danger of falling apart, the race against time was being lost. Things
were bad but not unrecoverable for the Brigade and Division as a
whole. Experience should have taught Sitwell that he should have taken
the advantage, but all he did was lose himself in the confusion and
resigned himself to do nothing in terms of an attack. Sitwell referred
the situation to Hammersley, who was in a worse situation, with three
brigades to sort out let alone one. Higher authority was in the shape of
Stopford, who lay offshore upon his headquarters yacht *Jonquil*.
However Stopford was reported to be asleep, nursing a recently
sprained ankle. He had previously reasoned that he could exercise more
control from aboard the *Jonquil*, but with limited communications to
the shore at this time it is difficult to imagine a commander being in
less control.

Hammersley, however, was still determined to push forward but had
received no news from his leading brigades since 5.30 am.

Communication had been established with Anzac and soon a message was received from Birdwood reporting to Hammersley that a number of wagons and a Turkish artillery battery had been sighted retiring back from the village of Anafarta Sagir. At about 7.00 am patrols sent out from 33 Brigade, who were entrenched southeast of the Salt Lake, reported a strong Turkish force still on Chocolate Hill. The officers of the Brigade wanted to attack this position from the southwest, and had the men to do it; divisional headquarters however refused such an attack due to the belief that the south western side of the hill was heavily wired. In fact only a few strands of rusty barbed-wire were *in situ,* which was nothing that would have hampered an advance; however, this was not known at this time. Stubbornly, Division was sticking to the original orders for an attack on the hills from the north.

Divisional Headquarters had issued three orders, each one overriding its predecessor. What should have been a fairly simple task was becoming confused. At 8.00 am, after hearing that Hill 10 had been captured, Hammersley issued an order that when 31 Brigade arrived, 32 and 34 were *to push on vigorously* to the Chocolate Hills. Hill's 31 Brigade would then protect the left flank of this attack by advancing southeast from Hill 10 towards the direction of Ismail Oglu Tepe (W Hills). It was soon reported that 34 Brigade and the majority of 32 Brigade had already advanced in a northeasterly direction from Hill 10. With this update Hammersley, who had just been badly shaken by a Turkish shell that burst over his headquarters on Lala Baba, killing one officer, two orderlies and wounding an aide-de-camp, then issued a second order to Haggard and Hill, cancelling the earlier one issued at 8.00 am. Realising that the situation had changed, the new order, written at 8.35 am, now ordered 31 and 32 Brigade *to push on vigorously* alone to the Chocolate Hills and W Hills. It was vague as to which Brigade was to capture what hill; but regardless, at least the Brigades were on the move. At 8.45 am Brigadier General Hill arrived at Lala Baba to meet Hammersley and voiced his concerns about being separated from the rest of the 10th Division if he were to advance now on the Chocolate Hills. Hammersley explained that there was no alternative and needed to ensure the early capture of these objectives. A third order was then issued at 9.05 am that instructed Haggard to

Aboard a Motor Lighter.

advance 32 Brigade on the left flank of 31 Brigade to capture the W Hills.

Now to the confusion. The time between when the orders had been written and the time when they were received is entirely different, as could be expected. At 8.45 am Hill was aware of the orders for his Brigade's advanced on the Chocolate Hills. However, also at this time, Sitwell had just received the first set of orders issued at 8.00 am that requested the same objective. Sitwell immediately wrote to Lieutenant Colonel Cathcart Hannay, 5/Dorsets, saying:

> *8.55 a.m. 31st Brigade of six battalions now on the way to Hill 10. On its arrival 32nd and 34th Bdes. will move on Yilghin Burnu. 31st Bde. proceeding with right on Ismail Oglu Tepe, protecting the left of 33rd and 34th Brigades from the direction of Baka Baba. Northumberland Fusiliers will attack Yilghin Burnu supported by Lancashire Fusiliers and 32nd Brigade. You will cover north flank of advance.*

Haggard received the subsequent two orders issued at 8.35 am and 9.05 am about the same time, and showed these to Sitwell. As Sitwell was senior brigadier and there was no mention in these latter orders to 34 Brigade, Sitwell unfortunately cancelled his earlier orders for the attack on the Chocolate Hills and took no further action. Not knowing what to do, and with also a weakened brigade and under the orders of Sitwell, Haggard reported this back to Hammersley.

At 10.30 am Hill issued orders to 6/Royal Inniskilling Fusiliers and 5/Royal Irish Fusiliers (RIF) of 31 Brigade and 7/Royal Dublin Fusiliers (RDF) from 30 Brigade for the attack on Chocolate Hills. He ordered these battalions to cross the Cut, skirt the northern rim of the lake, and then deploy for the attack. 32 Brigade were to advance simultaneously on their left flank to take the W Hills. Hill then went to see Haggard at 32 Brigade headquarters to ensure their support. Haggard would not move his men without Sitwell's sanction as he still came under his command, so Hill then went to see Sitwell. Sitwell would not help without new written orders from divisional headquarters and, anyway, told him that his responsibility was for the protection of the beach and, as his men were already engaged with the Turks to the north, he had none to spare for the attack this early. As Hammersley's orders were for a simultaneous attack on the Chocolate Hills, and without support from 32 Brigade, Hill decided to postpone the attack and refer to Hammersley. It was close to midday when Hill met with Hammersley, who was sitting on Lala Baba hoping to watch the advance. Hearing of the confusion amongst his brigadiers, Hammersley sent a message to Sitwell ordering the immediate advance on both the Chocolate Hills and W Hills.

Wounded awaiting evacuation on B Beach.

Upon receiving the order Sitwell, who remained reluctant to move, began citing many different excuses such as 'heavy casualties', lack of water and heat exhaustion. About the same time an officer from 34 Brigade reported to Sitwell that he had been on patrol for the last three hours and was convinced that the Turks had pulled back as very few were sighted. This was good news, but it did not stop Sitwell from complaining. Hill's battalions had just begun to resume their advance, and Sitwell was ordered to support them, excuses or not. There was an increasing amount of shell fire, and at about 1.30 pm Haggard himself was seriously wounded by a shell splinter. At 2.30 pm Hill, who had established his headquarters near the Cut, received word from his three battalions that they were on the northeasterly edge of the Salt Lake and were being harassed from the direction of Baka Baba and Tekke Tepe by rifle fire and shrapnel. There was no sight of 32 Brigade, who had been ordered to protect this flank. Hill quickly implored Sitwell to help, who then said he would send two battalions to the left flank. In the meantime Hill also sent forward 6/RIF to aid the situation. Hammersley, then hearing the earlier news that there was no support on the left flank, immediately suspended the attack, ordering it to recommence at 5.30 pm. The revised plan for 5.30 pm was now for Sitwell to assault only the Chocolate Hills and not the W Hills. The attack would have extra support from two reserve battalions (6/Lincolns and 6/Borders) from 33 Brigade and artillery support from

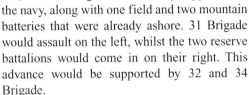

the navy, along with one field and two mountain batteries that were already ashore. 31 Brigade would assault on the left, whilst the two reserve battalions would come in on their right. This advance would be supported by 32 and 34 Brigade.

Hill's 31 Brigade, which had landed at about 8.00 am that morning, were to have a long and trying day. Slow getting ashore, they had to then cross the Cut. The Cut was S shaped, about 15 feet deep with sheer sides, over which Turkish artillery had carefully registered. Every minute it was swept by bursts of shrapnel, and the only way it could be crossed was by a section at a time rushing over it and trusting their luck. Lieutenant Colonel G. Downing, 7/RDF, *who was described as a man of unusual height and girth,* stood in the centre of this muddy, shrapnel-swept zone, quietly twirling his stick.

Lala Baba and the new Cut in 2010.

This site of fearlessness inspired his young men to cross. With almost overpowering heat, a blinding glare from the surface of the Salt Lake, tiredness and already lack of water; it took the Brigade two hours to make the crossing. They then moved onto Hill 10 and by 3.00 pm were beginning their march towards the Chocolate Hills. With orders to approach the hills from the north, the path would take them on a grueling five mile march around the top of the Salt Lake and then south towards their objective. As the crow flies, due east, the ground that would have been covered by a direct approach across the dry lake would only have been a mile and a half. The Brigade was being harassed by the enemy from a distance, which slowed their approach to the objective. When the British artillery barrage started at 5.15 pm, in preparation for the attack fifteen minutes later, they were still half a mile short of their objective.

> *On their right the glistening sheen of the Salt Lake stretched away to the hump of Lala Baba, with the crowded bay beyond, where the naval guns slid forward, flashed, belched, slid back, double-cracked, and rent the air sunder with screaming speed-sound of shells overhead. A few seconds later the hillsides quaked and threw up lumps of chocolate and chocolate powder. When the naval bombardment ceased, the field guns on Lala Baba opened up again.*[16]

Under the cover of the guns the Irish troops continued to edge forward until they were at the foot of the hills. With the light now fading, the 6/Lincolns and 6/Borders arrived, which added the necessary and fresh impetus for Hill's men finally to rush the hills.

With Turkish fire slackening, the Irish launched their final assault on the eastern half of the Chocolate Hill (later named Green Hill), whilst the Lincolns and Borders attacked the western half. Just before the assault Sergeant Robert Clayton, 8/Northumberland Fusiliers, found himself lost; finding another lost sergeant from another battalion, they went on to find their units together. Crossing the Salt Lake they:

> ... saw a Regiment lying in the open about 100 yards in front; we got up to this Regiment, which was the Royal Irish. I saw another Regiment on my left, so I left the Sergeant and doubled over to where it was and found out it was the Inniskilling Fusiliers, so I stopped with them and went on with them to the Hill. They started to charge and I found myself in the Border Regiment. I went up the Hill with them; when I got to the top every Regiment seemed to be mixed up with one another. We got to the top alright; I was with the Dublin Fusiliers when the trench was taken.[17]

The mix up did not prevent the hills falling and, after a stubborn rearguard action fought by a small party of Turks, the majority of the garrison having already withdrawn, both Chocolate and Green Hill fell. By 7.00 pm they were finally in British hands. Captain Percy Hansen, 6/Lincolns, who was to later win a VC, and an officer of the Borders patrolled forward onto the W Hills and found the area clear of Turks. Unfortunately the opportunity to move forward and hold this hill was lost in the chaos of the day and the faded light. Sprawled across their newly captured position, the men fell down exhausted, many slept where they collapsed, whilst others continued to work into the night collecting the wounded or establishing a defensive line of outposts to protect their new gain. At last the British were in possession of this objective, but unfortunately this was the sole gain for the first day ashore for IX Corps.

As had become the pattern, there had been considerable confusion during the attack on the Chocolate Hills. This was commented on in the final report of the Dardanelles Commission, which noted that none of the brigade commanders, Sitwell, Hill or Maxwell, accompanied their troops, remaining about two miles away from the action:

> In the absence of superior military control and guidance on the spot, a force of inexperienced troops, unacquainted with local

conditions and consisting of a number of battalions drawn from five brigades - namely, two from the 30th, three from the 31st, two from the 32nd, two from the 33rd and one from the 34th - must have been lacking in cohesion and co-operation, and the evidence discloses the confusion and delay which resulted from this cause.[18]

In the Official History, Aspinall-Oglander makes a reference to further confusion at this time: which hill was which? When Yilghin Burnu was reached it was understood that this was Chocolate Hill, and Green Hill was Ismail Oglu Tepe, hence the lack of advance later in the day on the real Ismail Oglu Tepe, as it was thought that this was Green Hill. With the earlier confusion of orders and the delays in getting 31 Brigade ashore and in position, this left Sitwell's and Haggard's Brigade's sitting helplessly on and around the beach waiting. Valuable time was being wasted when energy and speed was needed.

Brigadier General Hill arrived at the Chocolate Hills about midnight and began to reorganise the mixed group of battalions that were milling about the area. Ahead lay the prize of the W Hills, but instead of ordering an advance to take the hill, he withdrew 6/Borders and 6/Lincolns to the foot of Chocolate Hill, whilst the remaining battalions from 33 and 34 Brigade, which had not heavily been engaged in the action, were recalled by Sitwell to the beach. No one in IX Corps

Coming ashore on B Beach (Norman Wilkinson).

seemed to understand the need to keep the advantage and to advance to the high ground, not pull back to the beaches. This squandered opportunity was already a characteristic of this operation, if not of the Gallipoli campaign as a whole. Paralysis was firmly setting in with command, despite isolated successes against minimal Turkish opposition. The clock was preciously ticking towards the time that the Turkish reserves would be arriving, and then the high ground would not be uncontested. At this stage most of the Turkish defenders had not even been engaged, so at the end of the day the British were only in possession of the beaches whilst a few Turks remained unchallenged on the high ground, probably looking down in equal confusion across the Suvla plain, trying to understand what the British objectives were.

Kiretch Tepe Ridge

Because of the earlier problems with the beetles grounding, Commander Unwin came aboard the *Jonquil* at 4.00 am on 7 August to dissuade Stopford from making any further landings within Suvla Bay itself. This was reported to be the first news Stopford had of the landings. Unfortunately this change in plan had the effect of delaying the landings of Mahon's 10th Division. It was not until 11.30 am that the first battalion, 6/Royal Munster Fusiliers (RMF), began to disembark and, to add further to the confusion, this battalion would come ashore separated from the rest of 30 Brigade at a place called New A Beach (later named West Beach) near Ghazi Baba. The navy

had recently discovered this as a feasible landing place on the northern edge of Suvla Bay, which later became the main base at Suvla. The rest of 30 and 31 Brigade were landed two miles away on C Beach. From then on progress was slow. Small land-mines had been laid by the Turks on the beach that caused several casualties and added further delays. The second battalion to land, 7/RMF, was sent to a little cove further to the west, for disembarkation at about 1.00 p.m. The third battalion to land, 5/RIF, was not fully ashore till late in the afternoon and the last company of 5/Inniskillings did not land until the following day, and then had to be redirected to West Beach because of the increased Turkish fire on C Beach.

Brigadier General L. L. Nicol's 6/RMF were eventually joined by 7/RMF, who had been put

Kiretch Tepe Ridge, looking towards the Turkish positions.

ashore further south. Together they moved off in the direction of Kiretch Tepe ridge to join up and support the isolated 11/Manchesters, who had been holding the ground here since the night. Upon reaching the Manchesters' position, who were some 800 yards west of a Turkish strongpoint on the summit, a combined attack was quickly organised and led by Major Harry Bates. Already wounded earlier in the day in

the wrist and stomach, he led the battalions forward, crying, *Come on Manchesters, show the Munsters what you are made of!* They got to within 100 yards of the enemy strongpoint; Bates was hit again and killed.[19] No further movement forward was made, however ground on the northern slopes were secured down to the Gulf of Saros. The combined effects of heat, thirst and exhaustion meant that the Manchesters could go no further. At about 9.00 pm they were relieved

A machine gun section disembarking near Ghazi Baba.

by 5/Inniskillings. The 11/Manchesters had by then suffered fifteen officer casualties and the loss of nearly 200 men; a high price, but a valuable position had been won.

Unfortunately Nicol made no attempt to take the line forward, or extend down its southern slopes to the Dorsets' position at Hill 28. Second Lieutenant Ivone Kirkpatrick, 5/Inniskillings, wrote:

> *Having relieved the exhausted Manchesters, we began to dig in. There was no one in front of us but the enemy of whose whereabouts or number we had no knowledge and we must try to dig in, as the staff were of the opinion that we should be shelled in the morning. That night was one of the most arduous and uncomfortable I have ever spent. The soil was hard and rocky; our only digging implements were entrenching tools. We dug all night and when dawn broke had little to show for our labours. Most of the men had succeeded in digging shallow graves with a parapet of loose earth and flints, but some who had struck rocks had not even that... On Sunday everything was absolute peace and quiet, the Turks had in fact withdrawn all their guns, there*

was no shelling and very little rifle fire to be heard. Looking down you could only see a mob of our chaps all round the beaches trying to get water. We were fortunate in our position because the destroyer Grampus *cut one of its own water tanks loose and floated it ashore and supplied us from that. Of course the quantity of water was very little, you got about a pint a day, which with the temperatures verging on a hundred isn't very much.... We all knew that something very wrong was happening that we ought to be advancing not just sitting there.*[20]

IX Corps had suffered 1,700 casualties in the first twenty-four hours; this was almost as many men that Willmer had to defend the area. Major Willmer reported back to the commander of the Turkish *Fifth Army*, General Otto Liman Von Sanders, at 7.00 pm on 7 August, that *no energetic attacks on the enemy's part have taken place. On the contrary, the enemy is advancing timidly.*[21] Willmer begged for reinforcements to arrive as soon as possible, as he believed this lull would not continue and that the British would attack soon. Von Sanders had received the news of the landing at Suvla at 1.40 am on 7 August. As soon as it became clear that Bulair was not threatened and, sharing the same fear that the British would break through soon, he ordered both Turkish *7th* and *12th Divisions*, under the command of Colonel Feyzi Bey *(XVI Corps)* to the south. Ahead of these battle hardened units was a punishing thirty mile forced march, which they began soon after receiving

Major Wilhelm Willmer.

the order to move at 6.30 am. This force would be needed urgently for von Sanders to launch a counterattack which he wanted to happen as early as possible on 8 August. He directed the *7th Division* to go into the line north of the Sari Bair ridge where the Anzac offensive was threatening, whilst directing the *12th Division* against Suvla. As this attack could not happen for almost another day, this gave the British almost a whole day to take advantage of the situation. The British were only three miles away from their goal; the Turks thirty miles! No one stood in between.

1 War Diary: 32 Infantry Brigade Headquarters (National Archives: WO95/4299).
2 Priestman, E. Y., *With a B-P. Scout in Gallipoli,* (London: Routledge & Son, 1917), pp.161-162.
3 Hargrave, J., *The Suvla Bay Landing* (London: Macdonald, 1964), p.67.
4 Ferrers-Guy, M.C., *The Lancashire Fusiliers Annual,* (Dublin: Sackville Press, 1916), p.225.
5 The Naval Review, Vol.II, 1916, *Dardanelles Notes* – HMS Prince George, p.251.
6 Aspinall-Oglander, Brig-Gen C.F., *Military Operations Gallipoli,* Vol.I, (London: Heinemann, 1929), p.235.
7 The Naval Review, Op cit. p.251.
8 Notts & Derbys Annual, 1922 – Notes from Lt-Col Murray and Captain Loyd.
9 Poem by Signaller R. Ecclestone, 9/Sherwood Foresters.
10 Wylly, Col. H.C., *The Green Howards in the Great War 1914-1919*, (Richmond: Butler & Tanner, 1926).
11 Priestman, E. Y., *With a B-P. Scout in Gallipoli*, (London: Routledge & Son, 1917), pp.166-167.
12 Ferrers-Guy, Op. cit., p.226.
13 Kannengiesser, H., *The Campaign in Gallipoli* (London: Hutchinson & Co, 1927), pp.205-6.
14 National Army Museum: G. Boucher, 34th Brigade Collection, p.3.
15 Hargrave, J., Op. cit., p.95.
16 *ibid*, p.126.
17 National Army Museum: R. Clayton, 34th Brigade Collection, p.3.
18 *The Final Report of the Dardanelles Commission*, Part II, Section 86, (HMSO, 1918). The commission was an investigation into the Gallipoli campaign. Witnesses involved in the expedition were interviewed, with its final report issued in 1919. It concluded that the expedition was poorly planned and executed and that difficulties had been underestimated, problems which were exacerbated by supply shortages and by personality clashes and procrastination at high levels.
19 Major Harry Cecil Bates, 11/Manchesters, is commemorated on the Helles Memorial, panels 158-170.
20 IWM Document Collection: I. Kirkpatrick manuscript.
21 Sanders, Liman von., *Five Years in Turkey,* (US Naval Institute, 1927).

Chapter 3

DAY OF REST - SUNDAY 8 AUGUST

The goddess of victory held the door to success wide open

Following a quiet night, the morning of the 8th was absolutely still. Out of a cloudless sky the sun was shining fiercely. The enemy's guns were silent. Apart from an occasional rifle-shot on Kiretch Tepe there was not a sound of war. The sand-dunes near the Cut were crowded with resting troops. The shores of the bay were fringed with naked figures bathing... It was now broad daylight and the situation in Suvla Bay was verging on chaos.[1]

Major General Sir Alexander Godley later remarked to Admiral Sir Roger Keyes:

You can imagine my feelings when I watched my men fighting like tigers, doing practically the impossible, and at the same time could see, within three miles, the 10th and 11th Divisions loafing and bathing.

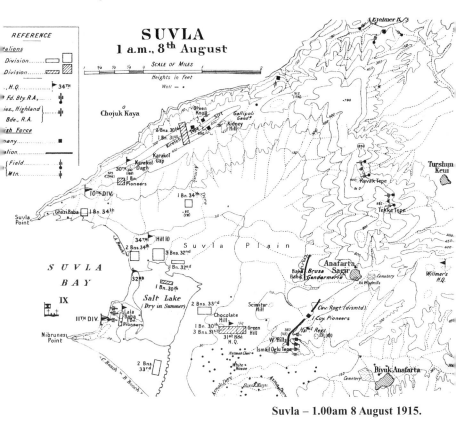

Suvla – 1.00am 8 August 1915.

These statements were not wholly true, for although some men were bathing, these were men from the ancillary units, as the infantry not in the firing line or supports were busy making up fatigue parties. British War Correspondent Ellis Ashmead-Bartlett, who witnessed the landing, recorded: *no firm hand appeared to control this mass of men suddenly dumped on an unknown shore.*[2] The Suvla landing was going astray, and crucial time was being wasted. Stopford and his IX Corps Headquarters had been landed overnight and established themselves near Ghazi Baba. The afternoon before Hamilton sent his first message to Stopford:

> *4.20 pm. GHQ to 9th Corps. Have only received one telegram from you. Chief glad to hear enemy opposition weakening, and knows you will take advantage of this to press on rapidly. Prisoners state landing a surprise, so take every advantage before you are forestalled.*

Very soon the Turkish reserves would be upon them; then the real fight would begin.

With the opportunity of the relative calm, Hammersley was keen to push forward. However Sitwell and Hill were keener to rest and reorganise before making any further movement into the surrounding hills. All should have known the urgency to get inland to secure the heights, but consolidation was the name of the game. Resigned to the fact that little could be done without rest and reorganisation, Hammersley, with no other reason than to clear the beach of the large

Lighters at Suvla Bay.

number of troops there, ordered Sitwell to advance two miles inland to occupy the line of farm buildings at the far end of the Suvla plain. This area was known as Sulajik, and rested on the lower foothills of the Tekke Tepe ridge, but once there they would still be two miles from its crest. At the worst, however, this put Sitwell in a better position to take the surrounding hills than where his Brigade was in the morning. Still, opportunities to continue an easy advance were needlessly being squandered.

On Kiretch Tepe there has been no movement forward from the time the 11/Manchesters had been relieved. With no orders or knowledge of the general plan, or who was out in front, Brigadier General Nicol, who now commanded the troops on the ridge, continued to dig in as best he could. Even though there was little Turkish resistance, Mahon believed that they could not advance any further without artillery support. He duly reported this to Stopford. There were in fact three companies of *Gelibolu Gendarmerie*, under the command of Captain Kadri Bey, on the ridge, who were placed in short lengths of hastily dug trenches with no barbed wire. These details were not known to Mahon, although what he did know was that whoever was in front had been putting up a determined fight the day before. The 10th Division actually landed without their artillery, which was either still in England or in Egypt, so any fire support Mahon needed had to be given by the navy or the few batteries of 11th Division that had come ashore the day before.

Stopford was aware that the Turkish reserves from Bulair could be on the high ground by the afternoon of 8 August, so he knew the

paramount importance to push forward along Kiretch Tepe and across the Suvla plain to take the heights of Tekke Tepe. However, after receiving reports from the divisional generals about the men being tired, the sheer length of the line that they were having trouble establishing and the concern about the lack of artillery support and stores which had been landed, he decided that his priority must be safeguarding the beachhead, the operation's primary objective. Even though Turkish defense was minimal or in some places nonexistent, Stopford would order no advance until the evening of 8 August at the earliest. He did not want to commit to a battle until his troops were suitably fed and rested, and even then the objectives detailed for capture came with the qualifying phrase, *if possible*. At 7.10 am he ordered Mahon to entrench the northern flank to protect against any Turkish attack; the offensive was becoming a defensive action far too quickly. Without the Tekke Tepe ridge in British hands, Suvla would be far from secure.

At this time Hammersley and most of his men were still just a stone's throw away from the beach and, apart from the early fighting at Lala Baba and Hill 10 and the capture of the Chocolate Hills the previous night, little movement inland had been made. Between the beach and Tekke Tepe the area was not only empty of British, but also Turkish troops who, with the exception of those on Kiretch Tepe, had pulled back the previous night. Willmer feared losing his artillery, so had withdrawn his guns the previous day.

Captain John Coleridge, 11th Division staff officer, was sent out early on the 8 August by Divisional HQ to make a general reconnaissance to ascertain the troops positions and impress the importance of gaining the W Hills before nightfall:

> *I left D.H.Q. about 9 a.m. and walked towards Chocolate Hill. En route I passed the line of trenches dug from the Salt Lake to the sea, and found the 6th Lincolns and 6th Borders coming into them, having been relieved north of Chocolate Hill by the 7th South Staffords. The men were quite cheerful, and I was told that the Brigadier (Maxwell) had gone to Chocolate Hill. On arriving there I found the place crammed with men, both 31st and 33rd Brigades. The men were tired and thirsty, but not depressed, and there was plenty of bully and biscuits to eat. I met Generals Maxwell and Hill, and we went to Hill 50 [Green Hill] together. The enemy was very quiet, just a casual bullet now and then. The Brigadiers both agreed that there were very few Turks on W. Hill, and that the men, given a few hours rest and some water, could well go on and attack W. Hill. I warned them to expect orders. I then went northward, and saw the South Staffords. The troops were in good order. They had, I think, got a little water from Ali Bey Cheshme. I believe, but will not swear to it, that the South Stafford were already on Hill 70, anyhow they were good fighting value. I then turned rather more westwards, and crossed the scene of the previous day's fighting. There were a few corpses and some equipment lying about (not in excess), but most of the dead had been buried. I then came to the 6th Yorks. The battalion only had five officers with it, and the men were distinctly demoralised. In my opinion the battalion wanted relief. I then visited the West*

Ridings, York and Lancaster (practically untouched) and the West Yorks. I stayed with them some time and watched the Dorsets have a set-to with some Turks and progress slightly. I did not see the Manchesters. I then went to Hill 10, and saw Colonel Minogue and Shuttleworth. They were both confident they could get on when ordered, provided they were not asked to cover too wide a front and that the troops from Chocolate Hill moved forward simultaneously. They agreed with me that the 6th Yorks were of no fighting value. I then went towards the Beach and saw the two Fusilier battalions, both somewhat shaken, especially the Lancashire Fusiliers. I did not see the Brigadier (Sitwell).[3]

Upon receiving Hammersley's order, during the morning of 8 August, to advance the line, Sitwell reluctantly ordered 31 and 32 Brigade forward to establish a line from where 30 Brigade were positioned on Kiretch Tepe, through Sulajik to Chocolate Hill. This would have the effect of establishing a connected line from north to south and at last filling the dangerous gap that had formed in the Suvla plain. For the advance, Sitwell verbally told Lieutenant Colonel Minogue, now in command of 32 Brigade after Haggard's wounding, that the troops were *not intended to fight* but merely to entrench their new position. Even though no pitch battles were expected during this advance it showed a mindset, from Stopford down to his brigadiers, of passive lethargy that was soon to spread throughout the Corps. Unfortunately, despite no Turkish resistance, the order was carried out exactly; the only movement that day was a general movement forward before the line stopped. Ahead the high ground still lay undefended.

Hill, who was still in position on the Chocolate and Green Hills,

Digging in near Chocolate Hill.

continued to entrench and improve the positions. This continued unopposed. In front of Hill's position the whole Anafarta Spur lay there for the taking; this opportunity would never present itself again. As Sitwell advanced across the Suvla plain to Hills northern flank, he too met no Turkish opposition, which was fortunate as he did not want a fight. In front of him the Tekke Tepe ridge also lay undefended, a prize that was also never to be won. The only enemy was the tiredness of the troops, many who had not slept for about fifty-two hours since leaving Imbros. Water had become very scarce and the main ration of bully beef caused more problems, as it did not react well to the heat, which turned it into a liquid, and the salt in the beef only made one even thirstier. With no or little water arriving in the firing lines at this time, men had to be sent back ladened with water bottles to the beach. Water now was being pumped ashore but at a slow rate, leaving men queuing for hours to get a bottle filled. Water would continue to be a logistical problem for the British until the end of the campaign.

Even without opposition the advance did not go well. Lieutenant Colonel Hannay's 5/Dorsets did not advance, as he was ordered to wait for Nicol's 30 Brigade, on the Kiretch Tepe ridge, to advance. However 30 Brigade had not received any orders to move, so remained where they were. On the right the 6/East Yorks advanced as planned to connect up with the troops on Chocolate Hill, securing a forward position by

Queuing for Water at Suvla Bay.

late morning on Hill 70. To their left a company of 9/West Yorks were in touch; however the rest of the Brigade was separated someway to the north. The 8/West Ridings were entrenching near the Sulajik huts, whilst 6/York & Lancs were halted on the plain between Sulajik and Hill 10. It is doubted if Minogue knew how advanced the 6/East Yorks and 9/West Yorks were, both of which were in dominant positions on the northern slopes of the Anafarta Spur. Scouts from both these battalions had pushed onto the high ground near the village of Anafarta Sagir, where they spotted a recently evacuated trench near Baka Baba, and small parties of Turks retiring in the direction of the village *apparently moving to escape the shell fire of the ships*, as Lieutenant Colonel Henry Moore of the 6/East Yorks recorded in his report written that day. He finished the report by saying, *nothing could be seen of any formed body of the enemy or any sign that the hill* [Tekke Tepe] *was occupied by him.* This valuable information was reported back by signal to Brigade HQ on Hill 10. Actually two officers and a signals corporal of the battalion claimed to have reached the summit of Tekke Tepe during 8 August, a fact not known by Hamilton at the time.

Lieutenant John Still, 6/East Yorks, wrote to Hamilton after reading his diary, published in 1920.

> *As you justly say, anyone with half an eye could see Tekke Tepe was the key to the whole position. Even I, a middle-aged amateur who had done a bit of big game shooting and knocking about,*

> *saw it at once. We reconnoitred it, sent an officer and my signaller corporal to climb it, and got through to Brigade H.Q. the message giving our results. I sent it myself. The hill was then empty.*[4]

Still's account was later confirmed by another young officer of the battalion. Still had forgotten that the hill had been reconnoitered by two officers at the time; one was killed in the main attack, but the second, Lieutenant James Underhill, 6/East Yorks, had survived and wrote to Still.

> *Being a qualified land surveyor, and experienced in the use and*

71

construction of maps and the knowledge of the country, I was well able to keep notes of our positions and was the officer mentioned in your letter who took the patrol up Tekke Tepe. In fact I still have your signal corporal's field glasses, which I took from him while on the hill, my own being smashed by a rifle bullet whilst using them on this patrol. Again, while you say Tekke Tepe was not occupied, it was held very lightly by patrols. We ran into two of them before reaching the top; out of one we bagged two Turks, the other escaped us. There were also three short lengths of partially dug trenches, unoccupied while we were there, but showing signs of most recent occupation.[5]

Even if Minogue was unaware of the situation ahead, he, as well as Sitwell, were both sticking by their orders not to advance any further regardless. At 11.00 am GHQ informed Stopford that an air reconnaissance by the Royal Naval Air Service had reported the encouraging news that there was no Turkish movement to the east of Tekke Tepe, ending the message by saying: *Hope this indicated you will be able to gain a footing early on the Tekke Tepe ridge, importance of which you will realise.* Now men on the ground and the air had confirmed some very encouraging news, so the advance should have

The ground lay for the taking – August 1915.

been straightforward to enable the capture of the Tekke Tepe ridge that morning. Stopford, acknowledging the promising news, forwarded this newly arrived information to his divisions, ordering them to continue the advance, but then he added the proviso only if the ground was proved to be lightly held. He did not want a fight:

> It is of the greatest importance to forestall the enemy on the high ground north of Anafarta Sagir and on the spur running thence to Ismail Oglu Tepe. If you find the ground lightly held by the enemy push on. But in view of want of adequate artillery support I do not want you to attack an entrenched position held in strength.

At noon Stopford then sent a message to GHQ:

> Heavy fighting yesterday and unavoidable delay landing artillery make me consider it inadvisable to call on troops to attack a strongly entrenched position without adequate support.

The mockery of this was that there were no strongly entrenched positions, as recent reconnaissances have proved.

On Imbros Hamilton was becoming troubled by the lack of progress at Suvla. Hamilton's earlier focus had been the Anzac attack on the Sari

Bair ridge, where he had been receiving regular progress communiqués; but from Suvla he had only received two messages. The last, sent by Stopford, at 5.10 am on 8 August, announced the capture of Chocolate Hill, this already being twenty four hours late. No other information of progress was sent, so no news was now being assumed as bad news. Golden opportunities were being lost due to the perceived lethargy at Suvla and intervention was needed. Hamilton had already dispatched Lieutenant Colonel Cecil Aspinall, one of his staff officers, to discover first-hand what was happening at Suvla; were the British now on the ridges? Aspinall was accompanied by Lieutenant Colonel Maurice Hankey, Secretary to the Committee of Imperial Defence, who was to report on the progress of the campaign to the British Cabinet. After nearly a four hour wait for a boat, they left for Suvla, arriving about 11.30 am, five and a half hours after receiving his instructions from Hamilton. About the same time that Aspinall and Hankey were coming ashore at Suvla, Hamilton had received another cable from Stopford that said:

> *Consider Major General Hammersley and troops under him deserve great credit for result attained against strenuous opposition and great difficulty. I must now consolidate.*

Stopford appeared satisfied with the first day's results and now was digging in; not the offensive spirit Hamilton probably wanted to hear.

It was now nearly midday; after reading Stopford's last signal about consolidating when he should have been on the heights, exacerbated by not having heard anything from Aspinall and Hankey at this time, Hamilton decided to see Suvla for himself. However there appeared no ships available to take him, Hamilton wrote in his diary: *it was not a question of convenience or inconvenience but one of preventing a Commander-in-Chief from exercising his functions during battle.* Excuse or not, as Hamilton was to receive blame later for not intervening at Suvla sooner, he used this time to signal Stopford back saying: *You and your troops have indeed done splendidly. Please tell Hammersley how much we hope from his able and rapid advance.* This was not the time to congratulate Hammersley. Yes, a landing on an unopposed shore had been achieved, but the new port was far from secure, with none of the major objectives having been taken. Hamilton really had no idea what was happening at Suvla, but he would soon be fuming when he eventually did reach its shores.

Aspinall and Hankey at first found the calm and inactivity at Suvla hopeful, assuming it meant the fighting was now far away in the midst of the hills. There was no shelling and only the occasional rifle shot high up on the Kiretch Tepe ridge. As they walked along the beach this optimism did not last; they were soon warned to keep their heads down as the front line was only a few hundred yards away! Leaving Hankey on the beach, Aspinall, now concerned, strode off to find Stopford, who was back aboard the *Jonquil*, apparently in excellent spirits, well satisfied with progress. He greeted Aspinall by saying: *Well, Aspinall the men have done splendidly, and have been magnificent.* When Aspinall pointed out that the men had not reached the high ground, Stopford replied: *No, but they are ashore.* Aspinall begged Stopford for an immediate advance to take the high ground before the Turkish reserve from Bulair got there first. Stopford agreed with the need for urgency but believed his Corps could not advance without giving men rest and also bringing ashore adequate artillery. Stopford was maybe over cautious, but he firmly stood by his and his Chief of Staff's belief that artillery was paramount in a successful advance and no attack would occur until his artillery was ready. But Stopford did not need to 'attack', as there were only a few Turkish piquets reported on Tekke Tepe at this time; it was a rapid advance, not firepower, that was needed to take the high ground. Stopford who, incidentally, was probably a little shaken by Aspinall's earlier visit, went ashore to visit the beach and divisional headquarters, only to find Hammersley was out. After a briefing from one of Hammersley's staff officers, it was reported that:

> *The various commanders were confident that an attack was feasible. He* [Stopford] *seemed very pleased and said that we must attack at once, lest the Turks forestalled us. The words he finished up with I remember; he said, 'It may cause us casualties, but not one tenth of those we shall suffer if we delay'. He seemed perfectly confident, and said General Hammersley was to go and see him on the* Jonquil *directly he returned to camp.*[6]

An order, ready by 5.30 pm, was drafted by Stopford and Hammersley for a night attack to capture the W Hills and Anafarta Sagir before first light on 9 August. At last Stopford was showing an offensive spirit that had been lacking so far. But was this going to be too late? Worried by their earlier meeting, Aspinall sent the following message to GHQ:

> *Just been ashore, where I found all quiet. No rifle fire, no artillery fire, and apparently no Turks. IX Corps resting. Feel confident that golden opportunities are being lost and look upon the situation as serious.*

This cable did not reach Imbros until the following day. In the meantime, at about 4.30 pm, Hamilton had arrived at Suvla aboard the

Triad. Boarding HMS *Chatham*, the flagship of Vice Admiral John de Robeck, who was in command of the landing fleet, Hamilton was able to meet Aspinall and the naval staff face to face. It was here, on that afternoon of 8 August, nearly two days after the landing had commenced, that Hamilton gained a clear picture of events. He was furious. Along with Commodore Roger Keyes they raced across to the *Jonquil* to challenge Stopford; it was now 6.30 pm.

Hamilton finally boarded the *Jonquil* to meet with Stopford. All were becoming increasingly aware of the clock ticking and the vital importance of gaining a foothold on the heights, but intervention was going to be too late. The meeting lasted five minutes. Stopford explained the reasons for the delay and, without adequate artillery, did not want to enter in *to a regular battle*. Hamilton then went ashore to meet up with Hammersley on Lala Baba, but without Stopford, who allegedly declined to join him due to his leg still hurting. Hamilton insisted that an advance be made immediately and that at least one battalion should be on Tekke Tepe by dawn. The Tekke Tepe heights were his priority; the W Hills and Anafarta Sagir could wait. Stopford's IX Corps had twenty two battalions at Suvla against approximately three Turkish battalions; the situation was quickly going to change and all the advantages that the British had had during the previous two days were to be lost.

As 32 Brigade was already thought to be concentrated at Sulajik, Hammersley thought this brigade was best placed for the immediate advance, along with the divisional pioneers, the 6/East Yorks, as

Vice Admiral John de Robeck and General Sir Ian Hamilton.

they were believed to be the freshest battalion. The focus of the attack would now be the Tekke Tepe ridge and not the W Hills and Anafarta Sagir as previously planned. Hamilton's intervention here actually resulted in further delays, as a new set of orders had to be sent out. It took the leading battalions of 32 Brigade until 4.00 am to begin their attack on Tekke Tepe instead of midnight. Still not knowing the exact whereabouts of all his battalions, which were spread across the plain, Minogue sent out runners to concentrate them all on Sulajik by 10.30 pm, before the advance. This would have a damaging effect, because 9/West Yorks were already 1,000 yards east of Sulajik, near Baka Baba and well placed to advance on Tekke Tepe early. The 6/East Yorks were also close by, on Scimitar Hill, and equally well placed for a direct advance on the heights. Well placed they may be, but not as well placed as they were to capture Stopford's original objectives of the W Hills and Anafarta Sagir. Here they were already on the undefended foothills of the spur which could have spelled the capture of both of these objectives that afternoon. Unfortunately another effect of Hamilton intervention was the unknowing sacrifice of these objectives that would cost so many lives trying to capture them in the coming days. With Scimitar Hill abandoned to the Turks, it would cost 33 Brigade 1,500 men to try and retake it the following day, and twelve days later IX Corps would lose over 5,000 trying to capture the same ground.

The 8/West Ridings were already at Sulajik and it was not long before 6/York & Lancs joined them from near Hill 10; however, due to the Brigade Major and the runners not being able to find them, it was many hours before the messages finally got to the 6/East Yorks and 9/West Yorks. Lieutenant John Still, wrote that *the Brigade Major was lost! Good God why didn't they send a man who knew the country? He was lost, lost, lost and it drives one almost mad to think of it. Excuse Me.* When the East Yorks were eventually found, sometime just before midnight, it was probably more by luck than guidance. Then, it took the battalion almost three hours to pack up and find their way in the dark across the difficult ground that separated them from Sulajik. The time was now 2.30 am. Waiting another hour for the 9/West Yorks to arrive, who did not show, Minogue eventually decided to issue the order to advance. The first objective was Tekke Tepe and then Kavak Tepe; the race had begun. Minogue ordered Lieutenant Colonel Henry Moore's 6/East Yorks, supposedly the freshest battalion available, to push on at once with half of 67 Field Company Royal Engineers, under the command of Major Francis Brunner. The 8/West Ridings would advance on their left flank. The remaining two battalions would follow as soon as 9/West Yorks arrived. Unfortunately the West Yorks had become lost in the scrubby ground around Abrikja and Baka Baba and were not found until a runner stumbled across them at 5.00 am, 9 August!

Major Francis Brunner, Royal Engineers, killed on Teke Tepe.

In half an hour the first rays of dawn would be showing; however it would be too late; precisely two hours too late. When the 6/East Yorks received the message to advance they were in an extended line, digging in again, as no one told them they were expected to lead an attack. The men were very tired and many were asleep after having had an exhausting night already. At about 3.30 am the company commanders received their orders and were told that the Battalion was to seize Tekke Tepe, whilst the West Ridings were to attack Kavak Tepe on the left. Lieutenant Colonel Moore, realising that it would take some time to reorganise his men and noting that time was of the essence, immediately started off with his headquarters and D Company, instructing the other three companies to follow as soon as possible. It was now eight hours since Hamilton insisted that at least one battalion was established on the

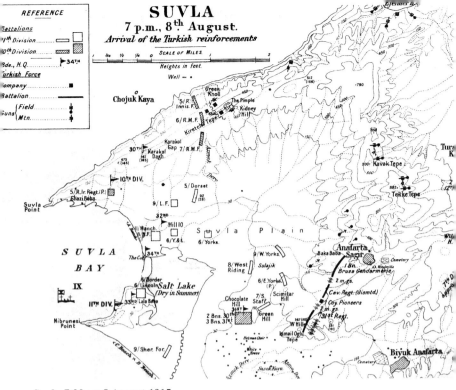

SUVLA

7 p.m., 8th August.

Arrival of the Turkish reinforcements

Suvla 7.00pm 8 August 1915.

crest. By the time dawn came Moore was only on the lower foothills, with the heights of Tekke Tepe still looming above. As he continued to climb Turkish resistance was soon woken; Moore losing one officer and several men to wounds. The advance, in the semi darkness over unfamiliar, rough and steep terrain, was difficult even without a hidden enemy firing at them. The scrub was dense and prickly and movement was severely impaired. The advance continued slowly, in single columns, so it was not until 4.00 am that Moore's men began to observe the summit, which then was still some way off. By 5.00 am, as the first golden rays of dawn were highlighting the summit, Moore's extended party of men had almost edged to their goal, reaching the head of a small ravine. It was then apparent that the Turks were appearing in larger numbers, and heavy rifle fire was opened up from the front and flanks, sweeping Moore back down into the twilight below. He had run into two lead battalions of Feyzi Bey's reinforcements. Overwhelmed, D Company withdrew in confusion. The remnants of the company made a couple of stands to try and stem the Turkish onslaught, but it was hopeless with so few men. Retreating down the slopes they were picked off one by one as they retraced their steps back down the twisting ravine. Tekke Tepe had lain virtually undefended for two days and now the prize was lost. The Turks had won the race. Colonel Hans Kannengiesser, commander 9th Division, wrote: *during the whole of the 8th August the goddess of victory held the door to success wide open for Stopford, but he would not enter*[7]; by the time Hamilton eventually intervened it was too late.

The leading elements of Feyzi Bey's reinforcements had began to arrive, near Büyükanafarta, a little earlier than the British expected, during the night of 7 August. However, the bulk of the troops did not make an appearance until the morning of 8 August. The Turks were equally exhausted, this was one of the hottest days of the summer and the men had been forced to march over thirty miles in an oppressive heat. Feyzi asked for time to rest his men, but von Sanders wanted them to counterattack immediately. Feyzi objected, because his men were tired and there was no available artillery support; however this stood him no good. Von Sanders immediately removed him from command, and replaced him with Mustafa Kemal, commander of the *19th Division.* By 9.45 pm on 8 August Kemal was now responsible for the whole Anafarta section. Kemal had a great advantage over Feyzi as he knew this area intimately, having fought in the Anzac area since 25 April. He rode out that night to view the Suvla situation for himself and to examine the condition of Feyzi Bey's men. He came to the same conclusion: that the troops were completely exhausted and suspended the attack until the morning of 9 August.

Moore's men were attacked by elements of Lieutenant Colonel Selahattin Adil's *12th Division*, who was sent forward to make contact with the British advanced line at Suvla, some two kilometres away from their positions. Adil positioned the Division on the high ground to the north, from Kidney Hill to Tekke Tepe. South of here Willmer remained by Baka Baba and the W Hills, whilst Colonel Halil's *7th Division* was pushed in south of Willmer to aid the Turks on the Abdul Rahman Spur, who were opposing the Anzac breakout. With the high ground around Suvla now seemingly secured by Adil's men, Kemal could focus on the threat to Sari Bair ridge, where the main Anzac attack was taking place.

The *12th Division* began their advance at 4.00 am on 9 August and did not expect to run into the British so quickly. Adil's experienced *35 Regiment* was the first to come into contact with the leading elements of 32 Brigade, namely Moore's 6/East Yorks. As the Turks streamed over the hill, shrapnel from his *12th Artillery Regiment* was opened on the leading groups of the British. Moore's men suffered heavily, as D Company got cut off. Of approximately thirty men who were nearing the top of Tekke Tepe, only Lieutenant Colonel Henry Moore, Major

Francis Brunner, Captain Richard Elliot, Lieutenant John Still, Corporal William Blanchflower and Private Edward Moor escaped. Captain Richard Elliot, wrote of the events:

We started about hundred strong and came under heavy rifle fire from both flanks as we approached the foothills and particularly from the position from which we had been withdrawn during the previous night. Captain Grant, commanding D Company, was hit and I took charge. At the foothills Colonel Moore gave me the necessary orders and the position I was to make for. We started up Tekke Tepe about sixty strong. Lieutenant Wilson, who was killed, was leading the party on my left and I leading the other party. Lieutenant Rawstorne was to collect men who came later and to join up on my right. When about half way up the hill we extended, having come under rifle fire from the higher ground above. Nearly at the top we found that a deep fold separated us from the top and the hill. It was impossible to advance further; the enemy was in large numbers round by on the east of the hill. I waited for reinforcements. We were now about thirty strong and under heavy rifle fire. Lieutenant Colonel Moore, Lieutenant Still and Major Brunner RE came up about fifteen minutes later with some more men and I reported to Colonel Moore that the enemy was above us in very superior numbers and, after considering, he ordered us to retire with the remnants. I took charge of a small party to cover the retirement where necessary. When nearly at the bottom of the hill we were surrounded and Colonel Moore ordered us to surrender. When we had surrendered Colonel Moore made an attempt to sit on the bank of the ravine and was bayoneted through the back; he died about ten minutes later. Lieutenant Rawstorne, who I did not see at all until we were at the HQ of General Liman von Sanders, appears to have taken up about ten men. The men captured consisted of about six taken with Lieutenant Rawstorne, a number of men who did not get beyond the foothills, some who did not get the order to retire and three or four signalers and other men who

Lt Col Henry Moore, 6/East Yorks, killed on Tekke Tepe.

arrived down safely with Colonel Moore, Lieutenant Still and myself. Whilst up the hill I could see the remainder of the Battalion being attacked so we could not expect reinforcements and I was powerless to help them.[8]

Another officer from the 6/East Yorks also witnessed the affair, Lieutenant Eric Halse, who was following on later with the rest of the battalion. By the tone of his letter, written in September 1915, Halse was obviously embittered about the performance of the staff, which was most probably shared amongst many. An example of poor Staff work was the way this 'brigade' attack ended up to be only a 'battalion' attack, which in turn filtered down to being just a company advance. Halse wrote:

We were supposed to attack before dawn, but owing to orders being late it was broad daylight. The attacked position had not been reconnoitered, the men were dead beat, having had no sleep since we landed and were utterly done. However we had to obey orders. We were allowed to reach half way up the slope by the Turks and there received it in the neck. The Turks were strongly entrenched and were about four to our one. They also had a machine gun enfilading us on our left and a party of men enfilading us on our right. They had us in a trap pure and simple. The regiments that were supposed to be on our left and right flanks had gone somewhere else. We lost 15 officers and 300 men in half an hour. Human nature could stand no more. One Company was captured all together and the rest turned and ran. I don't blame the men for it was their first time under fire and really men could not be expected to endure it. I collected a few men and we made a bit of a stand further back, but eventually had to retire back to the reserves who were a mile and a quarter behind instead of 400 yards. The staff work was damned rotten

and nearly all the Staff officers are incapable, inefficient fools. They take no interest in anything at all. The only thing they care about is their own damn skins, if they are safe it doesn't matter about the rest of us.[9]

Lieutenant James Underhill, 6/East Yorks, in a letter to John Still, wrote in similar vein:

The great fundamental point was that Tekke Tepe should have been taken on the evening of August 8. That this could and would have been done had there not been a lamentable failure of the Staff I think goes unquestioned by those of us who had an accurate knowledge of the conditions; it was the loss of the Gallipoli campaign. I am even of the opinion that had the staff work not been so rotten, and that the attack in the early morning of August 9 been by three battalions instead of us alone, it might have been successful. If you remember, the attack was to have been a brigade affair, three battalions in attack with one in support. The supports (the West Ridings) were there, but where the other two battalions were, God alone knows. I think all of K's Army who took part in this landing and the following few days felt it intensely that they were blamed by the Staff for the failure on the grounds of being green troops. Compared with later experiences in France, the 11th and 10th Division fought as well as any troops ever did, be they Regulars or otherwise, and I am sure that those of us who had the honour to belong to either the 11th or 10th Divisions feel grateful to you for coming out plainly and placing the blame where it so justly belongs.[10]

Limit of Moore's advance. Slope of Tekke Tepe near Baka Baba.

Suvla 7.00pm, 9th August.

So what of the other battalions? About this time 8/West Ridings, who also started off late, were approaching the foothills when the Turks begun their counterattack. Lieutenant Colonel Horace Johnston and his second-in-command were killed, and the supporting machine guns that belonged to the 6/East Yorks were rushed and captured. The resistance from the remaining men quickly collapsed, the survivors scattered back into the plain below. Over fifty men in the advance were known to have been captured during this action; the vast majority were from the 6/East Yorks. The 9/West Yorks were the next to feel the force of the sudden Turkish attack, as they fell back to Sulajik with heavy losses. They too made a stand by two stone huts, reinforced by two companies of 6/York & Lancs, where the line was held, although the Turks got within forty yards of overrunning 32 Brigade HQ. North of the West Yorks was a gap, but this was soon plugged by 159 Brigade, 53rd (Welsh) Division, who had landed on C Beach that morning. The Turks, luckily for the British, did not press home their attack.

Hamilton had observed the battle from the *Triad*. He wrote in his diary:

My heart has grown tough amidst the struggles of the Peninsula but the misery of this scene well nigh broke it. Words are of no use.

Hill 971

Short of water and blind for sleep,
After that night the men felt done
As we watched the dawn begin to creep;
But orders reached us on the run
To move and take Hill Nine Seven One.

By some mischance it reached us late,
So we lost the dark of a precious hour,
Lost first trick in the game with fate;
While against the sky the hill's black tower
Loomed with a sinister sense of power.

Time was short, and orders pressed;
D Company moved on alone,
While the major stayed to bring up the rest,
Across the fields where the bullets moan,
Into the rough of tumbled stone.

We marched across the twi' lit slopes,
Eight officers and some seven score men;
It looked the most forlorn of hopes,
And in my heart I wondered then
How many would ever come back again.

Two officers fell in the first half mile
To dropping shots from the eastern flank,
And sadly thinned were the rank and file
When we breathed in cover a little while
And left our packs on a rocky bank.

Then up, up by the winding ways,
Through streams of boulders and clumps of thorn;
The weary body its brain obeys;
And the men pushed up through the stony maze,
Pushed on in the grey of dawn.

Up! Up! while the bullets sing.
The fire comes faster as up we go;
Hitting the rocks with a vicious sting,
Echo re-echo the gullies ring,
And the plain looks flat below.

The line grew thinner and straggled wide
As one by one our fellows dropped
To a flanking fire from either side;

But the rest climbed on like a flowing tide,
And only the wounded stopped.
Still up and up, yet higher and higher,
Over the rocks, an endless climb,
Under an ever-increasing fire,
Hot with the glow of helpless ire,
Lost to all sense of time.

The enemy fired without a rest,
From right, from left, from straight ahead;
The bullets sang like a hornet's nest,
And swept our men from the open crest,
Till many were wounded and most were dead.

So we drew away and turned to go,
For we only mustered about a score;
And we looked right down a mile below,
Where the fight, like a moving picture show,
Sent up a distant roar.

Then down that dreadful mountain-side
The Colonel went with broken pride,
Finding a way with the handful left
Where a gully cut a winding cleft
That helped our path to hide.

The Turks fired down on the beaten men:
Half-way down we had shrunk to ten;
And they claimed as prisoners only five;
These were all who came out alive
At the foot of that winding glen.[11]

1 Aspinall-Oglander, Brig-Gen C.F., *Military Operations Gallipoli*, Vol.I., (London: Heinemann, 1929).
2 Ashmead-Bartlett, E., *The Uncensored Dardanelles* (London: Hutchinson, 1928).
3 Coleridge, J.D., quoted in Major Dudley Ward, *History of the 53rd Welsh Division* (Cardiff: Western Mail, 1927), p.23.
4 Letter by J. Still, published in *The Times*, October 1923, (King's College London - Hamilton Collection:7/2/62).
5 Letter by J.T. Underhill (King's College London: Hamilton Collection: 7/2/62). Published in *The Times*, titled *The Suvla Bay Failure – New Evidence*, 14 February 1925.
6 Coleridge, J.D., quoted in Major Dudley Ward, *History of the 53rd Welsh Division* (Cardiff: Western Mail, 1927), p.24.
7 Hans Kannengiesser Pasha, *The Campaign in Gallipoli* (London: Hutchinson & Co, 1927), p.220.
8 Elliot, R.D., Officers Capture Reports (National Archives).
9 The Great War Archive, University of Oxford http://www.oucs.ox.ac.uk/ww1lit/gwa; ©Jerome Farrell.
10 Letter by J.T. Underhill (King's College London: Hamilton Collection: 7/2/62). Published in *The Times*, titled *The Suvla Bay Failure – New Evidence*, 14 February 1925 .
11 Poem by Lieutenant J. Still, 6/East Yorks. The title Hill 971 is erroneous as this describes the attack on Tekke Tepe.

Chapter 4

SCIMITAR HILL – 9/10 AUGUST

Truly it was Valour of Ignorance!

When Stopford was met by Hamilton again, during the morning of 9 August, he was setting about the building of his headquarters near Ghazi Baba. Hamilton wrote:

> *Walking up the lower slope of Kiretch Tepe Sirt, we found Stopford, about four or five hundred yards east of Ghazi Baba, busy with part of a Field Company of Engineers supervising the building of some splinter-proof huts for himself and staff. He was absorbed in the work, and he said that it would be well to make a thorough job of the dug-outs as we should probably be here for a very long time. I retorted, 'Devil a bit: within a day or two you will be parking the best of the Anafarta houses for your billet'.*

Stopford appeared to be focused more on his shell proof dugout than what was happening to his men in the foothills. With hopes now dashed for 32 Brigade to establish themselves on Tekke Tepe, this was just another in a growing list of lost opportunities that had been there for the grabbing; now a real fight would be needed!

Typical splinter-proof headquarters at Gallipoli.

Both the 10th and 11th Divisions were utterly exhausted at this stage, demoralised by the lack of water and sleep. Along with a growing casualty rate and confusion, many of the units were still fragmented across the battlefield, where gaps in the line still needed filling. Stragglers were also becoming a problem as Captain Edmund Reidy, 11/Manchesters, recalled:

> *I was ordered by General Sitwell to extend and not to allow any men to pass through except the wounded. In some cases a soldier had a slight wound, and had a party of three or four to take him to the beach. I succeeded in collecting over one hundred which I placed on the left flank, which was reported to be threatened.*[1]

Scimitar Hill, so easily given up during the night, now became the focus of the fighting. This indistinct, curving, sandstone ridge, shaped like a scimitar, was to be the scene of a new chaotic battle, which would rage for the next two days. Maxwell had earlier planned to push forward over Scimitar Hill, which he believed was still held by the 6/East Yorks, to support the advance on Tekke Tepe. The information that the battalion had been withdrawn during the night was not passed on to Maxwell, as alas the news that Tekke Tepe was not in British hands, which he hoped would mutually cover his advance. Maxwell's

Scimitar Hill, August 1915.

33 Brigade advance would comprise of 6/Borders, 7/South Staffs and 6/Lincolns, leaving the 6/RIF and 6/RDF in reserve. Maxwell's men moved forward at 5.15 am. Progress began slowly, mainly caused by the thick dwarf-oak scrub that covered the slopes of both Scimitar and W Hills. This forced the men to take the narrow goat tracks, which funneled the advancing columns into single file. It was first made apparent to the Lincolns and South Staffs that Scimitar Hill was no longer occupied by the British when their advance was met by a deadly frontal rifle fire from the direction of the hill. They then attracted hostile shelling, soon followed by parties of Turks advancing towards them over the Anafarta Spur. These were the newly arrived men from Adil's *34 Regiment*. As 32 Brigade was being crushed a little further to

Major Jack Jennings, 6/RDF, killed at Scimitar Hill.

the north, it was now the turn of 33 Brigade to feel the force of the Turkish counterattack.

The South Staffs fared badly from the start and had losses of their

colonel, adjutant, second-in-command and all four company commanders. In fact every officer in the firing or support lines of this battalion were killed or wounded within the first ten minutes of the attack. The remnants of the battalion still pushed on and, with support from the Lincolns and Borders, they managed to fight their way to the northern end of Scimitar Hill; but here the advance stalled. Maxwell then sent up 6/RDF, quickly followed by 6/RIF, to support the troops on the hill, where the line continued to ebb back and forth across the crest. About 10.00 am, 2/4 Queen's and 1/4 Royal Sussex, part of Brigadier General Hume's 160 Brigade, 53rd (Welsh) Division, arrived to support Maxwell. Immediately the Queen's were ordered forward to support the hard-pressed troops on the slopes of Scimitar Hill, quickly followed by the Sussex. Lieutenant Colonel Frank Watney, commander of the Queen's, mentioned in his diary that he was told that under no circumstances was he to *go off into the blue*, but to maintain a supporting position by digging in on Scimitar Hill. This was fair enough to support the dwindling men trying to hold the hill, but was not the offensive spirit needed to turn the tide.

The rest of the 53rd (Welsh) Division, commanded by Major General John Lindley, was at this time still in the process of coming ashore. Put under the temporary command of Hammersley, who was sensibly instructed by Stopford to use the Division in such a way that it would be possible to reassemble them in the evening, under their own commander, to form a corps reserve, the Welsh went into the fog of war. This Division was not the strongest on paper; only three months before leaving England they had lost virtually all of their best trained battalions to the Western Front, only to have the ranks reconstituted from second line and home county units. The Division was also landed without their artillery; this was left in England; and had only one Field Ambulance, no transport, no stores and no signal company. Just before disembarkation, Lindley remarked in his diary:

> *I left England three weeks ago today and know no more than the most ignorant man in the Division. It seems rather funny, but I don't suppose they know from day to day what will be wanted. The only thing we pray is that we may stick together and not be broken up, and in that way we may be in time for the grand attack, if one is contemplated.*[2]

Unfortunately this was not to be the case.

Thrown immediately into the battle, the 53rd Division would be tested from the start. Most of the men had been at sea for three weeks and, upon landing on an enemy shore, were engaged straightaway. Lindley noted in his diary that *I had to help General Hammersley ... I had to put battalions in just as I could, as they had not all landed.* Worst still, Lindley, his staffs and regimental officers had not seen a map of Suvla and had no idea of the lie of the land or the current situation at the front; no one even knew where the front line was. It was a recipe for disaster. So this fresh but raw division was quickly lost into the chaos that had plagued IX Corps thus far. The Official History states that,

> *amongst the crowds of troops encountered on the beach there was a general air of depression, confusion, and indifference, which spread amongst the new-comers like a fog, and very rapidly.*

Inferno.

With little more than a couple of hours' notice, their first demand was to capture Scimitar Hill and the W Hills. The first scene to meet the leading elements of the Division was the hard pressed men of Maxwell's 33 Brigade retiring from Scimitar Hill.

Major John Meredith Hulton, 1/4 Royal Sussex, recalled the situation:

> We were to go forward and restore the line as the Dublin Fusiliers were falling back. When I asked whereabouts was the line, I was told that no one knew but if I went, pointing to a column of smoke caused by burning scrub, in that direction, we ought to find the 2/4th Queen's Regiment. That was all the orders it was possible to obtain (of course we had no maps). Anyhow, we got into a formation with plenty of depth to it and went off cheerfully towards the column of smoke. We met plenty of wounded coming back, all of whom advised us not to go on! Fortune however was on our side for, as we went forward, Colonel Campion and myself leading, we bumped slap into the left hand man of the Queen's, sitting in a sort of ditch.[3]

With the Sussex reinforcing the Queen's left flank, this would not be enough to help those on Scimitar Hill itself. Heavy Turkish shell fire, which was not helped by the additional British guns, whose shells were falling short, soon started to pound the crest, where casualties quickly mounted. There was little response to the Turkish shelling, but what covering fire could be provided by the navy and the few 18 pounders and mountain guns available proved inaccurate. Panic soon struck.

Running back from the left flank streams of men came, crying out: *The Turks are on us!* This had the effect of forcing the line back down to the western slopes of the hill. However the men, mainly from the South Staffs and Queen's, were soon rallied, with no Turks in sight, so that the advanced trench line could be reoccupied. Heavy shelling of the crest grew in intensity and accuracy and, with a fast dwindling number of men remaining, Maxwell reluctantly ordered a withdrawal to a trench 300 yards short of the crest.

Hamilton wrote:

> *At dawn on 9th I watched General Hammersley's attack, and very soon realised, by the well-sustained artillery fire of the enemy (so silent the previous day) and by the volume of the musketry, that Turkish reinforcements had arrived; that with the renewed confidence caused by our long delay the guns had been brought back; and that, after all, we were forestalled. This was a bad moment. Our attack failed; our losses were very serious. The enemy's enfilading shrapnel fire seemed to be especially destructive and demoralising, the shells burst low and all along our lines.*

To make matters worse, just after midday a scrub fire broke out that quickly engulfed the hillside. Private John Hargrave, wrote:

> *The gorse and dry holly-oak scrub, even the dead grass on the surface and the tough ilex and juniper roots beneath it, were ablaze, so that soon Scimitar Hill was a roaring, crackling mass of flames.*

The blaze soon forced the total abandonment of Scimitar Hill, as those who could made their way back through the choking smoke and flame. Unfortunately many of the wounded had to be left behind to their fate. This prompted Captain Percy Hansen, 6/Lincolns, to call for volunteers to assist him in rescuing the wounded, who were in danger of being consumed by the scrub fire. Along with Hansen, Lance Corporals Arthur Breese, Samuel Goffin and Ewart Clifton dashed back through the clouds of smoke and a stream of bullets into the burning scrub, which now gave off a terrific heat, and between them saved several wounded men from being burnt alive. Six times Hansen went into the inferno and rescued a total of six men. This was the first VC to be awarded for the Suvla operations. The non-commissioned officers who volunteered were each awarded the DCM for *conspicuous bravery and devotion to duty.*

Captain Percy Howard
Hansen VC, 6/Lincs.

Captain Hansen rescuing wounded on Scimitar Hill, also known as Lincoln Hill.

Percy Hansen and Ewart Clifton at work.

Corporal Ewart Clifton, 6/Lincs
who helped Hanson bring in the
wounded, but was later killed.

Ashmead-Bartlett, who was watching the attack from Lala Baba, witnessed the British wounded trying to escape the flames:

> I watched the flames approaching and the crawling figures disappear amidst dense clouds of black smoke. When the fire passed on little mounds of scorched khaki alone marked the spot where another mismanaged soldier of the King had returned to mother earth.

The attack was a failure; the Turks were now too strong, forcing the British to fall back to a line that ran approximately due south of Sulajik to Green Hill. Here the Sussex, Queen's and Lincolns remained. Whilst this was going on the 6/Borders had advanced towards the W Hills and entrenched to the south of Scimitar Hill at a place called Torgut Cheshme, which they held until 5.00 pm, when they too were eventually ordered to withdraw. Maxwell's attack was unsuccessful, resulting in the loss of about 1,500 men for no gain. Maxwell, looking for someone to blame, was unfairly scathing of the role played by the Queen's and Sussex. He wrote that

> ...neither of these battalions, as far as I can see, accomplished anything and did not appear able to go on after a few rounds of shrapnel and remained in the low ground northwest of Yilghin Burnu, and took little or no part in the operation.

Only leaving their transport a few hours before and after three weeks at sea, the Queen's did try their best to get to the crest of the hill but, by the time they were joined by the Sussex on their left flank, the whole hill in front of them was ablaze in a mass of flames and covered by a choking smoke, untenable by anyone.

The Sussex, on the left flank of the Queens, had a slightly better time. Major John Meredith Hulton, 1/4 Royal Sussex, continued:

> We extended to our left and eventually included the Sulajik Farm Houses in our line, with no one on our left. Having made ourselves secure and echeloned one company back on our left flank, patrols were sent out to our front to see what was to be seen through the dense smoke and fire that was still burning in the scrub. I remember they came back black in the face and frothing at the mouth with dryness! There was not much firing going on during our little operation ...and so ended the first day's war for most of us. It was a very great change from the comforts of the ship, this jump right into war, and I have always felt, apart from the lack of all orders, maps etc, that this sudden change of

British ambulance wagon near the Salt Lake.

surroundings had a lot to do with the lost feeling that undoubtedly existed. I don't think anyone can realise the hopeless feeling that existed. In the light of subsequent experiences one can now realise how hopeless it all was – a whole flock of more than willing sheep without a shepherd, going practically aimlessly along into a belt of burning bracken which raised clouds of choking dust enough to stop the attack of enthusiastic troops full of confidence. Truly it was Valour of Ignorance!

Whilst the fighting on Scimitar Hill was in full swing, the 9/Sherwood Foresters were advancing from the south of the Salt Lake, where they had been sitting idle for two days. Advancing towards the W Hills, it was hoped that the line could be joined up with the Anzacs in the area of Damakjelik Bair. The advance would have been unopposed if it had been made before 9 August; however now the Sherwoods came up against the Adil's *12th Division*, which were advancing quickly across both banks of Azmak Dere in an effort to drive a wedge between Suvla and Anzac.

Captain Francis Loyd, 9/Sherwood Foresters, who was wounded the following day, wrote:

On the morning of August 9th at 4.45 a.m. the order for a general advance received and we all advanced to the attack. Our Battalion advanced in the gap between Damakjelik Bair and Yilghin Burnu towards Chocolate Hill or, to give its correct name, Ismail Oglu Tepe.[Note: this shows the confusion with names, as Yilghin Burnu was in fact Chocolate Hill, Ismail Oglu Tepe was actually W Hill]. *The country over which the line allotted to the Battalion stretched was covered with scrubby undergrowth, with here and there patches of former cultivation and two orchards. Rough narrow paths ran in many directions. By 8 a.m. a satisfactory line of defence had been taken up at the cost of eight Officers and 150 rank and file, the Battalion having met a withering fire from enemy concealed in the scrubby undergrowth. At about 3 p.m. the Turks attacked and got in between A and B Companies on the right. By this time the sum total of officers in these two companies was two 2nd Lieutenants. Lt.-Col. L. A. Bosanquet, mobilising all possible signallers, runners, servants, etc., went forward and, counter attacking, succeeded in beating off the Turks and bringing off an orderly retirement of the Battalion to a much more secure and better placed positions in the dry bed of a river 400 yards in rear of the Battalion's original position. By this time seven Officers had been killed, eleven wounded, including the Colonel, and one missing, and the strength of the Battalion in rank and file reduced to about 300. At 5 p.m. the 1/1st Herefords came up to reinforce the Battalion. They arrived half battalion strong as they had been badly shelled on the way up, they said, the other half battalion was therefore remaining in the Salt Lake trenches, which the Sherwood Foresters had vacated that morning.*[4]

After heavy casualties the Sherwoods, now under command of Major John Blackburne (Lieutenant Colonel Bosanquet having been earlier wounded), managed to hold its ground, and by nightfall were supported by the 1/1 Herefords and entrenched a line that ran south as far as Azmak Dere, near Kazlar Chair.

When dark came the Herefords took over the right of the line, and the remnants of the two companies thus released were formed into a reserve. At midnight the Herefords were withdrawn, being required for an attack the following morning. The right of the line was therefore taken over by the 'reserve', under command of the Adjutant, Capt. F. F. Loyd. Between the right flank of the Battalion and the left flank of the South Wales Borderers (13th Div) there was an absolutely unavoidable gap of a mile. Altogether a pleasant position on a three days' empty stomach. There was some desultory fighting during the night, luckily no concentrated attack.

The southern flank of IX Corps had achieved little on 9 August whilst, in the north, Mahon's men were still holding the part of the Kiretch Tepe ridge that was captured by the 11/Manchesters during the first few hours of the landing. Since then little progress had been made and Mahon did little more than just look at the Gendarmerie for the last couple of days. When Hamilton had finished with Stopford earlier that morning he went in search of the Irish. He found Mahon after a walk of about two and a half miles along the ridge. He wrote that Mahon,

> *...is angry, and small wonder, at the chaos introduced somehow into the Corps. He is commanding some of Hammersley's men and Hammersley has the bulk of his at the far extremity of the line of battle. He besought me to do my utmost to get Hill and his troops back to their own command.*

Mahon was in a fighting spirit, which made Hamilton happier, and was confident he could clear the Kiretch Tepe ridge by a supporting attack on his southern flank. On Hamilton's return to Stopford's headquarters he told him *that the sooner the Kiretch Tepe nettle was grasped the less it would sting.* Stopford sanctioned Mahon's plan, hoping the capture of Kiretch Tepe would help a further attack on the Tekke Tepe ridge.

With Hill's absence, Mahon had attached two battalions from 34 Brigade, 5/Dorsets and 9/Lancashire Fusiliers; however Mahon was not in touch with them. Stopford had already instructed that a destroyer bombard the crest of the ridge to aid Mahon's attack. Down on the plain the 5/Dorsets had been ordered to start their advance upon the beginning of this bombardment and, exactly as planned, this began successfully. When the Dorsets were observed moving off, Nichol told Mahon that he was still waiting for his rations and water to be brought up; without waiting, Mahon ordered Nichol to carry on at once. At 7.30 am two companies of the 5/RIF advanced along the northern slope whilst the 6/RMF attacked along the crest, supported by two machines guns from a Royal Naval armoured car detachment.[5] On the southern slopes of the ridge, by the Dorsets, the 7/RMF began their advance without their water bottles, as they had not returned yet. They were not the only ones; the Dorsets too had to advance with no water. In support were the two remaining companies of the 5/RIF on the northern slopes, whilst the 9/Lancashire Fusiliers were held in reserve near to Hill 10.

Destroyer HMS *Foxhound* began the bombardment of the crest with great accuracy, which was continued by HMS *Grampus* when it took over the bombardment at 7.00 am. As the Turks had few supporting artillery or machine guns on this ridge, the 5/RIF advance began successfully on the northern slopes, with few casualties. Problems soon

An old trench marks the approximate position which the Inniskillings reached on 9 August.

began when the Turkish positions on the crest were neared. Here resistance from the *Gelibolu Gendarmerie* slowed the 6/RMF advance. At 1.30 pm *Grampus* renewed its bombardment on the Turkish strongpoint that was holding up the attack, which enabled the Munsters to continue their advance a little, finally capturing the Turkish strongpoint near the crest, to be named Jephson's Post after Major John Jephson, 6/RMF, who led the attack. But here the advance stopped again. It was not the Turkish defence this time but the utter exhaustion of the troops caused by lack of water and the oppressive August heat. The Official History noted:

> *The sun always struck more fiercely on the rocky slopes of Kiretch Tepe than on any other part of the Suvla front; the supply of water on that flank was still a difficulty; and there, too,*

maddening thirst was as much responsible as Turkish bullets for checking the Irish troops.

Second Lieutenant Terence Verschoyle, 5/Inniskillings, recalled the conditions:

The rocky ground made it difficult to dig trenches and sangars of rocks scraped out and piled up in front of the 'trench' were the result of much hard labour. All munitions, food and water had to be brought up the tortuous tracks right along the ridge to the front line and as the hillside positions were exposed to the blazing August sun the shortage of a nearby water supply soon became a prime consideration to all personnel. For my own platoon it seemed best to pool all the water in some large empty biscuit tins, buried in the earth for coolness' sake, in the neighbourhood of my so-called dugout, and to divide it among the men at certain definite periods of the day. Thus compulsory economy of water was inflicted upon the very thirsty that must have been extremely irritating. On the other hand, they could be sure of having a little left to mitigate their thirst at an advanced period of the day. The water-bottles were to be stacked at the same place, to be regarded as the property of the community and not of individuals, and to be filled by a fatigue party whenever opportunity was presented to replenish the biscuit tins. Meanwhile any derelict water-bottles, of casualties or fools, that might be found lying about were to be deposited there too; then, when there were enough water-bottles, and the habit of husbanding the water had been instilled, these would again become the property of individuals, which is what eventually happened. These details are dull and childish to read now but were at the time a matter of life and death.[6]

On the southern slopes the 7/RMF and 5/Dorsets made their advance towards Kidney Hill, a distinct kidney shaped mound on the southern

The southern slopes of Kiretch Tepe, August 1915.

slopes of the Kiretch Tepe ridge. Here too the ground was rough, which made the going difficult, the advance stalled about 700 yards short of the objective - not from Turkish action, as there was little, but from exhaustion. The line of advance, that lost all cohesion, faltered and then came to a standstill. The Munsters were suffering from acute thirst, as their water bottles had not yet reached them, and the Dorsets were no better off. Sergeant Gerald Boucher, 5/Dorsets, recounted: *many fellows I saw took out their rifle bolts and sucked them in the hope of cooling their parched throats.*[7] There was no recorded order for the halt and no counter order to continue. Confusion reigned and by nightfall, and still with no water, the Munsters withdrew, quickly followed by the Dorsets. All the ground that had been gained was relinquished without a fight, both battalions ending up on their original start line; it was another bad day for Mahon and his men.

Mahon was deeply disappointed with the lack of progress during the day and was equally surprised when he received a complimentary message from Stopford on his troops performance that ended with: *do not try any more to-day unless the enemy gives you a favourable chance.* Mahon was an angered man; as a senior lieutenant general he had to settle for the command of just one division, and actually had under his command barely three battalions. One brigade was seconded to the Anzac operation, whilst another was put under Sitwell's command, leaving Mahon one brigade, from which one battalion was still missing!

This was a bad day for the British in general and not just for Mahon. By nightfall on 9 August almost nothing had been achieved, leaving most of IX Corps in disarray. Lieutenant Edward Compton Mackenzie wrote in his diary:

This has been a day of disappointments. The IXth Army Corps failed to push on, and all our advantage seems lost. Sir Ian went off to curse the General commanding. It's really heart rendering. We still hope that they'll get to a certain ridge, but there is no news, and in military operations no news is bad news.[8]

Not only does 9 August mark the end of any real chance of success at Suvla, but it also signalled the end of the offensive at Anzac. Mustafa Kemal had left Suvla during the afternoon as soon as he was confident that the British were checkmated. On returning to the Sari Bair ridge, where he learnt of the loss of Chunuk Bair and Hill Q, he quickly set about organising an attack for the early morning of 10 August. This would be the turning point of the August offensive and the loss of all hope for Birdwood's breakout. The Turks had contained the threat at Anzac and now sealed the British into Suvla. Compton Mackenzie ends his entry for 9 August:

There is still no good news of the IXth Army Corps. I'm afraid they've ruined the show. It's absolutely damnable. Dawnay was almost weeping when he came back from Suvla today. There were only eight hundred Turks and we had more than fifteen thousand men. They actually bathed ... if this is Kitchener's Army (and the best three divisions at that), give me the good old Territorials.

Stopford received a message from Hamilton just after midnight, which read:

9th August
Despatched 11.25 PM.

I am in complete sympathy with you in the matter of all your officers and men being new to this style of warfare, and without any leaven of experienced troops on which to form themselves. Still I should be wrong if I did not express my concern at the want of energy and push displayed by the 11th Division. It cannot all be want of experience, as the 13th have shown dash and self-confidence. Turks were almost negligible yesterday ... today there was nothing to stop determined commanders leading such fine men as yours. Tell me, what is wrong with 11th Division? Is it the divisional general or brigadiers or both? ... You must get a move on or the whole plan of operations is in danger of failing, for if you do not secure Tekke Tepe ridge without delay the enemy will. You must use your personal influence to insist on vigorous and sustained action against the weak forces of Turks in your front, and while agreeing to the capture of the W Hills and spur mentioned in C.G.S. letter to you today, it is of vital importance to the whole operation that you thereafter promptly take steps to secure the Tekke Tepe ridge, without the possession of which Suvla Bay is not safe. You must face casualties and strike while the opportunity offers, and remember the Tekke Tepe ridge is your principle and dominant objective and it must be captured. Every day's delay in its capture will enormously multiply your casualties ...

Stopford replied:

I must regret that the force under my command has not succeeded in gaining the high ground east of the bay, the importance of which I fully recognize and have never ceased to impress on all concerned. It has been a great disappointment to me that an attack which I had fully expected would have succeeded yesterday turned into a defensive action in which it became a question not of pushing on but of holding the ground. I need not say that I have done my best to find out the cause of this. I hear the same thing from everyone; that it is due primarily to exhaustion from want of water. There is no doubt that there is a certain amount of water to be found, but it requires development, and in the meantime every drop of water has to be taken to the troops on mules, of whom very few are available, and which are also becoming exhausted from want of water.

I was most anxious to push on the day after landing, but was assured by everyone that without water it was an impossibility, and I had to stop landing guns and even rations to get mules landed for water purposes.

I don't think the men have had much training in field manoeuvring, though I hear they are well grounded in trench warfare. The officers are inexperienced in the work and cohesion gets lost. I must also point out that the troops are being asked, without adequate artillery support, to attack an enemy who is very clever in defence. The naval guns do not do much good against men who are extended and the moment their guns stopped yesterday morning, our men were being fired at from everywhere in their front. The only artillery available to assist in the attack was two field batteries, one of which was not horsed, and one mountain battery (I had to send the other mountain battery to the 10th Division), instead of the six to eight batteries which would have been the normal proportion for the troops engaged. I do not think the failure is due to want of energy on the part of the divisional and brigade commanders as they are as well aware as I am of the vital necessity of pushing on, but the fact remains that they cannot advance, or, when they do advance, hold their ground.

General Mahon made very slight progress yesterday and cannot push on without further artillery support, which is not available. He also reports his men are quite exhausted from want of water.

I have seen my divisional commanders and urged on them the necessity of a further advance today, but I regret to say that they are convinced that without more water and more artillery support they cannot hope for a successful advance and deprecate a further attempt.

I have, however, decided to make an attempt to push on and have ordered General Lindley to attack with his Territorials, supported by the 11th Division and have asked the navy to support me with every available gun and of course I will use all the fields guns at my disposal and I can only trust that the attack may be more successful than was the one yesterday.

Given water, guns, and ammunition, I have no doubt of our being able to secure the hills which are so vital to us but, for a success, more water and adequate artillery are absolutely essential ...

On 10 August, with the rest of Major General Lindley's men ashore, Stopford was now relying on the 53rd (Welsh) Division to change his fortunes. Pushing Lindley's remaining brigades piecemeal into a renewed attack on Scimitar Hill, which had already eaten up 160 Brigade the previous day, it was now the turn of Brigadier General Lloyd's and Cowan's men. Lindley was to join them; going forward just before the attack in an attempt to establish his headquarters, he found the area a little hotter than expected. He wrote:

Captain Basil Beadon, 7/RWF killed 10 August.

I went forward at 5.00 am to a place I thought from the general situation given us on Monday night was safe and retired. However our line was not nearly so far advanced as we were told and we (I and my staff) found ourselves much too near to the enemy. Luckily we found a sunken road and got into it, but lots of bullets passed over it and some hit some sandbags we got behind. We could not well move for some time, but eventually we walked back at about 10.00 am to a position on Lala Baba hill.

By 10.00 am the attack had been going for almost four hours! Lambs to the slaughter, Lindley's men were being sacrificed in front of him.

Under the orders of Sitwell, Cowan's 159 Brigade was the next to be punished. Just north of Sulajik 1/7 Cheshires with 1/4 Welsh went into the attack, whilst the rest of the brigade, namely 1/4 Cheshires and 1/5 Welsh, were put in support of 32 Brigade. From this early stage Cowan had lost his brigade! The attack started unopposed, but very soon Turkish fire fell on its targets, checking the attack quickly. At 8.45 am a message was received that the Turks were counter attacking, so part of 32 Brigade were sent forward to reinforce the line, only to be met by men from the 1/4 Welsh pulling back with no enemy attack in sight. This rout was stopped in its tracks and the line once again surged forward but, unsupported, these few disorganised troops achieved little and eventually pulled back to the start line. An eyewitness, Sergeant William Phillipson, of 8/Northumberland Fusiliers, who were ordered forward in support, wrote:

> We were surprised to see men of two regiments (one a Welsh Territorial Regiment) doubling back. One man shouted "You don't want to go up there!" Well, perhaps we didn't, but an order to get a move on settled the question.

When the Northumberlands were ordered to withdraw the following day, Phillipson continued:

> When we got out of the trench we were followed by some of the Welsh who didn't seem to like the idea of staying in the trench and seeing us come out. They were ordered back but hesitated to comply, showing great lack of discipline.[9]

It was a worrying start for the Territorials.

Brigadier General Lloyd's North Wales 158 Brigade fared little better, having advanced from Lala Baba over the Salt Lake with little trouble, apart from some sporadic shelling. The Salt Lake was crusted over, which made fairly easy going; however in parts the men sank up to their ankles and ambulance wagons up to their axles. Lindley had to attach the 2/10 Middlesex to the Brigade to make up for the loss of the Herefords, who had not yet returned from supporting the Sherwoods at the Azmak Dere. Forming up south of 159 Brigade, they began to advance in the direction of Scimitar Hill, under increased shrapnel fire, in support of Cowan's brigade. Lieutenant Colonel Basil Philips, commanding 1/5 Royal Welsh Fusiliers (RWF), led his battalion forward, passing through the positions of 1/4 Cheshires and 1/5 Welsh. Philips got to within 200 yards

**He Did What He Could –
Captain Edward Lloyd-Jones
1/7 RWF, killed 10 August.**

105

Lt Col Basil Philips, 1/5 RWF killed at Scimitar Hill.

of Scimitar Hill before he halted, requesting support to enable him to make the final rush of the hill. No support came and, and whilst waiting in the maelstrom of fire, Philips was killed[10] and many more of his fellow officers wounded; the troops fell back in disorder. Eventually support did arrive in the form of a platoon led by Second Lieutenant Malcolm Eve, later Lord Silsoe, 1/6 RWF. Eve actually reached the crest of Scimitar Hill but, with only about thirty men and with no support, had to withdraw.

The attack had clearly failed by 1.00 pm but Stopford, who was observing the movement from Lala Baba, ordered Lindley to resume the frontal attack at 5.00 pm. Lindley wrote:

The men were very tired, and it was piping hot and there was no water. I ordered a renewal of the attack about 5 pm. This gave the men some chance but from what my Brigadier tells me I did not expect it to succeed.

This view was also shared by Hamilton who, when he received the information for a renewed attack, actually advised Stopford to rest and reorganise his troops instead. This was almost a role reversal between the two generals. Now Stopford had the offensive spirit, he was now being told by Hamilton to rest. Ignoring Hamilton, Stopford allowed the attack to continue. When it started only two unsupported companies from 2/10 Middlesex appeared to make any movement forward and, after about a 500 yard advance, losing four officers and a number of men, they were forced to return to their original starting lines. Halfhearted, the renewed attack was over before it really began. Casualties amongst the officers had been high; 1/5 Welsh suffered the loss of nine, 1/4 Cheshires eleven and 1/5 RWF, twelve. Lindley noted in his diary that the attack was:

Disappointing but all worked well and did their best, but the men really had no chance owing to the hurried way the thing had to be done. I nearly asked Sir F. Stopford on Monday night to put it off for twenty four hours but I thought he knew the circumstances and I did not like to start on the first day by any objection and he, Sir Frederick, was extremely nice about the whole thing in an interview I had with him at his Headquarters when all was over.

The fighting at Suvla had ended for now. IX Corps, as well as the Turks, were utterly exhausted, having fought themselves to a standstill, which allowed 11 August to pass uneventfully for both sides. For the Turks they probably thought the offensive was over, but for the British they were planning another attack the following day. The Turks had retained the high ground, leaving IX Corps to their gains along part of Kiretch Tepe, Lala Baba, Hill 10 and the Chocolate Hills. To the right flank of IX Corps, Chunuk Bair had been captured and lost, with the Anzacs fighting themselves to a standstill. At Helles the diversionary attacks failed to keep the Turks in the area engaged. The plan had failed on all three fronts, with an estimated 25,000 British and 20,000 Turkish losses in four days of fighting. Compton Mackenzie wrote a diary entry for 10 August saying that some general would get *stellenbosched* over this business, but before this would happen there would be more suffering at Suvla.

Dressing Station near the Cut.

Suvla Bay

Old rose and black and indigo,
Saffron streaks in a spume-tipped grey,
Purple, laved in the dawn's wan glow –
God, how fair you are, Suvla Bay!

Spitting shrapnel and shrieking steel,
Brave men dead in their youth's noonday,
All the anguish their loved ones feel
Is your ambrose, fair Suvla Bay!

Stabbing sun from a brazen sky,
Choking dust from the corpse-strewn way,
Each one treads as he marches by,
God, how I loathe you, Suvla Bay!

Tanned men delving with laboured breath,
Stinking lighters discharging hay,
Grey-hulled battleships belching death,
God, there's work on at Suvla Bay!

Pale, pale moon and the cold north star,
You who watch while I kneel and pray,
Take to her in the northland far
One sobbing prayer from Suvla Bay!

One sobbing prayer that the dull heart-pain
God in heav'n Thou alone canst stay,
For her be stilled till I come again
Back to her side from Suvla Bay! [11]

1 National Army Museum: E. M. Reidy, 34 Brigade Collection, p.4.
2 Unpublished diary of Major General John Lindley (private collection).
3 War Diary: 1/4 Royal Sussex Regiment (National Archives: WO95/4323).
4 Notts & Derbys Annual, 1922 – Notes from Major A. S. Murray and Captain F. F. Loyd.
5 In 1914 the Royal Naval Air Service (RNAS) raised several British armoured car squadrons, five of which were dispatched to Gallipoli. After their Rolls Royce armoured cars proved unsuccessful during the Third Battle of Krithia, the crews were 'dismounted' and, along with their maxim machine guns, supported the infantry until the end of the campaign.
6 IWM Department of Sound Collection: T. Verschoyle, Interview 8185.
7 National Army Museum: G. Boucher, 34th Brigade Collection, p.5.
8 Compton Mackenzie, *Gallipoli Memories,* (London: Cassell & Co., 1929).
9 National Army Museum: W. Phillipson, 34th Brigade Collection, p.6.
10 Lieutenant Colonel B. E. Philips is buried in Green Hill Cemetery, grave ref. II.B.9.
11 Poem by William Henry Littlejohn, 1/10 Middlesex, who was killed during the Battle of Arras in 1917.

Chapter 5

BATTLE OF KÜÇÜK ANAFARTA OVA
– 12 AUGUST

Good old Sandringham

Hamilton had not admitted defeat yet. Although he realised that the Anzacs were in no fit state to continue the attack on the Sari Bair ridge, he put his hope in the newly landed 54th (East Anglian) Division to change the balance at Suvla. Unaware of the scale of the defeat so far, he still believed that there was a chance to pry Tekke Tepe from the grip of the Turks. Using his only immediately available reserve, Hamilton needed the 54th Division to get IX Corps off the Suvla Plain once and for all before the Turks had locked the British into Suvla forever.

Major General Francis Inglefield's 54th (East Anglian) Division began to come ashore during the morning of 10 August, whilst the 53rd (Welsh) Division's hurried and poorly planned attack was failing and

161 Brigade, 54th Division, packing the lighters.

109

Birdwood's troops were being pushed off the Sari Bair heights. The result of the Welsh's continued fighting around Scimitar Hill was to be another failed enterprise; all there was to show for it was a large butcher's bill. Hamilton did not want the 54th Division to be thrown into a similar piecemeal action. He wanted all the troops to be ashore and to be used only when sanctioned by GHQ; however this is exactly what did not happen. At 10.00 pm, on 10 August, concerned about a gap in the line to the right of the 10th Division on Kiretch Tepe, Stopford ordered forward six battalions of the 54th Division to plug the line.

> *It must not be thought, however, that this line comprised trenches like unto those in France. There was no such indication of its existence and even the first line only consisted of a dry ditch, out of which some of the earth had been scooped.*[1]

So, only having left England barely two weeks previously, the six battalions, representing units from all three brigades, tired and disorientated, found themselves in the line.

GHQ ordered Stopford to use the 54th Division to attack and capture the Tekke Tepe ridge during dawn on the 12 August, following a night advance to the foothills. Recent aerial reconnaissance showed that the ridge had not been entrenched or held in any great strength, so an attack delivered with speed and force was hoped to take the high ground once and for all. The attack was to be spearheaded by the 54th Division whilst Stopford's other forces would provide a supporting role. It is worth noting that, as this Division began to disembark at A Beach, it came ashore with no artillery, no divisional signal company, no field ambulances, no ammunition and no mules. Stopford went about on 11 August reorganising his own battered, scattered and demoralized units instead of preparing for the attack. Even when confronted by Hamilton again, he continued to make excuses, blaming everything and everyone but his own lack of resolve. He argued with Hamilton that both of his Territorial divisions were sucked oranges and that they were not up to the job. Hamilton wrote:

> *He tells me straight and without any beating about the bush: 'I am sure they would not secure the hills with any amount of guns, water and ammunition assuming ordinary opposition, as the attacking spirit was absent; chiefly owing to the want of leadership by the Officers'.*

Hamilton could not accept this assessment and insisted that the attack must take place. As to 'want of leadership' being absent, most of the

Welsh officers were already dead or wounded, lying on the battlefield from the last botched attack. Acknowledging that Stopford had made no preparations for the attack, Hamilton had to accept a further day's delay, so postponed the attack to dawn on 13 August. Stopford then raised the issue of snipers amongst the thick scrub that faced them in many places, especially on the western side of the ridge, so Hamilton sanctioned a hundred Anzac marksmen to be employed in helping Stopford's men clear them out. These men, drawn from the Australians, New Zealanders and Gurkhas, were all experienced snipers or acknowledged marksmen, and included most of their divisional scouts. They would go out in pairs for the whole day with rifles, haversacks, water bottles and ammunition, as if on a rabbit shoot. They were successful at playing the Turk at their own game, but progress was slow, and with the attack planned for the following day, their task would be far from complete.

What Stopford found on the morning of 12 August was a disorganised 54th Division that had been trying to organise itself during the night. With an attack about to start his Corps could not have been in a worst situation. This time Stopford was probably correct in his assumption that the assault would probably fail; however Hamilton had lost his patience with him. Stopford wanted the 53rd Division to begin the advance during daylight. As they were already closer, the Welsh would be in a good position to push the line forward into the foothills, thus making the 54th Divisional advance easier with less ground to cover. However Lindley's men were still badly mixed up after the earlier attack; he wrote in his diary that the following day there was:

> Great difficulty experienced all day in getting in touch with the brigades. The Cheshires and the North Wales brigades are in an awful muddle, owing to so many officers having been killed or wounded, and the men are lost without them. The NCOs seem powerless and carry no authority – the officers have done wonderfully well, freely exposing themselves to get their men on, hence the heavy casualties.[2]

When Major General Inglefield (54th Division) learnt that the 53rd Division were in no fit shape, he offered to use 163 Brigade (Brigadier General Capel Brunker) in this task. If Brunker advanced the line about 2,000 yards east of Hill 28 during the day, 159 Brigade (53rd Division) could then come up to consolidate the position. This would allow the rest of the 54th Division to make a night advance and to be ready for a dawn attack. On either flank both the 10th and 11th Divisions would cooperate in the attack.

Stopford was unsure about the follow-up, so sanctioned the daylight advance of 163 Brigade to proceed and, depending on the outcome, would then order a main operation. If successful, the follow-on attack would commence at dawn on the following day, but if the attempt failed, then an extra twenty four hours would be needed before the attack could continue. Hamilton was disappointed with a plan that potentially added further delay; however he had no choice at this stage, so chose to agree to it. He thought that if the attack did fail that there might be an opportunity to divert the resources to a new attack on the W Hills instead.

Hamilton dispatched his Chief of Staff, Major General Walter Braithwaite, to Suvla to review and, if necessary, cancel the Tekke Tepe attack in lieu of one on the W Hills. When Braithwaite heard Stopford's arguments, there was an agreement to cancel both attacks regardless of the outcome of the afternoon's advance. Reluctantly Hamilton agreed. An attack on the W Hills would be made as early as possible, but it would not be ready by 13 August. Back in London, Kitchener had been very concerned at the slow progress made so far and now Hamilton had to tell him that the planned attack to break out from Suvla was being delayed another twenty-four hours. The only positive news he could cable to Kitchener was that the afternoon's advance by 163 Brigade had started favourably and that Mahon's 10th Division had got tired of looking at gendarmes and had captured a trench – not much to show from a whole army corps!

The ground over which 163 Brigade's attack was to take place, across the Küçük Anafarta Ova (Ova meaning plain), an area that comprised a flat, cultivated plain interspersed by ditches and dry water courses, clumps of trees and scattered farm buildings; exactly as it remains today. Ideal for defence, the Turks used this to their advantage.

Herbert Peters, Sniper,
Australian Light Horse.

Beyond the plain a number of stunted oaks, gradually becoming more dense farther inland, formed excellent cover for the enemy's snipers, a mode of warfare at which the Turk was very adept. Officers and men were continually shot down, not only by rifle fire from advanced posts of the enemy, but by men, and even women, behind our own firing line, especially from the previous attacks. The particular kind of tree in this part, a stunted oak, lends itself to concealment, being short with dense foliage. Here the sniper would lurk, with face painted green, and so well hidden as to defy detection. Others would crouch in the dense brushwood, where anyone passing could be shot with ease. When discovered, these snipers had in their possession enough food and water for a considerable period, as well as an ample supply of ammunition.[3]

There is much dispute amongst historians today as to whether Turkey used women snipers at Gallipoli. There was much written at the time from the British perspective and used extensively in the press, but all is circumstantial and most probably a spin of the old yarn. Turkish historians are adamant that they were not used in the military and also that all civilians were evacuated from the area at the time of the landings. With no evidence to support or deny these stories, they will probably remain, although some do sound convincing, myth. The following are two stories relating to women snipers. In the first, Michael McDonagh wrote:

Some of the best Turkish marksmen, as it turned out, were markswomen. Among those discovered was a peasant woman – the wife of a Turkish soldier – who lived with her old mother and her child in a little house near the Irish lines. This particular woman was a good shot, who specialised in hitting stragglers on the many trails between the front lines and the beaches. Having made sure her targets were dead, she would then rifle their bodies. When she was finally identified and captured her house was searched. A large quantity of money was found but, more surprising, was the discovery of a number of identity discs. Either she was proud of her work or she was getting paid a piecework rate for the job![4]

Private Charles Crutchley, who served as a machine gunner with 1/4 Northants at Suvla, wrote of an Australian counter sniper patrol at Suvla:

An Australian patrol caught a Turkish woman sniper, who had the identity discs of several British soldiers hanging round her neck. They shot her and that shocked me, for I thought she was a brave person doing only what many British women would have done to invaders of our land. But I kept my mouth shut, for I knew that in war everyone is affected by its lunacy.[5]

To the left flank was Kidney Hill, and ahead were the scrub covered

Hill 28, with Kiretch Tepe as a backdrop.

foothills of the Tekke Tepe Ridge; both were held by the Turks, who could enfilade any attack across the plain. In front of the Brigade were two companies from *1/36 Regiment*, with two further companies in support. The *3/36 Regiment* was in reserve near the crest of Kavak Tepe. Having only arrived the previous morning, the Turkish dispositions were unknown to the Brigade, who, having themselves only just arrived, had no time to make any reconnaissance of the area. Maps were issued late and many were of other parts of the peninsula; all very confusing. Instructions were issued by Divisional Headquarters to advance and clear the ground of snipers up to Squares 118.I, N and S. The Brigade, who for the attack was under the command of Lieutenant Colonel Sir Horace Proctor-Beauchamp Bart. CB, was to advance at 4.00 pm. The assembly area, north of Hill 28, was under a fair amount of shelling and sniping, water was also short and the

ground unfamiliar, whilst added to this was the general doubt as to the location of the objective, all spelling disaster.

At 4.00 pm a bombardment by naval and field artillery begun punctually, but it turned out to be completely ineffective; firstly, high explosive was being used instead of shrapnel and, secondly, the infantry were not ready to advance. The Official History stated that: *the liaison between guns and infantry was very defective; the gunners had no definite targets, and they were not even sure of the position of the British front line.* No one knew the location of the Turks, let alone the artillery and infantry. One battalion, the 1/5 Norfolks, had received the order to advance only a couple of hours before the attack was to commence and, if this was not bad enough, the Suffolks and Hants had not received the message at all! Most of the Brigade were spending a relaxing morning with no prior warning; not a good start to the operation. It was not until 4.45 pm that the infantry started their advance. The 1/5 Norfolks were positioned on the right flank, under the

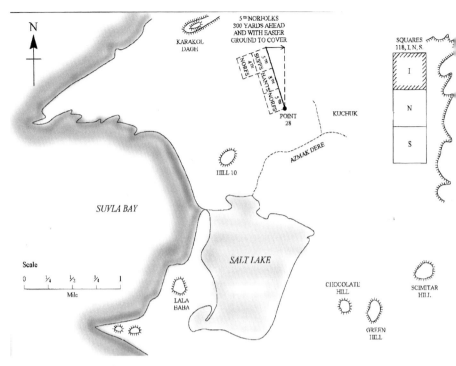

Attack of 163 Brigade on 12 August.

command of Lieutenant Colonel Sir Horace Proctor-Beauchamp. To their left were 1/8 Hants (Isle of Wight Rifles), commanded by Lieutenant Colonel John Rhodes, and to their left, on the northern flank, were 1/5 Suffolks, under the command of Lieutenant Colonel William Armes. Behind them were 1/4 Norfolks, commanded temporarily by their adjutant, Captain Eustace Montgomerie, as their colonel had been found unfit for command.

The advance started reasonably well and with few casualties; however, after several hundred yards the line began to falter, enfilade machine gun and rifle fire coming from Kidney Hill on the left flank and shrapnel fire from the direction of the Anafarta Spur over on right flank. The Brigade gained another 300 yards but then became disjointed, the 1/5 Norfolks veering over to the right and outpacing the Hants and Suffolks to their left. The Norfolks actually had a head start on the rest of the Brigade, as their start line to the east of Hill 28 was more advanced. Upon starting the advance the Battalion was ordered to move half right, an order that no other battalion appeared to have received. This movement was meant to align the Brigade up with Squares 118.I, N and S, as per the original objective, but only the

116

Norfolks took note. This soon caused a dangerous gap in the line as the Suffolks and Hants continued on in a more or less straight line. Two companies of the 1/5 Norfolks briefly halted to allow the Hants and Suffolks to wheel round but to no avail, as the order to press on was given.

Leading the 1/5 Norfolks was Proctor-Beauchamp and Captain Randall Cubitt, both men smoking whilst the Colonel spurred on his men, waving his cane and shouting: *on the Norfolks on, come on my holy boys, forward the hungry Ninth.*[6] After only 200 yards the order was then given to fix bayonets and to advance at the double. This brought upon them an almost immediate fusillade of bullets, as the glistening bayonets helped exposed their position. An eye witness wrote:

> *It was perfect hell. The hills were alive with rifles and machine guns. Still on they went, rushing forward. Men shouted 'Good old Yarmouth', 'Good old Sandringham', 'Good old Downham' and 'Good old Lynn'.*[7]

Casualties soon began to mount as the Turkish fire increased in intensity, but the advance continued in short rushes, as brave and keen groups of men rushed forward. Enemy rifle and machine gun fire appeared to be coming from all sides, including behind, where well concealed snipers shot at the officers and NCOs. Private John Dye, who was later wounded in the attack, remembered seeing Captain Frank Beck, from the Sandringham estate, leading C (The King's) Company forward[8]:

> *… walking with his stick just the same as he did at Sandringham, putting it down at the same time as he did his left foot. He might have been seen with his hat off or with his revolver in his hand when we were in the thick of it, but I did not see him that way.*

The heat and casualties continued to take their toll, causing the Brigade attack to soon break up. The ground also made it difficult to maintain cohesion, as the crisscross of dry water courses, hedge rows, scrub and dust all contributed to slowing it down. Some of the trees, scrub and fields had also caught fire, the rising smoke clouding visibility. On the right hand side of the attack, the Norfolks suffered less from rifle and machine gun fire and so were able to continue their advance as the Suffolks and Hants came to a halt. Although advances were still significant, in places up to 1,200 to 1,500 yards, the Suffolks and Hants could do no more, and fell back to a defensive line along a sunken ditch.

Over on the extreme right a party of fourteen officers and about 250 men, mainly from the 1/5 Norfolks, continued forward with their colonel but, unsupported and without protection on their flanks, their effort was to be doomed. An eyewitness wrote:

> *We tore ahead as hard as we could; it was blazing hot. The advance was rapid and there was an awful shortage of water. Men fell out exhausted by thirst. Many were wounded by the enfilading fire, but we got the Turks on the run. I saw Col. Beauchamp walking with the adjutant. He had a light cane in his right hand and a coat over his left arm.*

The advance was now in danger; Proctor-Beauchamp continued on regardless and soon the casualties began to mount. Men sought cover where ever they could, behind bushes, in ditches and hollows in the ground. Wounded tried to crawl back to their own lines whilst others continued forward to a cluster of stone farm buildings that offered some protection from the deadly fire. Upon reaching the buildings, Lieutenant Colonel Proctor-Beauchamp gave the order, *hound 'em out boys,* to clear the huts of Turkish snipers.

Second Lieutenant Roland Pelly, A Company, 1/5 Norfolks, in a letter to his father, wrote:

> *For some reason or mistake no regiment, of which there were loads, backed us up to shove us through. We were opposed by a wall of bullets and were knocked over right and left. I got too far ahead, lost my way and trying to find it again, was bagged by a Turkish sniper – which swarm – at very close range. The bullet broke my left lower jaw, tore my tongue in shreds and then out through my right cheek. Then after an awful wandering the RAMC got me; by 11pm they had carried me right back to expert*

Site of the Norfolks' Last Stand. One of the ruined buildings as it is today.

care... One or two wounded followed – Purdy, Oliphant, Seymour and told me we had been most frightfully cut up and almost wiped out... That was an awful night – absolute HELL – and surely if there had been someone behind we should have gone right through.

Pelly was correct; there was a mistake made. Proctor-Beauchamp allowed the 1/5 Norfolks to break away in direction from the rest of his brigade, and without allowing time to realign, he continued the advance unsupported. In and around these buildings, including a nearby vineyard, was probably the furthest advance that day, reaching about half a mile behind the Turkish front line.[9] At about 6.30 pm, as dusk was closing in, the Turkish *3/36 Regiment* launched a counter attack. The Turkish regiment had been collecting in a ravine towards the Norfolks' left flank and then, at the right moment, debouched from their cover, quickly bringing to an end Proctor-Beauchamp's survivors; few returned.

One survivor recalled his journey back to the British lines:

It was pitch dark, and I had lost all idea of direction. Suddenly I heard the sound of picks and shovels, and thought our fellows were digging themselves in. As we made our way along carefully an awful jabbering struck my ears and, peeping through the woods, we saw a large gang of Turks, digging like steam. 'One shot, sonny, and we all go west', I said to a man who raised his rifle. Absolutely no idea of direction; did not know if I was walking to Constantinople or to our camp. The Turks were burying the dead and, not wishing to give them another job, I eased off. After roaming in the gloaming for a good time, I got clear of the wood and fell in with an officer who was trying to find some of the boys. He led us to where some more of the crowd had taken up a position commanding three Turkish wells. We drank like horses, and then returned to duty.

A 1915 photograph inside one of the many buildings that are found over this area.

Lieutenant Ismail Hakki Sunata, *2/35 Regiment*, was in one of the burial parties, an experience he recounted in a diary entry for 13 August:

I got up in the morning, same stream, same dust and dirt, same people. The major sent for me. 'I am going to give you twenty men, bury all the British dead in our rear.' Burying the dead is an unpleasant thing. Nothing for it, orders are orders. We don't have picks either. We will try to get this done with entrenching tools and shovels. All the picks and shovels have been sent to dig trenches. They only gave us a few large shovels. The time came. It is still twilight. A terrible smell. A British body stretched out. The ground is hard, and can't be dug with the shovels. I say to the soldiers, 'Grab hold, let's take him to the ditch on our left.' Everyone cringes, saying I cannot hold him, I am afraid. This is not the place to be shouting and yelling at the men. Upon my insistence several soldiers grabbed the body by the trouser legs and began to drag it. We took it to the ditch, and shovelled some earth on top of it. So much for a human body. Off we go again. A few steps later another, then another. We can't take them all to the

ditch. We open a hole with the shovels, roll the body in, and shovel some earth on top. At one point someone said, 'A martyr'. One of our poor men. He is stinking like the British. And for days he has been lying in brotherhood with the British dead and had no quarrel with them. Hey Allah, so it is the thing called life that brings humans to fight. When they are dead they all lie quietly, calmly, without attacking each other. If only they could get along so well in health...

The weapons of the dead men have all been taken. The lack of picks renders the task difficult. One of them especially stank so much that one of the soldiers approaching him fainted. I tied a handkerchief about my nose. They grabbed the body by its leg, and it came off, by the arm and it came off. Is it that all men don't rot the same way? Why is this man in a hurry to rot? We threw some earth on him right there. Right there we found a machine gun tripod and its equipment. I loaded it on the backs of the soldiers. I returned to the major. 'Sir, we found these. We cannot bury the dead without picks. We

121

rolled the ones we found into ditches and threw some earth over them'. I thought maybe tomorrow someone else will get this job. The major said, 'All right, leave it till tomorrow, I'll give you picks tomorrow'. I thought 'Allah Allah, I am going to be stuck with this tomorrow again'.[10]

The 1/5 Norfolks have become the focus of this action mainly because of King George V's and his mother's, Queen Alexandra, personal interest in what happened to Captain Frank Beck, the Sandringham Estates Land Agent. Beck was also instrumental in forming the 'Sandringham' company before the war, which was made up of many of the grooms, gardeners, farm labourers and household staff from the King's estate. The Sandringham, or King's Company, was only one company of this Battalion, and this Battalion was only one of a four battalion brigade. Overshadowed by interest in 1/5 Norfolks, the Suffolks, Hants and 1/4 Norfolks barely get a mention. Another reason for the story getting fueled was due to so few men being reported as killed, most being posted as missing; so reports of the 'vanished battalion' hit the newspapers and the popular myth developed. Hamilton's Despatch sensationalized the event, which was written about again in the Official History, many newspapers, books, documentaries and in the television film *All The King's Men*. Stories of

Captain Randall Cubitt.

Lt. Victor Cubitt.

Lt. Eustace Cubitt.

2/Lt. Randall Burroughs.

the mysterious disappearance of the 1/5 Norfolks was also covered in some reports of the time, however, whilst as early as 1916 an article in the *Lynn Advertiser* stated that only 137 men were still missing – a big difference to that of a whole battalion!

The officer casualties were notable, as also were strong family ties between them. As with many locally raised battalions, there was a 'Pals' bond amongst the rank and file, and just looking at the officers we can see this was strong within the 1/5 Norfolks. Sir Horace's nephew, Second Lieutenant Montague Barclay Granville Proctor-Beauchamp served in the Battalion as did Frank Beck's two nephews, Lieutenants Evelyn and Alec Beck. There was the Cubitt family, including Captain Randall, Lieutenants Victor and Eustace Cubitt, Second Lieutenant Randall Burroughes, their cousin and also Lieutenant Roland Pelly, Randall's brother-in-law. To add to this the Cubitts were also distant relations of the Proctor-Beauchamp's. There were also the two Oliphant brothers, Lieutenants Marcus and Trevor, whilst Captain Arthur Mason was the brother-in-law of Captain Arthur Ward, the Battalion Adjutant. Apart from two identified burials in Azmak Cemetery, all the officers and men from the 1/5 Norfolks killed during this attack are commemorated on the Helles Memorial to the Missing (Panel 42-44).

An eye witness stated seeing a wounded Captain Pattrick, Lynn company, 1/5 Norfolks, and Sergeant Ernest Beart being disarmed and taken prisoner by the Turks. Both these men do not appear on any PoW lists, so are assumed to have been killed in action. Some men did survive captivity. Captain Cedric Coxon and Bugler Donald Swan were both wounded near the farm buildings and, whilst trying to make their way back to the British lines, were captured about a hundred yards from safety. In total the Turks captured at least two officers and thirty one other ranks during 163 Brigade's attack on 12 August. Two officers and fifteen other ranks were from the 1/5 Norfolks; eight of these were to die in captivity, whilst thirteen other ranks were from the 1/8 Hants and three were from the 1/5 Suffolks.

Second Lieutenant James Young, 1/8 Hants (Isle of Wight) kia 12 August (Helles Memorial).

The Brigade's casualties were heavy, especially amongst officers. The war diaries state that: 1/5 Norfolks lost twenty-two officers and 350 other ranks; the 1/8 Hants nine officers and 290 other ranks; and the 1/5 Suffolks, eleven officers (including Lieutenant Colonel William Armes) and 178 other ranks. The 1/4 Norfolks halted early on and so escaped casualties. Of those numbers, many wounded, disorientated and exhausted men returned back to the British lines over the next few days. The final casualty figure for the 1/5 Norfolks was adjusted to fifteen officers and 141 men killed on 12 August, of which only Captain Beck and sixteen men were recruited from the Sandringham **Helles Memorial.**

estate. Because of the Royal estate connection and interest and the fate of Captain Beck and the other men, this event, like so many others in the First World War, has become more myth than fact. Captain Beck's body was never found or, if it was, it could not be identified. After the battle a soldier found Beck's pocket-book and also his cheque book, but if this was found on the body or just lying on the ground is not known. The last sighting of Frank Beck was recorded in the *Lynn News & Country Press* in January 1916, when Private John Dye, from Beck's company, stated that he saw him later on in the attack *in a sitting position under a tree, with his head leaning over on to his right shoulder...I do not know whether he was then alive.* The next piece of news was received in late 1921 when Beck's gold Hunter watch was found to be in the possession of a Turkish officer who had fought in Gallipoli. The watch, along with some other items, including a small pocket knife, had been found during the war on the body of a British officer. The watch bore an inscription stating that the watch was given to Sir Dighton Probyn VC by Queen Alexandra. Probyn, who won his Victoria Cross during the Indian Mutiny, was a good friend of the Royal Family and spent his last years at Sandringham. The watch was subsequently given to Frank Beck by Probyn upon Beck's departure for Gallipoli in May 1915. The watch was purchased back and returned to the Beck family, with whom it remains as an heirloom.

In September 1919 the Reverend Charles Pierrepont Edwards MC went out to Gallipoli to establish what exactly had happened to the 1/5 Norfolks. Edwards was the chaplain to the 1/5 Suffolks during the war and had travelled out to Gallipoli with the Norfolks aboard the SS *Aquitania* in July 1915. He was awarded his Military Cross for rescuing wounded after 163 Brigade's attack that day. Whilst he was at Suvla with the Graves Registration Unit a report was released that stated *we have found the 5th Norfolks.* In total 180 bodies were found in the area of the attack about 800 yards behind the Turkish front line, of whom Edwards recorded that 122 were identified as 1/5 Norfolks. The rest were 1/5 Suffolks, 1/8 Hants and a few men from the Cheshires. One

Their Duty Done – Barnaby and Carter, 1/5 Norfolks.

man found had taken cover behind a stone and a large pile of empty cartridge cases round his skeleton showed that he had defended himself to the last. Edwards then came across the remains of about fifty men who had fallen in a grim hand-to-hand struggle; touching each other lay the bodies of Britons and Turks. Interestingly, the 122 figure is very similar to the earlier figure of 137 missing given in the *Lynn Advertiser.* This leaves fifteen missing from the 1/5 Norfolks, not the whole Battalion! Most were lying quite thickly around the ruins of a small farm, probably where most of the Battalion were surrounded and finally wiped out. When Edwards interviewed the Turkish land owner, he described returning to his farm after the war and finding many decomposing bodies of British soldiers, which he removed and threw into a ravine. These, and the remainder of the bodies in an area almost a mile square, were recovered and all buried in Azmak Cemetery; the unknown are commemorated on the Helles Memorial.

Support, in the form of 159 Brigade, was not contacted that day, so they remained ready in situ, awaiting the order to advance. Brigadier General Cowan did send forward 1/4 Cheshires and two companies of 1/5 Welsh, but by dusk they had returned, seeing little of the troops they were to support. The ground in this area was so difficult that it was not until 15 August that 163 Brigade and 159 Brigade found each other and joined up the line. With the exception of 163 Brigade's attack and the trench captured on Kiretch Tepe, 12 August was a reasonably quiet day for IX Corps, as were the following couple of days, which allowed both sides a respite. The earlier shortage of water had been resolved, as wells were discovered or dug across the Suvla plain, with water being found below ground without too much trouble. Stores were reaching the shore in greater volume and rations and ammunition were making their way by mule to the front.

With the line established and supply problems largely reduced, Hamilton prepared the next attack. This time he wanted the effort to be concentrated on the W Hills and Anafarta Spur. Hamilton was pushing for the attack but Stopford was concerned that, after the failure of 163 Brigade's previous attack, there would not be sufficient time to make the 54th Division ready. Stopford was worried that the 54th Division were a danger and might bolt at any minute, as he was also increasingly concerned about the loss of morale in 53rd Division who, under the shelling, were getting shaky to the extent that local commanders thought that they could break and seriously jeopardise the line. Major Thomas Gibbons, of the 1/5 Essex Regiment (54th Division), wrote:

It had been a trying ordeal for men who had no previous

experience of war; the want of sleep and fresh food, the constant strain, the blazing heat, the black plague of flies, the dirt and squalor of it all and, perhaps, more than anything else, the all pervading smell of death had proved too much for others more hardened than they, and it was no disgrace that the ordeal had proved too severe for a time for some sorely tried natures to bear.

Hamilton once again was forced to return to Suvla to see the situation first hand for himself. After the face to face meeting with Stopford and his subordinates, it led to Hamilton once again having to back down and accept a further postponement of an attack. There was a reliance on the two territorial divisions and if their commanders had no confidence in their ability without rest and reorganisation, beginning a new attack was doomed to failure. The criticism was probably over harsh of these divisions, as the officers and men in most of the units were in a position to fight, if handled properly. Up to this date they had lost heart because of ignorance of the situation and lack of intelligent orders. Senior command had failed them. That evening Hamilton cabled Kitchener to the affect that he thought the corps commander and the divisional generals were not fit to carry out a general advance. Now, with the fuse lit, he would await the response.

1 Burrows, J.W., *The Essex Regiment – Territorial Infantry Brigade*, (Southend: Burrows & Sons, 1932), p.48.
2 Unpublished diary of Major General John Lindley (private collection).
3 Loraine Petre, F., *The History of the Norfolk Regiment, 1914-1918*, (Norwich: Jarrold & Sons, 1953).
4 McDonagh, M., *The Irish at the Front*, (London: Hodder and Stoughton, 1916).
5 Crutchley, C. E., *Machine Gunner 1914-1918* (London: Purnell, 1975).
6 The 9th Regiment of Foot became the Norfolk Regiment in 1881 following the Childer reoganisation of the British Army.
7 Yarmouth, Sandringham, Downham and Lynn were the home towns of each Company of the Battalion.
8 In January 1915 E (Sandringham) and C (The King's) companies were merged when the battalion went from an eight to four companies, part of the general infantry reforms. The company was commanded by Captain F. R. Beck.
9 Described by Rev C. Pierrepont Edwards as British Map Reference, Square 118-I.
10 Hakki Sunata, I., *From Gallipoli to the Caucasus (Gelibolu'dan Kafkaslara)* (Istanbul: Bankasi Publications).

Chapter 6

DAY OF CRISIS: THE PIMPLE AND KIDNEY – 15/16 AUGUST

Their bayonets splinter from the sun's blinding rays

Now that there was time allowed to reorganise IX Corps, in particular his Territorial divisions, Stopford uncharacteristically decided to go on the offensive. Having mainly disregarded, until now, his left flank along the Kiretch Tepe ridge, Stopford decided that the recently reunited elements of Mahon's 10th Division were ready to advance. Since the first day Turkish defences on the ridge, in particular at Kidney Hill, had been a thorn in Stopfords northern flank. With attacks elsewhere failing, he now turned his attention to grasping the Kiretch Tepe issue. As Hamilton was making arrangements back on Imbros for Stopford's removal, Stopford, little knowing this would be his last action, had ordered Mahon to attack on 15 August and to capture the Turkish strongpoints of the Pimple and Kidney Hill, thus putting the British in a dominant position along the northern flank. Mahon had now got back his five battalions that Hammersley had borrowed, so was in a better position to continue the advance. Mahon's 10th Division, or rather what was left of his two battered brigades, were holding a line at Jephson's Post. The area from the sea up to the northerly slopes was being held by Brigadier General Nicol's 30 Brigade, whilst the southern slopes were now held by Brigadier General Hill's 31 Brigade. In support for this attack was Brigadier General Charles de Winton's 162 Brigade, which were camped near A Beach. It was planned for the Irish brigades to jump off from their current positions whilst 162 Brigade would attack Kidney Hill from the south.

It was believed that the area was only lightly held by the Turks, by the three companies of the *Gelibolu Gendarmerie* that had originally resisted the Manchesters' advance on 6/7 August and the Irish a couple of days later. This was now not the case. During the last few days two fresh regiments, a total of six full battalions with their machine gun companies, had come into the area. Commanded by Major Wilhelm Willmer from his headquarters close to the Pimple, he could also call upon two batteries from *11 Artillery Regiment*. The Turkish forces were deployed as follow: *2/127 Regiment* had moved on to the ridge in support after being transferred from the Asiatic side of the Dardanelles,

Irish in the trenches. One soldier attempts to draw fire from Turkish snipers as his mates catch up on sleep.

whilst Kidney Hill was defended by *3/19 Regiment* that had recently come up from Bulair. Further back *1/127 Regiment* were in reserve at Ejelmer Bay and *3/127 Regiment* behind Kidney Hill. Behind them the remaining battalions of 19 Regiment and the *1/39 Regiment* were also close.

With the new Turkish dispositions unknown, but in fact approximately seven times stronger than they were a week previously, Mahon issued his orders for a daylight attack at 1.00 pm. With last minute orders there was precious little time to plan properly for the attack and then to get all the men into position. Artillery support would be provided by 18 pounders from 58 Brigade RFA, four mountain guns, and two 60 pounders from the recently landed 15 (Heavy) Battery. Additional fire support from two naval destroyers, HMS *Grampus* and *Foxhound*, would be supporting the operation from the Gulf of Saros, thus making the artillery bombardment the heaviest so far employed at Suvla. Leading 30 Brigade, 7/RMF would clear the northern slopes whilst 5/Inniskillings would attack a small knoll on the southern slope, about 400 yards short of Kidney Hill. Supporting troops would advance along the crest to capture the two Turkish strongpoints before pushing across to support the attack on Kidney Hill, which was the main task for 162 Brigade on the southern flank.

After a successful bombardment on the northern flank, the attack started well, 7/RMF met little opposition and advanced steadily across the scrub covered slopes of the northern seaward ridge for almost a mile, capturing the Green Knoll and the Boot. Then 6/RMF, supported by two companies of 6/RDF, advanced along the crest towards the

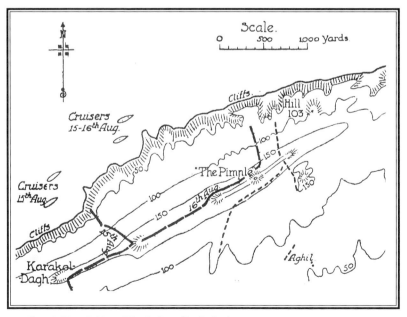

Kiretch Tepe Ridge (*The Pals at Suvla Bay*).

129

Looking towards the Pimple from the Jephson's Post cairn.

Turkish position, behind a rock strewn line known as the Pimple. The Turks continued to put up a determined defence of this strongpoint, which soon brought the advance to a standstill. At 6.00 pm Nicol, concerned that the advance had stalled, ordered the Irish to fix bayonets and charge.

Private John Hargrave, 32 Field Ambulance, who was a stretcher bearer on the ridge at the time, described the charge:

With the blazing sun setting at their backs, they stood up, fixed bayonets, and charged! Their sudden raucous outcry made me straighten up and turn my head sharp left. It was uphill for the first few yards. The Irish seemed to have been shot like rocket-men out of the sun itself, their bayonets splinter from the sun's blinding rays. Most of them were great strapping fellow, and there was a fair sprinkling of redheads among them. These, with flaming carroty stubble bristling their chins, mingled with the black eight-day growth of the majority, gave the charge a ghoulish frightfulness. They stormed up and over the crest at a bull-heavy canter, heedless of the thudding torrent of hissing lead that swept them. Many fell, but there was no wavering. The trusting bayonets flashed, blinked, and flashed again as they streamed forward along the hogsback. Few Turks stayed to meet them.[1]

This determined and heroic effort, despite heavy casualties, won the Irish this rock, and along with the successes on the seaward slopes, this put the British in a strong position that began to threaten the whole Turkish northern flank.

What was not so successful was the advance on the southern flank. The bombardment was not as effective as the northern slopes; the few shells that fell only alerted the Turks of the pending attack. The initial advance by 5/Inniskillings, however, began well but, lacking support and confronted by a strong defence, the attack here also stalled.

Second Lieutenant Ivone Kirkpatrick, 5/Inniskillings, who was wounded in the attack, wrote:

If the fire had any effect it must have been to warn the Turk to rise from his siesta. At 1.15 we started off at a brisk walk. My platoon was on the extreme left, that is to say the highest up and nearest to the crest on our side of the hill. In front of us the ground undulated downwards for some 200 yards; then came an even stretch of some 800 yards running up to the foot of Kidney Hill. Gullies, of irregular shape and size, ran at right angles to our line of advance and the ground was covered with scrub, very thick and prickly in places, whilst here and there were bare patches of sand and rock. We came under fire at once. Owing to the invisibility of the enemy it was not practicable to retaliate with rifle fire and our only course was to push on. My chief care and anxiety was to convey this to the men and to keep my platoon in line with the rest of the company. This was not as easy as it sounds. In the first place the scrub and the broken nature of the ground made it impossible often to see more than two or three men on either side of one. Secondly the rate of advance varied necessarily in various parts of the line. Whilst a section were racing across a bare sandy patch, the men on each side of them would be slowly pushing their way through dense clumps of scrub. It was only by dint of much labour and running hither and thither that it was at all possible to keep in touch with one's platoon let alone the rest of the company.[2]

The broken nature of this ground is still to be seen today, where it is easy to get lost in the tangled web of scrub, losing sight and sound of others if you are not careful. Battalion casualties were heavy (twenty officers and 336 other ranks), which included their commanding

Turkish view of the British lines from Kidney Hill, 2010.

officer, Lieutenant Colonel Arthur Vanrenen.[3] Without hope of continuing the attack and with no reinforcements, the Battalion was withdrawn across the same bullet swept ground they had just come. So what happened to their support, namely Brigadier General de Winton's 162 Brigade?

The three battalions in this brigade: 1/5 Bedfords, 1/10 Londons and 1/11 Londons[4] had reached the Irish flank at 1.00 pm, just fifteen minutes before the advance began. The Official History states: there had been no time to reconnoitre the very difficult ground over which the battalions were to move, and General de Winton had no information about the probable whereabouts of the enemy. During these early days at Suvla this was not unusual and indeed more the norm. Although the Bedfords began the advance with great enthusiasm, the ever increasing rifle and machine gun fire that met them with every step forward, coupled with the appalling nature of the ground, caused the advance to slow. The Bedfords first objective was strongly held by the Turks, but the leading companies:

Went to their work with a will and with that extraordinary verve which is so often characteristic of troops receiving their baptism of fire, and who do not as yet know the real meanings of wounds, and also of war seasoned veterans who have seen so many wounds that they have become fatalists. Well, as the leading

companies attacked, however, it became obvious that after a time their strength was not sufficient for them to crown the hill and establish even a temporary position without further aid. D Company was at once flung in to support the charge. The whole line went at it again and this wave of brave, intrepid and well disciplined men, only too anxious to blood their steel, soon cleared the position at the point of the bayonet.

With the first trench taken, the Bedfords reorganised and formed up for their next task, the capture of Kidney Hill. As soon as the Battalion

Turkish *Cheshme* on Kiretch Tepe.

continued on a very heavy fire immediately fell upon them. The casualties amongst the officers and NCOs were so high that one company was reported as being led by a private. Support from the two London battalions was sent forward to reinforce the Bedfords, but any momentum that had originally carried the Bedfords forward had already been lost.

Lieutenant Warren Hertslet, 1/10 (Hackney) Londons, wrote in a letter before the attack:

I hope my regiment will make a good show. Of course it is a tremendous moment in the minds of us all. None of us know how we shall stand shell and other fire in the attack. I personally feel very doubtful about my prowess in the bayonet charge. Well, by this time tomorrow I shall know about it or shall be unconscious of that or anything else.

He was to pay the supreme sacrifice that day. Hertslet is buried in Green Hill Cemetery (Special Memorial C5).

Lieutenant Allan Harding, 1/11 (Finsbury Rifles) Londons, was ordered forward from reserve in preparation for the renewed attack on Kidney Hill:

I hoped that I felt very brave and warlike. I had an alpine stick in one hand and a revolver in the other and on I went with my platoon. We went some way and then dipped down into a small, low valley where there were a whole lot of troops standing around really under cover. I said to one officer: 'Are you the firing line?' He said: 'Well, I suppose we are'. 'Well you've got to come with me. My orders are to go forward to capture the hill and to carry you with me.' I took my platoon on, we went over the slope and rifle fire started to knock around us. But there was no sign of the others following at all. They stayed in the valley. I was out on

Royal Irish Fusiliers, September 1915.

my own with my platoon deployed and my chaps started getting hit. I thought: 'Well, I don't know about this, it's not much cop!' I halted and thought I'd better try and get a message back to my company commander to say that I'd halted, to say what the position was. I got my orderly, wrote out the message on a field service message pad and told him to go back and find company headquarters. He didn't get more than about ten or fifteen yards and he was shot down. I thought: 'Well, that's not much good; I shall lose the lot if I go on like this.' So I decided to stay where I was. When darkness came we decided to go back as there was nobody on our flank at all. We started to withdraw, carrying our wounded and left two or three dead on the floor. We came to a line of troops who said they were the front line, they were all mixed up together and we joined forces with them. It was a mixture, a muddle, a mixture. Despite all their brave efforts, they could not maintain their hold on Kidney Hill and were forced to retire that night. That night the aftermath of battle was terrible. I remember the tremendous crash of rifle and machine gun fire close to and the 'thump' 'thump' of bullets and sparks flying from the stones while an officer, sergeant and six of us pushed through the scrub towards the curve of a hill which showed up darkly against the night sky. Between the bursts of fire the silence was broken by agonizing cries which will always haunt me: seemingly from all about that hill there were voices crying 'Ambulance' 'Stretcher-bearers' 'Ambulance' 'Oh damn you my leg's broken' and then again 'Stretcher-bearers'. It was horrible, we would start for a voice and it would cease and another far away would begin. That hillside was a shambles: evidently there had been a fierce hand to hand fighting there a few hours ago, rifles, kits, water-bottles, khaki, Turkish tunics and headgear were strewn everywhere among the scrub.

The Irish fight a desperate defence.

136

Some Territorials did manage to reach the forward slopes of

Kidney Hill, but here the advance stopped. De Winton went forward to try and inspire his men to advance, but was quickly wounded; the advance stalled again. They held this position, hoping for support to carry the hill, but none came and, with mounting casualties, a withdrawal during the night was forced. Thirty-seven officers and 900 men from the Brigade were lost in this attack, neither battalion managing to gain but a brief footing on the hill. The Bedfords alone lost fourteen officers and over 300 men that day.

Watching the battalions go into the maelstrom of rifle and shell fire were the 1/8 Hants (Isle of Wight Rifles). Ordered forward with the 1/5 Suffolks to support the hard-pushed Irish on Kiretch Tepe, the leading waves of the battalions soon advanced. The area they had to cross was devoid of cover and still under Turkish observation and, as in the previous advances, any movement was met by shrapnel fire. Waiting their turn to cross the open ground, and watching the men before them become victim to the shell and sniper fire, Captain Cecil Ellery's company refused to go forward. Whatever the reason, be it fatigue, lack of water, training, experience or confidence in their ability or leader, this had now become apparent. Facts are unclear of the exact circumstances, although we do know that there was an earlier incident before Gallipoli when Ellery was reprimanded in front of his men by Brigadier General Brunker. What now happened was Ellery, along with his mutineer Riflemen, were sent back to the beach by Brunker, but no further disciplinary action appeared to have been taken. Ellery's record was not tarnished for long; he ended the war commanding the battalion. It was also not long before Brunker departed; only days later he was invalided out of the army for good. The whole command structure was disintegrating at all levels, through casualties, through sickness, inexperience or sheer incompetence.

With the gains still held along the northern slopes, although no one side possessed the Kiretch Tepe crest line, the southern slopes continued to present a problem. Willmer had seen an opportunity and ordered forward both *1/19* and *1/39 Regiments* from reserve to join *2/19 Regiment* in a night counterattack. Thus started a series of ferocious bomb and bayonet attacks that began just before dawn on 16 August. The Irish and English troops resisted gallantly and, with grim determination, held back the Turkish onslaught. Additionally helped by the Munsters' 'guardian angel', a British destroyer in the Gulf of Saros, which kept its searchlights trained on No Man's Land, the Turkish attack was beaten back each time. Soon, however, the meagre supply of jam tin bombs that the Irish had been using ran out. This critical point in the defence witnessed men bravely trying to catch and throw

The Boot   The Green Knoll

The Boot and Green Knoll, 2010.

back the Turkish bombs. Many events of such bravery are recorded, such as that of Private Albert Wilkin[5], 7/RDF, who was mentioned in despatches for such a deed. Five times he performed this feat before his luck ran out; on the sixth attempt he was blown to pieces. Many more men followed suit; their names today lost to history. In the intensity of the battle, and without bombs, some men out of frustration even resorted to throwing rocks and stones followed up by bayonet charges to help safeguard their gains. The Irish position was one of hopelessness; blood and brawn would not be enough.

At 8.00 am on 16 August, Willmer increased the pressure on the Irish by ordering forward the *2/17 Regiment*, which had just arrived from reserve. The Irish still held on, but by 9.00 am the continued fighting prompted an urgent call for support, but this fell on deaf ears. Whilst the Irish were fighting for their very existence, Hamilton was fully immersed with the removal of Stopford and his generals. At this time Hamilton was actually unaware of the action on Kiretch Tepe but, worse still, Mahon, the divisional commander, had just resigned. At the

Gulf of Saros

Hill 103
(Northern
Redoubt)

height of the battle, when the Division needed him the most, he threw his hat in (the reason will be explained later). The Irish held on bravely, fighting throughout the day until 7.00 pm. Now in the dark, and fearing a complete collapse of the line, and giving up on any hope for reinforcement, Nicol reluctantly ordered a withdrawal from the Pimple and conceded most of the Hogsback to the Turks. The Pimple was never recovered, although the ground on the northern slopes, namely The Boot and Green Knoll, were retained. By dawn on 17 August the Irish and Territorials were back in the trenches whence they had started the day before. The cost, for little gain, was about two thousand men. The Turks also lost close to that number.

Even if Hamilton was not aware of this attack, von Sanders and Mustafa Kemal most definitely were. Still fearing a British breakthrough here, and concerned by the threat of the earlier advances, the Turks sent the *2/1 Regiment*, *3/1 Regiment* and the complete *126 Regiment* to help Willmer. They were not required, as early on 17 August the Turks were already back occupying their original positions and outposts on the top of the ridge. What was not known at the time

Taking the wounded down from Kiretch Tepe.

was how close the British came to victory in this attack. Firstly, the capture of Kiretch Tepe could have led to the outflanking of the Turkish forces and loss of the Tekke Tepe heights. Secondly, at Ak Bashi Bay the Turks had positioned their main ammunition storage depot, completely unknown to the British. If the attack had carried as far as Ejelmer Bay, this depot, which supplied the Turkish army on Gallipoli, would be under serious threat. Von Sanders feared an attack in this area and wrote in his memoirs, *Five Years In Turkey* (1927), that 15 August was a day of crisis, that if *the British had taken the Kiretch Tepe they would have out flanked the entire Fifth Army and final success might have fallen to them.* Von Sanders did not need to fear, as the advance on this ridge had no real objective and had no real support. Ak Bashi was never an objective and the attack could be described as an afterthought of Stopford's. Ironically Stopford's last order was for an attack; however this was too late and insignificant and achieved little more than the futile waste of life and a few more yards of scrub.

1 Hargrave, J., *The Suvla Bay Landing*, (London: Macdonald, 1964), p.216.
2 IWM DOCS: I. Fitzpatrick, Typescript account, pp.27-28.
3 Lieutenant Colonel A. S. Vanrenen is commemorated on the Helles Memorial, panels 97-101.
4 1/4 Northants only landed at noon on 15 August.
5 Private Albert Edward Wilkin, 7/Royal Dublin Fusiliers, is commemorated on the Helles Memorial, panels 190-196.

Chapter 7

STELLENBOSCHED – THE BRASS HATS GO

This is a young man's war

Even with the reinforcements of the 53rd (Welsh) and 54th (East Anglian) Divisions, both now ashore, giving Stopford the best part of four divisions, albeit with limited artillery, there was still limited progress. Stopford now blamed the reason for his paralysis on the Turks, claiming they were inclined to be aggressive. Did Stopford think it was going to be a walkover, without the need for a real fight? Many of his men did get into a real fight but, despite their brave efforts, this was not exploited. There was a general feeling that they had been let down by their own senior command.

Hamilton did nothing of substance to intervene. All he did was hope for a breakthrough and keep Kitchener up to date with the situation. On 9 August Hamilton cabled Kitchener:

> *I can find no sufficient reason why we were not in possession of the country from Ejelmer Bay to Biyuk Anafarta early yesterday morning except that just as no man putteth new wine into old bottles so the combination between new troops and old generals seems to be proving unsuitable except in the case of the 13th Division.*

That said, Hamilton still did nothing to change the situation. In this telegram he was open with his praise of the 13th Division, which was fighting under Birdwood's direction at Anzac, and thus critical of the 10th and 11th Divisions performance under Stopford. The performances of the 53rd and 54th Divisions were no better.

Hamilton's view of Stopford and his generals were further cemented by a report from a staff officer, Major Alexander Hore-Ruthven VC, who stated:

> *I found the 53rd Division in a line of lightly dug trenches, with men standing about on the parapet and even cooking in front of the trenches. No work was going on, and there was a general air of inaction. I was astonished to find that this was the front line. There*

Major Alexander Hore-Ruthven VC.

141

were no Turkish trenches or Turks in sight, and only some occasional desultory shelling and sniping. While I was there it was discovered that some troops in trenches in bushes on our left front, which for some days had been thought to be Turks, were in reality British. Every visit to Suvla discloses confusion, inertia, and magnification of difficulties, due to the pessimistic attitude of higher commanders and staffs, which filters down to the troops.

Hamilton finally cabled Kitchener on 14 August, reporting that the IX Corps generals were unfit for command. He had finally had enough of Stopford and his divisional generals:

The result of my visit to the IX Corps, from which I have just returned, has bitterly disappointed me. There is nothing for it but to allow time to rest and reorganize unless I force Stopford and his divisional generals to undertake a general action for which, in their present frame of mind, they have no heart. In fact, they are not fit for it. I am exceedingly reluctantly obliged to give them time to rest and reorganize their troops.

Kitchener swiftly replied:

If you should deem it necessary to replace Stopford, Mahon and Hammersley, have you any competent generals to take their place? From your report I think Stopford should come home. This is a young man's war, and we must have commanding officers that will take full advantage of opportunities which occur but seldom. If, therefore, any generals fail, do not hesitate to act promptly. Any generals I have available I will send you.

Kitchener immediately made available Lieutenant General Sir Julian Byng for the command of IX Corps. But this was a week too late. If Hamilton had had Byng originally the August campaign could have had a different outcome. Byng was the complete opposite to

Sir Ian Hamilton.

**Lieutenant General
Sir Frederick Stopford – relieved.**

**Lieutenant General
Sir Bryan Mahon – resigned.**

**Major General
Frederick Hammersley – relieved.**

**Field-Marshal
Horatio Herbert Kitchener.**

Generalleutnant **Otto Liman von Sanders and the Duke of Mecklenburg-Schwerin setting off to view the latest position at the front. Turkish continuing success could be attributed to the decisiveness of command by Sanders.**

Stopford and possessed the qualities of a commander that Hamilton so sorely needed at Suvla. On 15 August the old Suvla command began to disappear. Hamilton dismissed Stopford and, while Byng was travelling from France, temporarily replaced him with Major General Henry de Beauvoir de Lisle, commander of the 29th Division at Helles. Hamilton intended to retain Mahon in command of the 10th Division, as he was probably the only general in IX Corps that was *fit for it*. However, Mahon was infuriated that de Lisle, whom he disliked, was appointed above him and quit, saying: *I respectfully decline to waive my seniority and to serve under the officer you name. Please let me know to whom I am to hand over the Division.* He abandoned his Division while it was in the thick of the Kiretch Tepe fighting and was immediately sent to Imbros to cool off. The 10th Division was then put under the temporary

Major General de Lisle, temporary GOC IX Corps.

command of Brigadier General Hill, who was only to last another week himself before he was evacuated with acute dysentery. On 17 August the commander of the 53rd Division, Major General Lindley, voluntarily resigned, *on the grounds that his Division had gone to pieces and that he did not feel it in himself to pull it together.* The 53rd Division was then put under the command of Major General Herbert Lawrence. The following day Brigadier General Sitwell was relieved of his command and replaced by Lieutenant Colonel Hannay as commander of 34 Brigade. Command as well as the general situation was quickly collapsing.

The culling of the Suvla generals was going to be a little too late. Arguably the battle was lost after 9 August and the only hope left now was that the experience and leadership of Major General de Lisle, with the reinforcements of both the 29th Division and the 2nd Mounted Division, could produce a miracle. It is worth noting that both these divisions were not at full strength; the 29th Division had been badly mauled since the April landings and could only send two brigades

Lieutenant General Sir Julian Byng, appointed to command IX Corps, but too late to make a difference.

whilst the Mounted Division was really only brigade strength, with about 5,000 men. The 'Immortal' 29th Division from Cape Helles was likened to Napoleon's Old Guard, a body of men who could be relied upon, deciding the fate of a battle. However these regulars were a shadow of their former self and, like the Old Guard, it was to retreat in the face of overwhelming odds.

A lot rested upon Major General de Lisle's shoulders. He was not liked by many and had a reputation for a brute force approach, a complete contrast to Stopford. He was arriving to strange surroundings and in command of a disorganised and exhausted Corps with officers and men with whom he was unfamiliar. Casualties had been heavy, morale was low and what they had to show for themselves was little more than an exposed beachhead and partial gains along the Kiretch Tepe ridge. De Lisle's immediate task was to organise the Corps quickly so that it was in a position to continue the battle. What in reality faced de Lisle were positions that had been steadily reinforced by the Turks. If they were not able to be captured when lightly held, the demands for the same men to capture the heavier fortified positions were not going to make things any easier. For every minute of delay the Turks were getting stronger. The *Anafarta Group*, still under the command of Mustafa Kemal, now consisted of seven divisions and a cavalry regiment. Deployed from the north at Kiretch Tepe to the south at Battleship Hill, the group was supported by their divisional artillery, amounting to approximately a hundred guns, the majority of which were positioned in and around the W Hills, ironically the area de Lisle was to attack next.

Chapter 8

THE LAST GREAT SHOW – 21/22 AUGUST

Great Scott! This is a bloody business

Major General de Lisle's plan was to capture the heavily defended W Hills and Anafarta Spur, by a sweeping motion that would begin to push the Turks from the high ground and thus secure Suvla Bay. This was nothing original and why it was thought that it could succeed now when it had failed earlier goes to show the lack of tactical thought and almost an ignorance of command. Remember, these were the objectives that were obtainable during the first days of the Suvla landing, when they were practically undefended, not now when the Turks were there in force. Supporting IX Corps' depleted brigades were 5,000 fresh, dismounted, yeomanry from the 2nd Mounted Division and a brigade from 29th Division. The Yeomanry were to arrive from Egypt on 18 August, followed shortly afterwards by the 29th Division from Helles. Also supporting the attack would be an Anzac brigade, which would cooperate on the immediate right flank, in the vicinity of Hill 60. The 29th Division would be used to capture Scimitar Hill and the 11th Division would try again, after its last failed effort, to capture the W Hills, leaving the Yeomanry in reserve, to be called upon when needed.

Even with this injection of manpower, de Lisle could only muster 10,000 rifles for the attack and realised quickly this would not be enough to capture and hold both the W Hills and the Anafarta Spur. There were also concerns that to capture and hold the Anafarta Spur, Tekke Tepe would also need capturing. He thus amended the plan to capture the W Hills only. De Lisle soon became confident of success and planning began. The attack was to commence at 3.00 pm on 21 August, to take advantage of the setting sun. This time of day would allow the infantry to advance with the sun at their backs, thus aiding the artillery, whilst also blinding the defenders with the glare. This fine detail was refreshing for Suvla, but would it be enough to make a difference, a difference that could give the British a new hope?

The hard task ahead of him was not only apparent to de Lisle, but also to Hamilton, who had now acknowledged the failure of Suvla and the general August offensive. Hamilton cabled Kitchener on 17 August to inform him that his *coup had so far failed* and any hope of surprise on the Turks had passed. Not only this, but the Turks now outnumbered

147

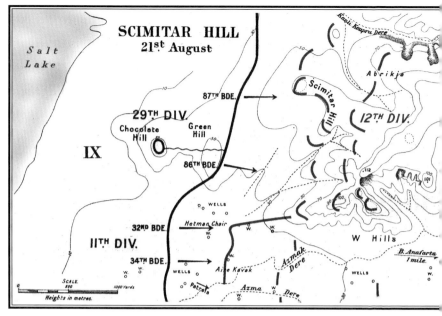

Scimitar Hill, 21 August.

him, their morale was good, they possessed all the advantages of position and ammunition supply did not appear to be a problem. Without an extra 95,000 troops, which would give Hamilton superiority, the offensive would be a failure; with no reinforcements Hamilton would be forced to reduce the Suvla perimeter to an area only slighter larger than Anzac. Hamilton would have to wait for a reply as there was another crisis brewing back in London; the Western Front was the priority again.

During the evening of 17 August the first of the 29th Division brigades arrived from Helles, two battalions of which were attached to the 53rd Division to help them consolidate the line. Now de Lisle had more seasoned troops to hand and had spent a couple of days assessing the Suvla situation, his confidence of success increased. He realised that the Turkish trenches, although obviously now defended, were not as heavily fortified as those at Helles and few, if any, were wired.

On 18 August Major General William Peyton's 2nd Mounted Division began to land. In April 1915 the Yeomanry had been sent to Egypt as possible reinforcements for Gallipoli, now it was their time to be

148

tested. The Yeomanry were formed into a brigade and initially attached to the 10th Division. Now that Mahon was gone and Hill sick with dysentery, Peyton was given temporary command of the Division, whilst Brigadier General Paul Kenna VC was given command of the Yeomanry in Peyton's place. Coming ashore at dawn, the Yeomanry were directed up to the Karakol Dagh to dig in.

Captain William Wedgwood Benn, 1/1 County of London Yeomanry:

> It was only a matter of ten days since the first landing had been made at Suvla Bay, so that the arrangements for disembarking were of an elementary kind. There was a pier, but it was not completed, and the road from it up the hill hardly existed. The skyline, which was only faintly illuminated with the early glow of the dawn, was jeweled with bursts of artillery, and occasionally a shell would fall in the water near our ship. Our disembarkation

A Squadron, The City of London Rough Riders, prior to their shipping to Gallipoli.

was effected by means of big dumb barges, covered with shell-proof hatches so as to protect the troops in their short passage from the transport. The ship kept as far as needful from the beach, which was well within reach of the Turkish guns. When we landed we were planted in a position which gave some shelter from the artillery fire, but our men were enjoined to get to work at once and dig themselves in for the next night. This was not an easy job for, with a small entrenching tool, working on ground which is little else but rock lightly covered with soil, it is hard to make a bank big enough to afford adequate protection ...With the help of my batman I dug a splendid hole behind a rock ...Our joint efforts produced a luxurious and well-protected villa residence on which we proudly carved in stone the name 'Battle View'.

With the new blood at Suvla there was an air of optimism about, with positive efforts to improve the situation. During 18 August the line was pushed forward in many places. The 54th Division had straightened the line south of Jephson's Post whilst the 53rd Division had filled a gap on their flank. It did not always go to plan. At dawn on 19 August, 34 Brigade tried to push their line forward near Hetman Chair. They soon met strong resistance and, in the movement forward, suffered a devastating casualty toll. One battalion, 8/Northumberland Fusiliers, continued to edge forward but without support, and lost nearly all its officers and 400 men in doing so. This damaged the Battalion to the extent that this unit had to be temporarily replaced in the line. As seen from Lindley's earlier remarks, and not uncommon of the period, the plan of attack was only shared with the officers, as NCOs held no authority. Sergeant William Fenwick, 8/Northumberland Fusiliers:

> *I personally knew nothing of the movement except we were to deliver an attack, although in charge of a section. Everything seemed to be in a rush at the last minute. Our casualties for the whole of the Regiment would be about 450 in about forty-five minutes. I think if the NCOs had been given a little of the programme before going into action, probably the casualties would have been lighter, as we lost all the officers except one.[1]*

Efforts were made to bring in the wounded during the day, but often this resulted in further sacrifice. Lieutenant Thomas Peel, RAMC, attached to 5/Dorsets, volunteered to go out at about midday. Initially he was not fired upon, allowing him to help several men, but then a sniper spotted him. Mortally wounded, Peel dragged himself back to the trenches, dying a few days later.[2] During the night further efforts were also hampered due to the Turkish fusillade that swept No Man's Land, allowing only a few to be rescued. The following morning Captain Ferrers-Guy, 9/Lancashire Fusiliers, went forward to support the action of 'straightening the line' and wrote of an interesting incident in his diary:

> *August 20th – Turkish officer came about armistice. Turks'*
> *Medical Corps good to our wounded. Brought in five*
> *Northumberland wounded. They were only allowed to come to*
> *within 200 yards of our trenches and our stretcher bearers*
> *fetched the wounded in. One Turkish officer passed through*
> *Brigade to Divisional Headquarters, and found he did not want*
> *to return, and surrendered. The Turks were shouting for us to*
> *return the officer. I honestly believe they thought we would not let*
> *him return.[3]*

The Yeomanry digging in after landing.

A further account, by Captain Arthur Gregory, 5/Dorsets, also described this remarkable episode:

> *Two Red Crescent men came out, Second Lieutenant George went and met them half-way between the trenches. George saluted them and they saluted, placed their hand to forehead and heart and bowed very profoundly. George offered his hand, at which they were delighted; a limited conversation then took place in French. They offered to carry all our wounded in, but on refusing that they stood by while our own stretcher-bearers went out and fetched then in; when they arrived in the trenches all of them had received first aid at Turkish hands, so the firing we had experienced the previous night had evidently been used to cover the work of their medical men. This episode was carried on in full view of both sides, men standing in the parados on both sides, and the greatest friendliness was shown by the Turks to Lieutenant George and to the stretcher-bearers that went out.[4]*

The following day, in the big attack, Captain Arthur Gregory would be wounded and Second Lieutenant Frank George killed. George is commemorated on the Helles Memorial, Panels 136-139.

To add extra weight to de Lisle's attack, Hamilton ordered up the remaining brigades of the 29th Division; but of these 86 Brigade arrived on 20 August whilst 88 Brigade, which was holding the front line at Helles at the time of the order, were only able to embark during the night of 20/21 August; the 2/Hants did not arrive until the battle had begun. De Lisle now wanted to make a broader attack with this added support, but this was flatly refused. Hamilton needed certainty for the capture of the W Hills without undue risk caused by trying to achieve too much with too few troops. If this operation was successful, the idea of capturing the Anafarta Spur and Tekke Tepe ridge was not even

Waiting for battle – Dugouts on Chocolate Hill.

mentioned, and in Hamilton's eyes it was not necessary anymore. Hamilton faced a dilemma of mounting casualties through combat and disease and no hope of any early reinforcements. It would weaken his forces if they were stretched too far. On the other side the Turks were steadily being reinforced to an extent now that at Suvla the British command believed that they faced 75,000 rifles against Hamilton's 50,000. Capturing the W Hills and, hopefully, Scimitar Hill and Hill 60 would therefore allow the line to be shortened, if necessary, thus allowing sufficient troops to hold the area from Lala Baba, Chocolate Hills through to the W Hills. The Kiretch Tepe ridge, Suvla Bay and the open Suvla plain could then be sacrificed for this stronger line, which would widen Anzac, to be shared by both Birdwood's Anzacs and IX Corps. The writing was already on the wall before the battle began.

The plan was for 11th Division to capture the W Hills whilst the 29th Division would simultaneously take Hill 112 and Scimitar Hill. These objectives were the priority and, if taken, there was flexibility in the plan for the Yeomanry Division, the corps reserve, to go forward and take Hill 101, due east of Hill 112, giving IX Corps command of the northerly area of Abrikja. The plan was left fluid enough for the 53rd and 54th Divisions, if opportunities permitted, to make an advance. In support of the attack was to be a brief thirty minute bombardment. This was kept short mainly for lack of shells, but it was also hoped that it would give no time for the Turkish reserves to reach Hill 112 before the 29th Division got there. At the same time the Anzacs would capture Hill 60, which had been a menace to the Anzac-Suvla line of communication. This attack was commanded by Major General Herbert Vaughan Cox, who had put together a composite brigade of about 3,000 rifles, a mix of British, Australian, New Zealand and Gurkha battalions.

In reality opposing the attack at W Hills and Hill 60 were two Turkish divisions; the *7th* and *12th*, whose boundary was astride the Azmak Dere. The *12th Division*, including the *Bursa Gendarmerie* and other units under Major Willmer's command, faced de Lisle's attack whilst the *7th Division* stood in the way of Major General Cox. The Turks also had in reserve twelve battalions from both the *6th* and *9th Divisions* within a five mile march of Suvla. Major General de Lisle faced no easy task in a battle that the Turks would remember as Second Anafartalar.

As the build up to the battle commenced, much of it in plain view of the Turks, it was not long before a desultory shelling began to fall on

29th Division battlefield.

Kavak
Tepe

Sulajik

Tek
Te

the British. By the morning of 21 August the Turks definitely knew that something was afoot; fire then begun to increase as targets were spotted. By midday a haze blanket rose up from the Suvla plain as the sun disappeared into the cloud. The weather was hot, the atmosphere tense and now this eerie haze began to mask the area, including the Turkish positions. Hamilton later wrote:

> By some freak of nature Suvla Bay and plain were wrapped in a strange mist ... this was sheer bad luck, as we had reckoned on the enemy's gunners being blinded by the declining sun and upon the Turkish trenches being shown up by the evening light with singular clearness, as would have been the case on ninety-nine days out of a hundred. Actually we could hardly see the enemy lines this afternoon.[5]

The omens were not good. At precisely 2.30 pm the British artillery bombardment began but, with lack of shell and little knowledge of the Turkish positions, this proved useless. On paper the eighty five artillery pieces allocated for the bombardment, with additional naval support from a battleship, three cruisers and two destroyers, may have looked impressive, but with poor visibility and shortage of ammunition the numbers gave no advantage. Midshipman Harry Denham wrote a worrying note in his diary: *our shooting was pretty bad; I know for a fact that one casemate had 7 on their fuse instead of 27 and hence wasted shrapnel on our own troops.*[6] If matters could not get worse, several of the larger calibre 60 pounders, which de Lisle needed for counter battery work, soon developed defects and had to be withdrawn from action. The bombardment achieved little and had the result feared

Baka
Baba

Scimitar
Hill

Anafarta
Sagir

of alerting the Turks of the pending attack; a heavy retaliatory bombardment now pulverised the British trenches, packed with troops waiting to attack.

To achieve a heavier concentration of artillery, de Lisle had made a last minute change to his plans. This was to delay the Anzac attack, which was originally planned to correspond with 11th Division's advance, by half an hour. This would allow the Anzac artillery to add their weight to the shelling on the W Hills and Scimitar Hill before they would switch to shelling Hill 60. The 11th Division would begin their attack at 3.00 pm, whilst the 29th Division and Anzacs would attack at 3.30 pm. As the 29th Division front was at least 700 yards away from the Turkish positions, the assaulting battalions of 86 and 87 Brigade were ordered to send forward one company 500 yards forward of the British trenches. This movement was also hoped to give the appearance that the whole line in front of Scimitar Hill and W Hills was advancing in conjunction with each other, thus reducing any concentrated fire on the 11th Division alone.

Lieutenant Ismail Hakki Sunata, *2/35 Regiment*, recalled the lead up to the British attack:

> *Two howitzer shells whined over our heads. They fell on 5 Company a little to our left. One shell fell in front of the trench, and another behind it. There was a tremendous explosion that filled the air with dust and smoke. Howitzers are different from other guns. We can't hear the gun fire. It's coming from somewhere on the right flank. The shells make a strange whistling noise as they pass over our heads. Then they land and explode with a great noise. They destroy where they land. May Allah help those who happen to be there. They are using Chocolate Hill as an aiming point. The trenches on the other side of it are under heavy artillery fire. This is turning into a major battle. The shelling goes on and on. The howitzer shells are coming so fast they seem like a constant thunder. Fortunately very few are*

11th Division battlefield. Approximate position of the British trenches.

Chocolate Hill   Green Hill   Scimitar Hill

falling in my area. The closest is about 30 metres away, on the far end of my platoon. From there to the left is dust, smoke, noise, confusion and terror. Nothing can be seen for the dust and smoke. I cannot see how far the bombarded area extends. A while later the 3rd Battalion companies, who were in reserve, began to arrive. They are sent to fill the gaps in the shelled trenches, but the shelling is still going on, so they pack into our trenches. There is hardly room to move. With great difficulty I was able to get some of them out and moving. Anyway, it is pointless to send more troops to be killed there. They can wait in readiness a little in the rear. It appears that the enemy will attack.[7]

Hetman Chair – 11th Division Attack

The first objective of the 11th Division was a trench that ran from Aire Kavak, near Azmak Dere, to Hetman Chair. Behind this trench was another at the base of the W Hills, joined by a communication trench; these were first objectives for the leading waves. This area consisted of wide open, cultivated fields, as they still are today, crisscrossed with irrigation ditches, lines of hedges and patches of scrub, all ideal for defence. 32 Brigade would send two battalions (6/Yorks and 6/York & Lancs) to attack the northern end of this line at Hetman Chair, whilst 34 Brigade would attack the southern section with two battalions (5/Dorsets and 9/Lancashire Fusiliers). To protect the divisional flank, patrols would be sent out to meet up with the Anzacs on the southern side of the Azmak Dere, towards Susak Kuyu and Kazlar Chair. Supporting the attack twenty-two machine guns had been amassed from the 11th Division, 2nd Mounted Division and the Royal Naval Armoured Car Division, that would fire down from Chocolate Hill. Once these trenches had been captured the remaining battalions of these brigades would push on to capture the W Hills themselves. Defending this position was a single battalion, *1/34 Regiment.*

With the attack planned for that afternoon, by 8.00 am 11th Division's orders had still not reached the brigades in the front line. The operation orders were written seven hours previously, but apparently the orderly who carried them was either shot or lost his way. It was not

etman Chair   Hill 112   W Hills   Azmak Dere

Some of the twenty-two machine guns amassed for the attacked.

until 10.00 am before duplicate copies finally got through to the Brigade HQs and, as one Brigade Major said: *the orders were lengthy ones, and it took some time to master the details and to draft Brigade Orders.* The result was that some commanding officers were only able to inform their battalion officers of the scheme at the last minute, leaving little if no time to digest what was required. This would have a direct bearing on the attack.

One officer with 6/York & Lancs was Second Lieutenant Priestman who, in a letter home, described the moment before the whistle blew:

You must try to imagine us squatting on our haunches in a shallow and dusty trench, listening to the most appalling uproar you could dream of. Behind us our big guns are roaring, above us the shells are tearing through the air, and in front of us, all up the long valley ahead, the crash of their bursting is simply deafening. Somewhere (all too vaguely described to us) are three lines of Turkish trenches which must be taken today. But the valley is broad and thick with bushes, and the enemy is cunning to conceal his position. No matter! This terrific bombardment

will surely overawe him and make our advance a simple matter. So we sit and listen and wait for the hour to come when we are due to hurl line after line of British Tommies against those trenches. Can you picture the feelings of all of us as we watch the minute hand slowly creep towards three? Ten minutes only now. Now only seven. And what of us all when that hand shall have touched the half-hour... ? And now the moment has come. A whistle sounds – a scramble over the trusty parapet we have learned to know as a shield for so many hours, and the valley is before us. The air is full on every side with invisible death.

Priestman was soon to find out that the bombardment had failed in most places, leaving the Turkish lines relatively untouched. As the 6/Yorks and 6/York & Lancs rose in attack they were met by an immediate fusillade of bullets. The ground they had to cover was flat and open and with over 500 yards to cover, the Yorkshire men became easy targets. Priestman continued his account:

'Whisss! phutt!' A bullet kicks up a little spray of dust from the dry, grey earth underfoot, another and another to left and right. The sensation of terror is swallowed in an overwhelming conviction that the only possible course is forward – forward at any cost. That is what we have been telling ourselves all through the long waiting, and that is our only clear impression now. Forward - and we instinctively bend as one does to meet a hailstorm - and rush for it. Beyond the rough ploughed ground over which we are advancing lies a low, thick belt of brambles and bushes. Here, for a time, we can lie under cover and regain our breath for a second rush. The man on my left stumbles and comes down with a crash and a groan. Only an instinctive catch of the breath and the old conviction – forward at all costs – swamps all other sensations. Down we go behind the kindly shelter, and the bullets fly over us. Telling the men to be quiet, I crawl through the brush to try and find our direction for the next

Scimitar Hill   Hetman Chair

Hetman Chair and the Turkish positions.

rush. Satisfied of our direction once more, our line bursts through the bushes and rushes over the open for the next hedge. A few piteous bundles behind us tell of our lessening strength – and now a new horror discloses itself, 'Boom! whirrrrr-crash!' On every side the ground is torn up by the heavy leaden pellets as the shrapnel bursts above us. And to left and right of me fresh sounds break out – dreadful human sounds which I won't describe. Hotter than ever this time, but there's another friendly hedge ahead. Strange how one notices details too. The straws that cover the hard, dry furrow, the broken rifle, carefully cleaned and oiled that morning, the old plough under the hedge where we throw ourselves down breathless. 'Boom – whirrr-crash! zzzzzrrrr!!' Sand, stones, earth fly in all directions through a yellow cloud of smoke; that was high explosive, ten yards behind us! Surely we must be near the first line of trenches now and that bayonet-charge which I have been dreading more than all. We were told it was only five hundred yards from our trench to the enemy's – and none of us realize that we have left that trench far on our right, from where the Turks are getting our lines broadside on, where a bullet can do double or treble work.

32 Brigade's attack at Hetman Chair was faltering. The initial waves of the attack soon lost direction, moving almost in a northeasterly direction. Realising their mistake, the lead battalions still attempted to carry the communication trench, however they never succeeded in correcting the original error, which made this task almost impossible. Both the 8/West Ridings and 9/West Yorks were quickly sent forward in

support, but they too ran into similar problems, first swinging too far left and from a northerly position then came under enfilade fire from the same Turkish communication trench. This loss of direction, largely due to the loss of the officers, left the men not knowing exactly what was expected of them. The attack was rushed; orders were late and in the most part vague as to their objectives. The men continued the advance as best they could, but they were quickly forced to ground, some finding cover in a shallow ditch that helped protect them against the incessant Turkish fire. As more survivors of the attack gathered here it was clear that the plan was failing.

33 Brigade was now sent forward from their reserve position at Lala Baba to support 32 Brigade. Their open formation was met with heavy shelling that had the effect of separating the formation, so two of its battalions actually ended up with 34 Brigade instead. The remaining two battalions carried on towards 32 Brigade's positions, which were floundering around Hetman Chair. The 9/Sherwood Foresters, led by Lieutenant Colonel Lionel Bosanquet, immediately assaulted the Turkish position at Hetman Chair. Bosanquet, who had been previously wounded here on 9 August, had only just rejoined the battalion. His reunion was not to last long and with his second-in-command, Major John Blackburne, was killed. Bosanquet is commemorated on the Helles

Major John Blackburne, killed at Hetman Chair.

161

Memorial, Panels 150-152 whilst Blackburne is buried in Green Hill Cemetery. From a letter it was said that Bosanquet,

> *must have done well, for he was close up to the enemy, ahead of most of his men, who were stretched out behind him, never a one with his back turned, and all in perfect alignment.*

The 6/Borders suffered a similar fate to its sister battalion when they attempted to assault the same position, also losing their commanding officer, Lieutenant Colonel George Broadrick, who is also commemorated on the Helles Memorial, Panels 119-125. The majority of the resistance again was coming from the Turkish communication trench that had been loop-holed. Without its capture, 11th Division was prevented from reaching the slopes of the W Hills. The shelling was so intense, and the scrub so dry, that the brush caught alight, hampering the attack as it tried to edge its way forward.

One senior NCO in the 6/Borders, CQMS Albert Victor Prosser, a veteran of the Boer War, was recommended for the VC for rescuing wounded, but was instead awarded a DCM and immediate commission. The *London Gazette* citation reads:

> *For conspicuous bravery and devotion to duty on the 21st August, 1915, at Suvla Bay (Dardanelles). During an advance over a bullet-swept area a fire broke out in the scrub, and a number of wounded were in imminent danger of being burnt to death. Quartermaster-Sergeant Prosser went out under very heavy fire to bring in a wounded officer, who was, however, killed by a second bullet before he could be put into shelter. He immediately returned and brought in another wounded man and continued going out and dragging the wounded out of the burning scrub and carrying them into safety on his back. Owing to his bravery and total disregard of personal risk he undoubtedly saved many lives. He was under heavy shell and rifle fire throughout.*

In a letter of congratulations dated 12 November, Brigadier General Robert Maxwell wrote:

> *...my very best congratulations both on your DCM and commission...I had hoped that it might have been a VC but I daresay with the promotion the other would suit you better; I did my best for you...*

Second Lieutenant Prosser DCM was killed on the Somme in November 1916 and is buried in Mesnil Communal Cemetery Extension.

Further abortive attempts were made into the evening to take the objectives by Maxwell's 33 Brigade, but to no avail.

The attack further south had a little more success, although initial Turkish resistance from the undamaged front line, missed from the earlier bombardment, inflicted heavy losses on the first wave. Losses amongst officers in 5/Dorsets and 9/Lancashire Fusiliers were particularly heavy. Even so, 34 Brigade managed to capture a portion of the Turkish front line, about 300 yards in length at Aire Kavak, and secure the adjoining part of a dry stream, namely the Azmak Dere. Attempts to capture the second Turkish trench failed. A sandbag barricade was quickly built across the streambed to help safeguard this gain and protect against the deadly fire the Turks were pouring into the nullah.

> *It was a pitiful sight now, the trenches being crammed full of dead and wounded and the cries of the wounded must have touched even the stoutest of hearts. Evening was now closing in and it was decided to stay here for the night although it was a nasty position to be in, as we were enfiladed and many were hit. The place was full of bodies of our own troops and the stench was awful.*[8]

The Lancashire Fusiliers were detailed to send out a patrol, commanded by a sergeant, to make contact with the Gurkhas from Cox's brigade, who were expected on the right flank. However, the patrol soon returned after meeting parties of Turks in the area instead. At one stage a body of troops was reported crossing their front who shouted: 'Don't shoot, we are Gurkhas'. These were probably Turks just trying their luck. What had not filtered down to this battalion was the last minute change in orders that delayed the Anzac attack on this flank; there were no Gurkhas, just open space, which was now filling quickly with Turks readying themselves for the counterattack.

The 6/East York, now commanded by Major M. G. Cowper, were sent up in support. To reach the captured trench they had to cross over 500 yards of open ground. Cowper wrote:

Sergeant Wilfred Mather, 9/Lancashire Fusiliers. Killed on 21st August (Commemorated Helles Memorial).

163

we got it pretty hot ... you could see the shells burst and feel bullets whistling through the air, could see the dust kicked up and the grass beaten down as though a severe hailstorm was going on.

Reaching the beleaguered Dorsets and Fusiliers, Cowper arrived with only about half a company. They would have to wait until further supports would arrive before the next line of trenches could be attacked. This was not to happen, as no more supports could get through. So Cowper set about consolidating the newly won trench. The Turks were now determined to recapture the lost ground and directed concentrated fire along the parapet, pinning the British down. Little did the 6/East Yorks seem to care. One man was reported as being so excited that he stood up waving his arms about like a madman and shouting incoherent things at the Turks. He was quickly hit, a bullet cutting his cheek, which only made him more furious, until at last someone pulled him down, still shouting, to the bottom of the trench.

In and around the Azmak Dere the Turks held back any further advance. Lieutenant George Mee, of the 6/East Yorks, led a small party of men forward to try and outflank the Turks, but this failed; the young subaltern was shot through the heart and died instantly. Mee is

Azmak Dere in 1915.

commemorated on the Helles Memorial, panels 51-54. This corner of the battlefield soon became too dangerous to hold, prompting Cowper to take up a less exposed position farther back in the nullah. A message was sent back to 34 Brigade HQ, asking where support from 33 Brigade was. The runner returned with a message that said they had gone in a different direction to that ordered. Only one lieutenant and twelve men of the South Staffs eventually came into the trench, reporting that they were all of 33 Brigade that had made it. No further advances could be made, although two companies from the Manchesters also managed to reach this precarious position, but with insufficient numbers to renew the attack; any continued advance would be futile.

A message was sent back asking for more ammunition, food, water and stretchers. Only ammunition arrived. Lieutenant Edward Sanders, 5/Dorsets, wrote:

> *It was already dusk. They were running short of ammunition in the battle line. All night long we worked, bringing up boxes from the dump and loading up parties with cotton bandoliers. It was a very dark night and you never knew whether you were going to step into a nest of Turks or your own men.*[9]

In the meantime stretchers had to be improvised for serious cases and the lame and slightly wounded had to get back as best they could. Night came without any cessation in the volume of rifle, machine-gun and shell fire. Cowper later stated that throughout the hours of darkness of that awful night there was not five minutes when there was a real lull in the firing. The situation in the nullah had grown gradually worse. The ground in front of the trench sloped rather steeply down, and was covered with thick bushes and small scrub. Through this the Turks crawled up close to the defenders and threw bombs over the barricade and into the trench. A lookout had to be posted on a bank, where he could overlook this bit of ground; he was given a revolver, and fired whenever he saw some dark object moving in the scrub. This helped the situation a little; it was a tense night.

After a sleepless night, dawn broke on these utterly worn out men. First light brought a renewed Turkish artillery bombardment and then a counterattack using bombs. The East Yorks, Lancashire Fusiliers, Manchesters and South Staffs fought on bravely, but it proved difficult without any bombs themselves. Lieutenant Sanders wrote:

I had taken up ammunition to a small party of East Yorks and Lancashire Fusiliers, about early dawn, who were holding on nobly to a sandbag parapet which was constructed across the Azmak Dere about 200 yards in front of our line; they were being badly bombed and had to retire later owing to the sandbags catching fire.

Highland Barricade in the Azmak Dere after August 1915.

Above right: Highland Barricade Today.

At this time a general withdrawal was ordered back to the original front line: the time was about 7.30 am, 22 August. All the ground so bravely fought over during the last sixteen hours was relinquished.

Lieutenant Eric Halse, 6/East Yorks, wrote:

During the night we held the captured trench in spite of counter attacks but in the morning we were turned out of it. We retired to our support trenches and, expecting to find nobody, you can imagine we were surprised to find that it was full of men of the 10th Division. Yet we had been told that there were no troops available to reinforce us, and here were the fellows, three battalions of them, 500 yards behind us. Result of the attack: nil. We (the East Yorks) lost another 200 men and seven officers out of eleven. It is a scandalous, wicked shame. If things had been properly managed we could have had a ridge of hills (which was the idea of our landing) at half the cost. Now we are no further forward than the day we landed and yet we are losing men and have suffered so much. Oh it is wicked and somebody ought to be made to suffer for all the mistakes. I can't express all I want to, it is beyond me; but if I live to get home I shall just say what I think.[10]

Scimitar Hill – 29th Division Attack

As the 11th Division began their advance at 3.00 pm, the leading companies of the 29th Division were sent out ahead of the British front line. Heavy shellfire was already descending upon the British by this time, and it was not long before the dry, scrub covered, slopes of Green Hill caught alight. Although this hindered the movement forward in some places, the smoke generated had the effect of helping to cover the advance of the leading companies into No Man's Land. Casualties were minimal at this stage; the advance appeared to be going to plan. 86 Brigade's task was to capture Hill 112, which lay on the end of the Anafarta Spur, approximately 1500 yards east of the front line on Green Hill. 1/RMF would lead the attack, supported by 1/Lancashire Fusiliers. The 2/Royal Fusiliers would follow in reserve, whilst the 1/RDF would remain in the British front line. Opposing 86 Brigade were two battalions; *2/34 Regiment* and *2/31 Regiment*, both commanded by Colonel Mehmet Ali.

At 3.30 pm the main 29th Division advance began. The Munsters began their attack but quickly came under fire from the Hetman Chair,

168

The British reserve lines south of Chocolate Hill, 1915.

the same trench that had caused the failure of the 11th Division's advance. The fire was so devastating that very few men from the Munsters even managed to reach the leading company that was waiting 500 yards in front. The Battalion moved off with 700 men; nine officers and 400 men quickly became casualties. Captain Guy Nightingale, 1/RMF, recalled:

> *They all got mown down by machine gun fire ... The Turks shelled us very heavily and the whole country, which is covered with gorse, caught fire. This split up the attack and parties got cut up. Many of our wounded were burnt alive and it was as nasty a sight as I ever want to see.*

Nightingale remained in the front line with the battalion headquarters, but still came close to becoming a victim of the blaze.

> *Our Headquarters was very heavily shelled and then the fire surrounded the place and we all thought we were going to be burnt alive. Where the telephone was, the heat was appalling. The roar of the flames drowned the noise of the shrapnel, and we had to lie flat at the bottom of the trench while the flames swept over*

The gentle slopes that were fire swept in 1915. Scimitar Hill, with Tekke Teppe in the background.

> *the top. Luckily both sides of the trench did not catch simultaneously, or I don't know what would have happened. After the gorse was all burnt the smoke nearly asphyxiated us! All this time our Battalion was being cut up in the open and it really was very unpleasant trying to send down calm messages to the Brigade Headquarters ...the telephone wires finally fused from the heat.*[11]

Within minutes the Munsters' advance had come to a standstill. The Lancashire Fusiliers, who followed shortly afterwards in support could

Scimitar Hill engulfed in flame.

achieve no more, so that an hour later no part of 86 Brigade had got any further than the leading companies, and these were pinned down in No Man's Land. To their north 87 Brigade had a little more success assaulting the northern slopes of Scimitar Hill, defended by *2/35 Regiment*. Lieutenant Ismail Hakki Sunata, was positioned north of Scimitar Hill and described the scene:

> *Suddenly the howitzers shelling the trenches fell silent. The naval guns and shrapnel shelling the rear continue. When the howitzer fire stopped the dust and smoke over the trenches slowly began to clear. From the right the word was passed by mouth: "The enemy has risen to the attack, let the left flank take care!" Indeed, behind the slowly clearing dust and smoke, from our position we began to see masses of British advancing. We immediately opened fire on them from the flank. The enemy is not attacking our front, but that of the units to our left. Our flanking fire is very effective. As the dust and smoke cleared from over them the units to our left also opened fire. Now it's up to the infantry. All the reserves and other idle forces began to move in that direction, towards the area under attack. The infantry fire is getting stronger and stronger. I doubt the enemy can succeed when all is up to the infantry rifles. But I don't know how much damage the artillery fire did. The British keep coming. We see this and fire incessantly. Now all the artillery sounds are dying away.*

The leading company of the 1/Inniskillings had advanced just after 3.00 pm to gain a position on the lower slopes of Scimitar Hill. This was achieved with very little loss. At 3.30 pm the remainder of the Battalion launched themselves forward through heavy enfilade fire to capture the

crest of the hill and the Turkish trench on its eastern edge.[12] However, as soon as they reached this position, they were immediately subjected to heavy machine gun fire which cut down the Inniskillings in their tracks. Most of this fire was coming from the direction of a knoll on map reference 105 D8, the importance of which was not realised at the time of launching the attack. With severe losses, the line broke and withdrew further down the hill to a ledge about hundred feet below the crest. The attack was carried forward again with the support of the 1/Borders and 2/SWB, but the crest was not reached again.

At 5.15 pm de Lisle, believing that Hetman

Turkish troops manning their defences.

Turkish field gun crew in action, in a blatantly posed photograph.

Chair had now been captured by the 11th Division, ordered the renewal of Major General Marshall's 29th Division attack.[13] This attack would now be supported by what was considered the cream of Britain's rural volunteers, the 2nd Mounted Division. There would be no exploiting success of the earlier attack, as there was not any to exploit; the Yeomanry were expected to push through and capture the same objectives that had held up 86 Brigade and then, with 87 Brigade, sweep along Scimitar Hill and across the end of the Anafarta Spur to capture Hill 112. If these hills were taken, this would allow the 11th Division to advance again on W Hill. It was now the turn of the Yeomanry to try where the regular troops had failed.

Another new division had been offered up on the altar of expediency. With no battle acclimatisation, no briefing, no maps, no idea what was happening, they were sent into the burning scrub on the hills.[14]

The Yeomanry's Baptism of Fire
At 3.30 pm the 2nd Mounted Division, under the temporary command of Brigadier General Paul Kenna VC, was ordered to advance from their reserve position at Lala Baba to Chocolate Hill. Once there, they would be in a position to push through the 29th Division to capture their assigned objectives. One by one the five brigades, each consisting of just under a thousand men, began to cross the open expanse of the dry Salt Lake. Reminiscent of a parade, they advanced; regiments followed each other in squadron order, each squadron then in line of troop order at set regular distances, advancing with echoes of the Charge of the Light Brigade minus the horses. *Theirs is not to reason why, Theirs is but to do and die* goes Lord Tennyson's poem, just before *canon volley'd and thunder'd, Storm'd at with shot and shell, Boldly they rode and well, Into the jaws of Death, Into the mouth of Hell.* Captain Wedgwood Benn, 1/1 County of London Yeomanry:

After about half-an-hour's progress we reached the enemy's shrapnel, through which, of course, we were bound to pass if we were to attain Chocolate Hill. As each line of the Division advanced into the beaten zone, the shells did their part, being timed to burst just ahead of our march. Casualties began, but our orders were strict, and forbade us to stop for anyone. When men fell they had to be left for the stretcher parties, which were following. As adjutant I was to and fro with Colonel "Scatters", who, though slightly injured in the foot, was marching in front of the line. Suddenly I saw with horror my troop hit by a shell and eight men go down. The rest were splendid. They simply continued to advance in the proper formation at a walk, and awaited the order, which did not come for another quarter-of-an-hour, before breaking into the double. Some men exhibited extraordinary calm. I remember one picked up a tortoise, surprised to see it running wild, and another, an NCO, observing a man drop his rations, bent and gathered them up for him, an act which just brought him in reach of a splinter which wounded him. Everyone was intensely excited, but all were bravely self-controlled.

Their morale and enthusiasm was high, this would be their first action, in fact the first time under fire for most.

The spectacle of the Yeoman of England and their fox-hunting leaders, striding in extended order across the Salt Lake and the open plain, unshaken by the gruelling they were getting from shrapnel, which caused many casualties, is a memory that will never fade.[15]

The yeomen were a target that the Turkish gunners could not miss, however the shrapnel was set to burst too high and casualties were not as heavy as they might have been. Major Aubrey Herbert viewed their advance from No.2 Outpost at Anzac:

The Yeomanry never faltered. On they came through the haze of smoke in two formations, columns and extended. Sometimes they broke into a run, but they always came on. It is difficult to

Advance Across The Salt Lake.

Turkish machine gun team.

describe the feelings of pride and sorrow with which we watched
this advance in which so many of our friends and relations were
playing their part.[16]

By 5.00 pm the whole Division had reached the cover of Chocolate
Hill, an advance of almost two miles, where the task ahead was
explained to the brigadiers. For this attack Brigadier General Lord
Longford's 2 (South Midland) Brigade was to take over the old front
line from 87 Brigade, to the north of Chocolate Hill. From there they
would renew the attack on Scimitar Hill, now known to the troops as
Burnt Hill. To the south Brigadier General Arthur Taylor's 4 (London)
Brigade, followed by Brigadier General Edgar Wiggin's 1 (South
Midland) Brigade, would take over 86 Brigade's line at Green Hill and
assault Hill 112. Lieutenant Colonel Edward Cole's 3 (Notts & Derby)
Brigade was to be in support, whilst Brigadier General Julian Tyndale-
Biscoe's 5 Brigade would be in reserve. Within half an hour the
brigades were on the move to their new jumping off positions, with
little knowledge of the task ahead of them or of what had already
befallen the 29th Division. All the brigadiers had been briefed; however
two of them still did not know exactly what they were meant to do. If
the brigadiers did not know, this left little hope for their officers and
men. Captain Wedgwood Benn, 1/1 County of London Yeomanry:

During the next advance we had no shell fire to meet, only rifle
and machine-gun fire, a new experience for us, and one which
inspired more fear than it really merited. We ran across the first

175

THE WARWICK YEOMANRY IN GALLIPOLI.

"A HORSE, A HORSE, MY KINGDOM FOR A HORSE"

'My Kingdom for a Horse.'

field and jumped into a line of trench supports of our own, then out again and forward into the next trench, leaping in on top of the men of the Division ahead of us, whose reserves we were. They nearly all, I recollect, shouted to us as we approached to take cover and get down, but almost always tried to wave us away from the particular part they themselves were occupying. The fact was they were packed tight, I should say one man to every fifteen inches. From here we got into a communication trench filled with men of the Irish Division [probably Irish troops from the 86 Brigade] *whose gallant attempt earlier in the day had failed. We had to stand aside to let pass a pitiable, ghastly procession of maimed, most of* whom had been half-stripped to have their wounds bound by their friends. The horror of that scene will bear no describing. Fearing the effect on the morale of our men if we stayed a moment longer, we decided to jump out of this trench altogether and to run across the field in front to a small hill a little ahead of us. As far as we could see it provided good cover, for there appeared to be a number of reserves lying there in perfect quiet and safety. Out we sprang with a shout and ran forward to the selected spot, only to find that it was under brisk machine-gun fire. The reserves were quiet indeed, for they were dead!

The Mounted Division was now firmly

committed to the chaos of the last attack; bodies were lying all over the ground in front, whilst wounded continued to dribble back from the mist ahead. The scrub was still aflame in many places and the acrid smoke added to the general haze that still covered the battlefield. The continuing din of battle only added to the confusion. All knew that there was only an hour of daylight left; progress had to be made quickly. Captain Wedgwood Benn, continued:

> We lay down flat, and then crawled a little higher up the hill, hearing all the time the terrifying rattle of a Maxim which we, of course, thought was the cause of all the killing. We assured one another for our better comfort that it must be one of our own guns covering the advance, and this, in fact, turned out to be true. We saw nothing for it now but to get up and shift our position. For one thing the bushes in front of us were alight and the fire was steadily advancing on to the corpses at our side. It was from this incident that the hill became known on the maps as 'Burnt Hill'. Having made up our minds, we rose, leaped over a low communication trench, across another field, and into the advance support trench we tumbled, despite the fact that it was already full. We were now behind the spot which came to be known later as 'Yeomen's Knoll'. ... it was getting dark, and we began to arrange our forces on the left and right to try to make

The terrible fires around Scimitar Hill.

up the line in order to hold it for the night ... We were all in a state of the greatest uncertainty, not knowing who was who, or where the enemy was to be found.

Sir Ian Hamilton, who had sailed over from Imbros to watch the battle from the Karakol Dagh, wrote:

By 6.30 it had become too dark to see anything. The dust mingling with the strange mist, and also with the smoke of shrapnel and of the hugest and most awful blazing bush fire formed an impenetrable curtain. As the light faded the rifles and guns grew silent.

Brigadier General Lord Longford – died leading his men into battle.

Just before 6.00 pm, Lord Longford's men, which consisted of 1/1 Royal Bucks Hussars, 1/1 Berkshire Yeomanry and the 1/1 Dorset Yeomanry, reached the old British front line by 87 Brigade. As they arrived, 2/South Wales Borderers (SWB) made a renewed advance towards Scimitar Hill, with instructions for one company to assault the knoll (105 D8) to the north of Scimitar Hill which had been giving trouble to the earlier attacks. It was not a positive sight that met the Battalion. The SWB's adjutant, Captain Aubrey Williams, noted that: *an endless stream of wounded Inniskillings and of the Border Regiment testified to the reception awaiting us.* The 2/SWB attack began at 5.30 pm. The late afternoon haze provided some cover for the initial advance, but the sheer volume of the Turkish musketry and shell fire fell upon them, testifying to the enormity of the task which could not be achieved alone.

Lord Longford personally led his Brigade forward, *walking about as if the storm of bullets had been hail*[17], in support of 2/SWB, to attack the northern parts of Scimitar Hill. There was initially confusion amongst the SWB, who expected the Yeomanry to attack on

178

Dorset Yeomanry Officers before leaving for Gallipoli.

their right, not through the middle of them; however the muddle surged forward. Ashmead-Bartlett described the attack:

> *The mob surged upwards. The roar of the guns, the crackle of rifle fire, the burr of the machine guns, was incessant, and then these blurred khaki figures disappeared into the darkness and were lost to view.*

Even though casualties soon mounted, the lie of the ground in this area afforded some protection from the deadly Turkish fire, enabling the advance to gain some ground. The crest of Scimitar Hill was once again captured, but also, once again, when the troops gained the top, Turkish enfilade fire was so accurate that the position could not be held.

The Turks, as described by the War Diary of the 1/Inniskillings, *were now standing on their parapets and firing from the hip and throwing hand grenades. The enemy shrapnel is very accurate and inflicted heavy casualties.* At 7.00 pm Captain Gerald O'Sullivan VC[18] 1/Inniskillings, collected together about fifty men, mainly from the Yeomanry, who were sheltering in a small nullah just below the crest line and, made another charge up the hill. This attack had some success and the first Turkish trench was reached, although already abandoned by the Turks. An attempt by O'Sullivan to reach the second Turkish trench failed; it was here that he fell, along with virtually all of his men; only a wounded sergeant returned. This detachment, so far in advance, and with no supports, had little hope of success. At least eight Yeomen were captured by the Turks during this action. Amongst those that survived the war in captivity were three members of the 1/1 Dorset

Yeomanry: Captain Douglas Pass, Corporal Ernest Hunt and Trooper Archibald Poole.

As the light faded the trench line along the crest was evacuated, either by order or panic, as witnesses wrote of Yeomen running back, shouting that they had the order to retire. This in turn took with them other units who were clinging to the top of the hill, the line soon withdrawing to a position further down the slopes, whence the battalions had earlier advanced. It proved impossible to retain Scimitar Hill whilst Hill 112 and W Hills remained in Turkish hands; the concentration of these combined strongpoints was too great. Lieutenant Ismail Hakki Sunata, *2/35 Regiment*, noted:

> *It is getting dark. With the ceasing of the artillery fire some calm has descended on the scene. But the infantry fire continues. The sound of the artillery has given way to other sounds. From our left come shouts, moans, groans and screams, and orders are given. The rear of the trenches is full of wounded and moaning men, there are dead also. In the twilight some are coming, some are going, total confusion. Nothing can be understood of what is happening. A medical orderly has been raked across the stomach at the level of his navel by a machine gun, his wounds are exposed.*

> *The word came an hour later. The British had broken into the trenches of the 34th Regiment on the hill [Scimitar Hill] to our left. Our battalion's 6th Company got there, joined by some forces from the 3rd Battalion. They drove the British back and retook the trench. Later the 64th Regiment came up as reinforcements. There are many dead and wounded. The enemy wounded are also calling out in front. The enemy was completely repulsed. The night passed with carrying the wounded and burying the dead. We were all awake. The day's events had made us so nervous we had forgotten even what sleep was. Some prisoners had also been taken. These rumours went around by word of mouth. We had suffered heavy casualties for lack of defensive equipment. The enemy had heavy losses because they were attacking, and because of the incompetence of their attack.*

Captain Aubrey Williams, 2/SWB, and his orderly went forward to find out the situation for themselves, as no information was forthcoming as to the situation ahead. Williams passed groups of wounded men from different regiments, none knowing what was happening or even where the enemy was. He wrote:

I could find no proper firing line so moved up to the top of the hill to reconnoitre. I found nothing there but a large number of British and Turkish dead. The orderly and I crawled over the crest and about thirty yards down the other side could make out a line of Turks. Many of them were kneeling in the open, firing at the top of the hill. Every few minutes bursts of MG fire swept the crest; most of it seemed to come in enfilade from the right [Hill 112]. It was obvious that there was no hope of being able to hold the crest. We crawled back and started to organize a line about thirty yards below the crest.

It was getting dark and a rough organised line just below Scimitar Hill was created, with the few survivors of the Yeomanry in the middle, 2/SWB to the left, 1/Borders to the right and the 1/Inniskillings in support at the bottom; the hill was prepared for the night.

The Turks must have heard us moving about as they suddenly advanced to the top of the hill and both lines faced one another, kneeling in the open at about 30 yards distance. The Turks showed up against the skyline whilst we were in the shadow. They soon had enough and withdrew and we went on with our reorganisation.

The remains of 87 Brigade could have occupied the crest during the night, but the problem would be at first light, when flanking fire would start again. For now they rested on the lower slopes, which gave them some protection. Captain Wedgwood Benn, recalled what happened that night:

About half-past one, in reply to several requests that we might be permitted to go on, a young officer ran along the trench, shouting that the orders were to retire at once. I can remember how foolish I thought his conduct, for the effect on our troops, under fire for the first time and completely fatigued by ten hours of fighting, was of the worst. However, I had to carry the order to the regiment on our left, and gradually the whole of what remained of the Brigade was withdrawn and began to form up in a road some two or three hundred yards to the rear. I was then sent back to inform whatever troops I could find on our right that the Brigade was moving. For me this was the most unpleasant hour I had had during the day. The moon seemed suddenly to be extinguished, and the rifle fire to redouble in vigour and the flashes all to become visible, though up to then I had hardly noticed them, I was suddenly convinced that the Turks now were

actually coming on. I found the regiment on our right, and shouted out my instructions in much the same style as the officer I had been blaming. I was pulled together by the conduct of a very young person in charge, who rose from the trench and most strenuously damned me for giving orders direct to his men, adding that as they did not belong to our Brigade he intended to ignore the orders and remain where he was. I shall always admire that exhibition of grit.

An onlooker of the day's events was Captain John Gillam, Army Service Corps, who noted:

We had not advanced our position, which was the same as before the battle. The gorse is burning fiercely on my right, lighting up the immediate neighbouring country. Several wounded were caught in it and burnt to death before they could be rescued, but many were saved, and some gallant deeds were done in their rescue.[19]

Captain Frank Hurndall, the adjutant of the 1/1 Berks Yeomanry, in a report written on 22 August, described the attack:

On reaching our own front line trenches and passing over them, the line of attack moved somewhat to the left to avoid the Salient SW of Hill 70, which was swept by machine-gun fire. Our advance still continued, though under heavy fire; and the fact that none of the enemy or his trenches could be seen owing to the scrub rendered the return of fire with any degree of accuracy impossible. About 100 yards short of the Turkish trenches the Regiment got some cover under a slight ridge and here the Brig-General, Lord Longford, ordered the charge. In the meantime some of the Dorsets and Bucks Yeomanry had prolonged our left. On the order to charge what remained of the Regiment swept over the ridge into the enemy's trench. At this point I would draw your attention to the gallant conduct of the Regiment and Major Gooch, who was first into the trench, closely followed by 2nd Lieutenant H.C. Blyde, the point captured formed the apex of a triangular trench. Owing to enfilade fire down the left the trench could not be held and after about ten minutes had to be evacuated. The remnants of the Regiment, together with parties

Ambulances on the Suvla Plain.

from various other Regiments, assembled in the cover afforded by the gully to the south of Hill 70.

This was held by a party of South Wales Borderers and Border Regiment. During the night the enemy counter-attacked, and it was eventually decided by Major Nelson, of one of the Infantry Regiments present and the senior officer there, to evacuate the position at about 4.00 am, 22nd August as it was considered untenable by daylight. All the wounded were removed to the rear during the night and the retirement was conducted in good order and without confusion. Being the senior officer left, I collected the Regt under cover of Chocolate Hill about 6.00 am on the 22nd and then reported to Colonel Grenfell, Commanding the Brigade. I regret to report a large number of casualties. The Regiment went into action with nine officers and 312 men, of these five officers and 165 other ranks are reported killed, wounded or missing.

Major Edward Gooch, wounded in the head during the attack, was evacuated from Gallipoli but died of wounds exactly a month later, and is buried in Fort William Churchyard, Scotland. Second Lieutenant Hubert Blyde survived the war. Lord Longford and his Brigade Major, Major Henry Watkin, both reported as missing, were later presumed killed. Longford's body was later found and is buried in Green Hill Cemetery (see tour section); Watkin's is named on the Helles Memorial to the missing, Addenda Panel 204. Also to die was Lieutenant William Niven, 1/1 Berks Yeomanry, the father of actor David Niven. He is also buried in Green Hill Cemetery as detailed later.

In a report from another squadron, Captain Philip

Major Edward Gooch, gallantly led his men in the capture of a trench.

Wroughton, later killed in Gaza in 1917, described the action he saw and mentions Niven:

> My Squadron reached Chocolate Hill with no casualties. I there received orders from Major Gooch to advance to attack Hill 70. My orders were to keep in touch with 1st Squadron Berks Yeomanry (Captain Hurndall's) and to keep the right of my squadron on the path running East from Chocolate Hill. The advance was to commence immediately. I ordered Lieutenant H Crosland to proceed with two troops extended in advance, and followed with the remaining two troops in Troop Column. I halted in our first line trenches until Major Gooch gave the order to proceed. This we did in Troop rushes until we reached a ridge that afforded some cover under the top of Hill 70. To get to this point it was necessary for Lieutenant Crosland to swing his left round somewhat to keep the direction. I then advanced with one troop (Lieutenant Niven's) to the gully at the top of Hill 70, where some of the 29th Division were holding on gallantly under a heavy fire. We remained here until the 1st Squadron came up on my right and the Dorset Yeomanry came up in support. The charge was then ordered by the Brigadier. We got to the 2nd line of the enemy's trenches. Whilst here I received a verbal message from the Brigadier to Major Gooch (who was here wounded) to support the left of our line if possible, followed almost immediately by another verbal message to retire to the ridge. Our position at that moment was quite untenable and the left of our line was already retiring. We retired behind the crest of Hill 70 once more, where the Bucks Yeomanry came up in support. Time 7.30. I have no farther knowledge of what happened, being shortly afterwards rendered unconscious.
>
> As far as I could see every man in the squadron did his duty gallantly throughout the attacks and I find it impossible to single out men for your notice where all were doing well. But I think that the four troop leaders, Lieutenants Niven and Crosland, and Sergeants Hewer and Horne deserve great credit for the skill with which they brought their troops up to the attack without losing place or direction in a particularly difficult piece of country, and without unduly exposing their men. Private... brought the first message from the Brigadier down the line under exceptionally heavy fire and after the retirement I particularly noticed Corporal Chasney (wounded) Private How and Private ... who helped me to try and collect the men who had become scattered

184

Lieutenant Niven (right), just after landing at Suvla (Berkshire Yeomanry Museum).

Inset: Lieutenant W.E.G Niven, killed on Scimitar Hill.

BELIEVED TO BE BURIED
IN THIS CEMETERY
LIEUTENANT
W. E. G. NIVEN
BERKS. YEOMANRY
21 AUGUST 1915 AGE 37

THEIR GLORY SHALL NOT
BE BLOTTED OUT

in the darkness and confusion.

Another of Lord Longford's men was 22 year old Private Frederick William Owen Potts, from B Squadron, 1/1 Berks Yeomanry:

> *We began to ascend Hill 70 in short spurts, halting from time to time. We had fairly good cover, because the scrub was not on fire, though several parts had been burnt out. During one of these halts we were ordered to fix bayonets. We had found shelter in a bit of a gully, and were pretty well mixed up with other regiments – the Borderers, Dorsets, and so on. We first got the idea that we were going to charge from an officer near us; but he was knocked out with a broken arm, I believe before the charge came off. He was just giving us the wheeze about the coming charge when a bullet struck him. An officer shouted, as far as I can recollect, "Come on, lads! We'll give 'em beans!" This is not exactly according to drill-books and regulations as I know them; but it was enough. It let the boys loose, and they simply leapt forward and went for the Turkish trenches. It was not to be my good fortune to get into them, however; in fact, I did not get very far after the order was given. I had gone perhaps twenty or thirty yards when I was knocked off my feet. I knew I was hit. I had a sort of burning sensation; but whether I was hit in the act of jumping, or whether I jumped because I was hit, I do not know. What I do know is that I went up in the air, came down again, and lay where I fell.*[20]

Potts had been shot through the thigh, the bullet luckily missing a major artery and the groin by a fraction of an inch. He lay, helplessly, in a little thicket of scrub, watching the advance continue. The Berkshires had some success forcing the Turkish defenders from their trench, but, when reduced to little more than a dozen men, they were also compelled to withdraw. Potts, observing the advance from further down the hill, was soon joined by another wounded Berkshire lad, a trooper named Arthur Andrews.

> *We lay there, perfectly still, for about ten minutes. Andrews had been shot through the groin, a very dangerous wound, and he was suffering terribly and losing a great deal of blood. We had been together for a few minutes when another trooper, a stranger to me (a Bucks Hussar), crawled up to our hiding place. He had a wound in the leg. We were so cramped for space under the ticket that Andrews had to shift as best he could, to make room for the newcomer. That simple act of mercy saved his life, for the*

stranger had not been with us for more than ten minutes when a bullet went through both his legs and mortally wounded him. He kept on crying for water; but we had not a drop amongst the three of us, and could not do anything to quench his awful thirst.

That fearful afternoon passed slowly, with its grizzling heat and constant fighting, and the night came quickly. The night hours brought us neither comfort nor security, for a full moon shone, making the countryside as light as day. The cold was intense. The stranger was practically unconscious and kept moving about, which made our position worse, because every time he moved the Turks banged at us ... I lay absolutely as flat as I could, with my face buried in the dirt, for bullets were peppering the ground all around us, and one of them actually grazed my ear. This wound covered my face in blood. Was I scared or frightened? I can honestly say that I was not. I had got beyond that stage, and almost as a matter of course I calmly noted the details of everything that happened.

Throughout the night Potts and Andrews hung on, but the unknown Bucks Hussar had died of his wounds. They had suffered terribly during the day, from incessant Turkish sniping as well as the heat of the sun, thirst, hunger and the pain of their wounds. As daylight replaced moonlight and with firing still going on, they could observe stretcher bearers further down the slope, but they were too far away for their help. They chose to remain hidden upon the upper slopes of Scimitar Hill until night fall again. During the night they decided that they had to move, as staying would mean certain death. Painfully they covered about 300 yards towards the British lines, using water bottles from the dead to help quench their thirst. Under cover of some scrub they rested until the following night before making another effort to continue their journey. Andrews had gone as far as he could, begging Potts to leave him. Potts refused and with the aid of a shovel, to which he fastened Andrews, he dragged him very slowly towards the British lines. The Turks observed this movement and fired at Potts who, carefree, continued to drag Andrews down the hill. Potts knew he had reached safety when he heard a challenge from an Inniskillings' sentry. Both survived their forty-eight

Private Frederick William Owen Potts VC.

187

hours ordeal on Scimitar Hill and were soon evacuated to Malta for hospital treatment. Potts' gallant act of selfless devotion resulted in the award of the VC, the first yeoman to be given the award. He said that he felt that he had done no more than any other British soldier would have done for a comrade. His London Gazette citation reads:

> For most conspicuous bravery and devotion to a wounded comrade in the Gallipoli Peninsula. Although himself severely wounded in the thigh in the attack on Hill 70, on the 21st August, 1915, he remained out over forty-eight hours under the Turkish trenches with a private of his regiment who was severely wounded and unable to move, although he could himself have returned to safety. Finally, he fixed a shovel to the equipment of his wounded comrade, and using this as a sledge, he dragged him back over 600 yards to our line, though fired at by the Turks on the way. He reached our trenches at about 9.30 p.m. on 23rd August.

So what of the renewed attack by 86 Brigade from Green Hill; why was Hill 112 not captured? Brigadier General Claude Perceval, 86 Brigade commander, was informed that the mounted division would be arriving to storm Hill 112; 86 Brigade reserve, which consisted of 2/Royal Fusiliers, was got ready to advance with them. By 6.00 pm there was no sign of the yeomanry. At 7.30 pm darkness had fallen and still there was no sign. Without the support of the Yeomanry, the Fusiliers' attack would be pointless, so the order went out to withdraw what was left of the Munsters and Lancashire Fusiliers who was still holding an advanced position out in front. So where were the missing Yeomanry brigades? Approaching the rear of Green Hill, 4 and 1 Brigades had stopped to await further orders, as neither commander knew what was required of them. In the confusion some smaller detachments actually went on blindly, some reaching the 2/SWB position on the southern slopes of Scimitar Hill. Others found

Brigadier General Paul Aloysius Kenna VC (Omdurman).

themselves in the area of Hetman Chair, where they became lost and pinned down in the open fields, and amongst the myriad of ditches, sunken lanes and hedgerows that crisscrossed the area.

'Great Scott! This is a bloody business!'

Brigadier General Kenna VC, even though it was now dark, wanted 3 (Notts & Derby) Brigade to capture Hetman Chair and then Hill 112. Lieutenant Colonel Sir John Peniston Milbanke VC, commanding officer of 1/1 Nottinghamshire (Sherwood Rangers) Yeomanry, and a friend of Winston Churchill, received his orders for the attack. He told his fellow officers: *We are to take a redoubt, but I don't know where it is and don't think anyone else knows either, but in any case we are to go ahead and attack any Turks we meet.* The attack went ahead and Milbanke was killed. His last words were, *Great Scott! This is a bloody business.*[21] There was nothing to show for this attack, apart from

Dead Man's Gully.

Lieutenant Colonel
Sir John Peniston
Milbanke
VC (South Africa).

a trail of bodies leading back to the British lines. Veterans later referred to this area as the Valley of Death.

> *In front of the trench in the gully* [Dead Man's Gully], *and up the hillside were thousands of unburied and rotting bodies, lying in fantastic attitudes, there seemed to be at least one a yard and in many places they were piled into little heaps. The stench was appalling, and the flies from all these putrefying corpses came over in their swarms and settled everywhere.*[22]

The general attack was now over and it had obviously gone badly wrong. Early successes offered a glimmer of hope, but inexperience, poor generalship and a strong Turkish defence finally sealed any hope the British thought they had. 21 August was a disaster for de Lisle and the last of Hamilton's gambles had ended yet again in dreadful failure. Limited gains along Scimitar Hill had been made and the situation initially looked promising, but these positions retained at nightfall were precarious, to say the least. The summit could not be held. The area from Hetman Chair to Azmak Dere remained in Turkish hands; the only success was the capture of a small portion of Turkish trench near Aire Kavak. As soon as the failure was recognised by IX Corps Headquarters, de Lisle reluctantly allowed Major General William Marshall to withdraw back to the old British front line, as the positions on the lower slopes of Scimitar Hill were worthless and any night advance to hold the top would only be enfiladed from Hill 112 in the morning. No general wants to relinquish ground unless absolutely necessary. Hamilton wrote in his diary: *I am confident he* [de Lisle] *will be able to give good reasons for his act.* He could for, if Hill 112 was not captured, Scimitar Hill could not be held, and to attack Hill 112 a simultaneous attack was needed on the W Hills. All gains were evacuated during the night and early morning, whilst efforts concentrated on collecting the wounded and retrieving equipment. The Anzac attack by Major General Cox on Hill 60 was also a failure, although he would fight on for another two days before a renewed attempt to capture the hill, on 27 August, would again fail.

British dead near Hetman Chair, August 1915.

Captain Teichman, a Yeomanry medical officer, wrote of the aftermath that confronted him on the Salt Lake:

> *What a scene of desolation – dead men, mules, rifles, ammunition, helmets and emergency rations lay everywhere. As we marched slowly along, we came across some of our dead and hastily buried them while it was possible. Most of these had not fired off any ammunition, as they had been killed by shell fire long before they were within rifle range of the enemy. It was sad work, burying these men, mostly yeoman farmers in the prime of life and of splendid physique – the senseless slaughter of war seemed appalling when viewed calmly after the excitement of battle was over.*[23]

The last chance for any progress at Suvla had ended in failure, and a very costly failure at that. This was probably the least successful of all the Gallipoli battles - and there were a few. IX Corps' losses for the day

The stench was appalling.

were 5,300 killed, wounded and missing out of 14,300 who had taken part, whilst Turkish losses were about 2,000. The Turkish *12th Division* had to be withdrawn from the line on 22 August by Mustafa Kemal, although their casualties were nowhere near those of the British. Hamilton begins his diary entry for 22 August with *Suvla gone wrong again.* He casts blame on the gods: *the ancient Gods fought against us yesterday – mist and fire, still hold their own against the inventions of man.* Maybe Hamilton should have looked more closely at home for the cause of the failure. The Official History was less poetic, stating that, *despite the show of distinguished bravery, the task had proved wholly impractical. Without more troops any attempt by frontal assault against an entrenched position of great natural strength, manned by a determined and victorious enemy*, with flanking machine-guns, was bound to fail.

On 23 August Lieutenant General Sir Julian Byng arrived to take over command of IX Corps. Byng, the general that Hamilton had originally requested back in June for the Suvla operation, had arrived too late. Aspinall remarked: *the experienced pilot has arrived but the ship is already on the rocks.* De Lisle returned to the 29th Division and Mahon returned to resume command of the 10th Division. Also on Byng's ship were Major General Edward Fanshawe and Major General Sir Stanley Maude. Both were highly respected generals, Fanshawe took command of the 11th Division in place of Hammersley, who had collapsed from what was reported as a blood clot in his leg[24], and Maude would be appointed to command the 13th Division at Anzac. The day prior to this, Brigadier General Hill, commander of 31 Brigade, was invalided from the Peninsula, suffering from acute dysentery. The enemy was not just the Turks, the terrain and the generals; sickness was going to be the new cause of attrition. Six Suvla generals had now been removed from command in nine days, probably a record in the annals of British military history, but Suvla, if not the whole Gallipoli campaign was now beyond recovery.[25]

By now Hamilton had heard from Kitchener that there would be no more reinforcements unless Lieutenant General Sir John Maxwell in Egypt had any spare, which he did not. The swing had moved back to the Western Front, where all focus and resources were now being directed. The writing was on the wall; the last great battle had been fought and lost at Gallipoli, and already there was talk of evacuation. As the August offensive came to a close, so did the career of Hamilton, who received his recall on 16 October. His recall is best described in his own words:

> *From this date onwards, up to the date of my departure on 17th October, the flow of munitions and drafts fell away. Sickness, the legacy of a desperate trying summer, took a heavy toll of the survivors of so many arduous conflicts. No longer was there any question of operations on the grand scale, but with such troops it was difficult to be downhearted. All ranks were cheerful; all remained confident that, so long as they stuck to their guns, their country would stick to them, and see them through the last and greatest of the crusades.*

The seed had already been sown by Kitchener for evacuation, which Hamilton thought was unthinkable; Hamilton remained optimistic of success until the end. Andrew Bonar Law put it into words on 19

August: *General Hamilton is always nearly winning*. His last chance was the big attack on 21 August, now all his life lines were gone. Many of his generals had already gone, as were his once enthusiast volunteers, many of which were now lying buried; a testament to Hamilton's failure. Kitchener replaced him with Major General Sir Charles Monro. The age of miracles were passed for Hamilton, as was the whole Gallipoli campaign. Monro arrived on the Peninsula towards the end of October to review the situation for himself. Even with reinforcements, he ruled out any success of turning the tide at Gallipoli. He said:

> *Even had we been able to make an advance on the Peninsula, our position would not have been ameliorated to any marked degree, and an advance to Constantinople was quite out of the question... Since we could not hope to achieve any purpose by remaining on the Peninsula, the appalling cost to the nation involved in consequence of embarking on an Overseas Expedition with no base available for the rapid transit of stores, supplies, and personnel, made it* [the evacuation] *urgent.*

1 National Army Museum: W. J. Fenwick, 34th Brigade Collection, p.3.
2 Lieutenant T. A. Peel, RAMC is buried in East Mudros Cemetery (grave II. H. 143).
3 Ferrers-Guy, M.C., *The Lancashire Fusiliers Annual*, (Dublin: Sackville Press, 1916), pp.237-238.
4 National Army Museum: A. W. Gregory, 34th Brigade Collection, p.12.
5 Hamilton, I., *Ian Hamilton's Final Despatches*. (London: George Newnes, 1916).
6 Denham, H.M., *Dardanelles, A Midshipman's Diary 1915-16* (London: John Murray Ltd, 1981), p.154.
7 Hakki Sunata, I., *From Gallipoli to the Caucasus (Gelibolu'dan Kafkaslara)* (Istanbul: Bankasi Publications).
8 National Army Museum: G. Boucher, 34th Brigade Collection, p.10.
9 National Army Museum: E. Sanders, 34th Brigade Collection, p.10.
10 The Great War Archive, University of Oxford http://www.oucs.ox.ac.uk/ww1lit/gwa; ©Jerome Farrell.
11 Letter written 25 August 1915 by Major G. W. Nightingale, (IWM collection).
12 This was probably the trench that the 6/East Yorks dug before evacuating Scimitar Hill on 8 August.
13 Reports had been received by de Lisle's HQ erroneously reporting that 11th Division *were doing magnificently* and were in possession of Hill 112. War Diary: 1/RMF (National Archives: WO95/4310).
14 Steel, N., & Hart, P., *Defeat at Gallipoli*, (London: Macmillan, 1994), p.292.
15 Keyes, R., *The Naval Memoirs of Admiral of the Fleet Sir Roger Keyes*, (London: Thornton Butterworth, 1934), p.421.
16 Herbert, A., *Mons, Anzac and Kut* (London: Hutchinson, 1919).
17 Thompson, C. W., *Records of the Dorset Yeomanry 1914-1919*, (Bennett & Co, 1921) p.19.
18 Captain G. R. O'Sullivan was awarded the VC for actions at Gully Ravine, near Krithia (Helles), in June/July 1915. He is commemorated on the Helles Memorial, panels 97-101.
19 Gillam, Major J., *Gallipoli Diary*, (Unwin Hyman/Tom Donovan, 1989), p.209.
20 Hammerton, Sir J., *The Great War, I Was There*, Vol.1, (London: Amalgamated Press. 1916-21), pp.505-508.
21 Milbanke was awarded his VC during the Boer War. His widow actually went on to marry Lieutenant General Bryan Mahon, the then 10th Division commander, in 1920. He is commemorated on the Helles Memorial, panel 16.
22 Hatton, S. F., *Yarn of a Yeoman*, (London: Hutchinson, 1930).
23 Teichman, O., *The Diary Of A Yeomanry M.O.*, (London: Fisher Unwin Ltd, 1921).
24 Hammersley may not have been in good mental health at the time, which was not helped by the shock suffered when his headquarters was hit by a shell. It was also known, at one stage of his life, that he had been committed to a lunatic asylum, suffering from a severe nervous breakdown.
25 Two brigadier generals also died during this period, Lord Longford (GOC 2 Mtd Brigade) on 21 August and Kenna VC (GOC 3 Mtd Brigade) on 29 August. A further seven were wounded or invalided during the month of August: Brigadier General Haggard (GOC 32 Brigade, 11th Division), was wounded on 7 August; Brigadier General Granet (CRA, 11th Division), was wounded on 13 August; Brigadier General Cowan (GOC 159 Brigade, 53rd Division) was wounded on 14 August; Brigadier General de Winton was wounded on 15 August; Brigadier General Lloyd (GOC 158 Brigade, 53rd Division) was wounded on 17 August; Brigadier General Brunker (GOC 164 Brigade, 54th Division) was invalided on 18 August and Brigadier General Hume (GOC 160 Brigade, 53rd Division) was invalided on 31 August.

Chapter 9

AFTERMATH

Lieutenant General Frederick Stopford was made the scapegoat for the failure, not only of the Suvla operation but of the whole August offensive. Stopford was an easy target to blame, as he had little if no support. Aspinall was damning when he wrote the Official History but of course was protecting his part in the planning, as well as the reputation of his friend, Sir Ian Hamilton. Birdwood was also to blame Stopford, in a way to mask the deficiencies in the August plan and his Corps' failure to secure their primary objectives. Of course Hamilton was blamed for not intervening sooner, which all goes back to who appointed Stopford, if he was to blame, in the first place? This

A well near Chocolate Hill, October 1915.

responsibility must ultimately lie with Lord Kitchener who, as Secretary of State for War, had appointed an elderly and inexperienced general to an active corps command. Hamilton had no choice but to accept Stopford's appointment, but then he failed to impose his will on his subordinate. On 13 August Hamilton had written in his diary: *Ought I have resigned sooner than allow generals old and inexperienced to be foisted up on me?* By then it was too late and Stopford's departure soon led to Hamilton's downfall.

On the whole Stopford had many negatives, and Suvla many problems, but these have become over exaggerated in subsequent years. What must not be forgotten is a landing on an enemy shore was achieved and a port, although it remained far from secure, was established. The whole August offensive was undoubtedly flawed; Suvla, being an important part of that, failed in its aspirations – but so did the main Anzac attack. Both Suvla and Anzac relied on at least one of the offensives breaking through; however both fell short of the mark. Turkish fighting prowess was ignored and the challenges of the terrain were overlooked. Hamilton wrote in his diary: *we have won a good stake but we have not broken the Ottoman Bank.* Unfortunately this won stake in the great gamble was worthless: the British were no nearer to their objectives than they were during the April landings, or even after the naval attempts at forcing the Dardanelles. There was genuine anger after the failure of the August Offensive, as high expectations were dashed as opportunities were seen frivolously thrown away. There will always remain doubt as to the margin between failure and success, points that are still debated between historians today.

What has almost been forgotten is the ferocious fighting that took place at Suvla and the horrendous casualties thus suffered. It was not a

Azmak Dere Barricade, Winter 1915.

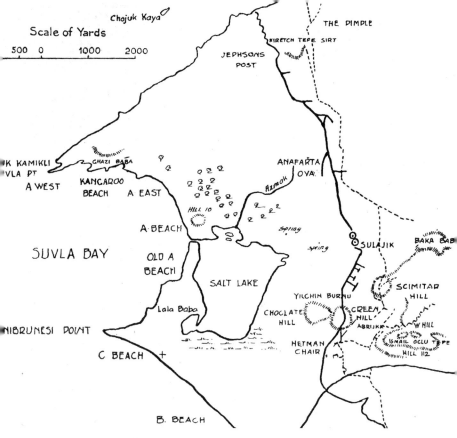

The line at the end of August 1915.

scene of men bathing and drinking tea on the beaches, as popular myth may tell. The Suvla fighting finally climaxed on 22 August as the botched Scimitar Hill attack came to an end, the last great battle of the Gallipoli campaign. When this failed it was clear that the earlier opportunities lost, could not be reversed by the continued sacrifice of blood. It was stalemate again. On all fronts the Turks had retained control of the high ground, and thus held all the aces in the pack; the game was undisputedly lost for the British.

The political scene had also changed; the focus was back on the Western Front, where Britain was coming under pressure from France to mount a major offensive at Loos. Even closer to Gallipoli was the new commitment to Salonika. Bulgaria, which had remained neutral thus far, sided with the Axis powers in September 1915, which threatened the Greeks. To aid Greece, Kitchener agreed to the sending of an Anglo-French army to Salonika, which robbed Sir Ian Hamilton of the 10th Division and the 2nd French Division, a major blow to Hamilton's Gallipoli plans. Actually there were no plans, but Hamilton

197

Yeomanry in the trenches.

was still confident of success, regardless of the writing on the wall. Back in London there was much anti-Dardanelles feeling and the likes of Ashmead-Bartlett and Keith Murdoch, two correspondents who had earlier visited Gallipoli, were now scathing of the campaign and how it was being run. This feeling was only strengthened when Stopford arrived home. When the Dardanelles Committee met on 11 October 1915 the fiasco at Suvla and the failed August Offensive could only mean one thing; the end of Hamilton and the campaign. On 14 October Hamilton was sacked, and on 20 December Suvla and Anzac were evacuated.

Lieutenant Eric Halse, 6/East Yorks, wrote an uncensored letter home that has survived. It was delivered by one of his sergeants whilst on leave, and ends by summing up the Suvla operation from his eyes, a view shared by many:

I have written a little diary day by day. It is true, every single word of it, and if anything does happen to me will be sent home to you; I shall see to that. I just want you to make full use of it for I think things are wicked out here and people at home shall not see how they are being deluded and being fooled by the people in charge. They are drawing heavy salaries and want to keep them. We are up against a big, tough proposition the biggest we ever had as a nation and if people in England don't wake up to the fact that lives are being wasted out here because of the incompetence of Staff Officers who get their positions not on merit but by influence. It is not right, for they have the lives of all the men out here and we want the best brains to beat the lead. Isn't there a man at home who is big enough and strong enough to take things in his own hands and guide the nation through these turbulent times? I can't believe there is not, but all this petty strife amongst the politicians at home is costing the nation hundreds and thousands of lives of the best and bravest that she can produce. It isn't right, it isn't fair, a man should be willing to fight for his country, but why should he be asked to throw his life away because of the idiocy of these asses at the head of things. Would you believe it – I know for a fact that Major Bray and myself are the only two officers alive who have actually been in the Turkish trenches that we attacked on August 21st and 22nd? Yet when we tried to tell the Divisional Staff about them we were told that they didn't want to know. Why? They ought to have been too thankful to get information that we could give them – but no! As long as their dug outs are the best that can be made that is all they care about. They are afraid to come any nearer the trenches than the beach and, if they could, I believe they would stay at Imbros. We never see a Staff Officer up in the trenches and there ought to be at least one somewhere to see how things are progressing, but no, all the staff are here for is a jolly good picnic and to get a few DSOs and VCs etc for things they have never done. They ought all to be made to take their place in the firing line so that they can see exactly what is happening ...

My heart is too full of anger to say more except to give praise to the men. They are the bravest the pluckiest and the best that the world can produce. It is glorious to fight with them and I feel proud to think that I am an officer of such a plucky lot. They have the cause of the country in their heart and no sacrifice is too great for it or for a comrade. Why, if only they had been properly led they would have shown the world that there is no finer soldier in the world than the Englishman who is fighting for his country.[1]

1 The Great War Archive, University of Oxford http://www.oucs.ox.ac.uk/ww1lit/gwa; ©Jerome Farrell.

Sir Ian Hamilton departing Gallipoli after his recall – 16 October 1915.

Chapter 10

BATTLEFIELD TOURS

1. The Landings
2. The Northern Sector
3. The Southern Sector

The three tours are designed to allow you to visit the Suvla battlefield over a period of three days. If you are short for time you could cover most of these areas by car or similar vehicle in a single day, but this would mean sacrificing most of the walking. On the maps the tracks marked with a dash can be driven or walked; those marked with a dotted line are walks only.

Suvla is the least visited and most remote area of the Gallipoli battlefield, but at the same time is also one of the most naturally beautiful. You will find that the four Commonwealth War Graves Commission cemeteries in Suvla are different to those on the Western Front. Because of the nature of the ground they have small tilted sandstone tablets for grave headstones. The Stone of Remembrance and white stone Cross of Sacrifice, a slightly different and more subdued style than those found in Europe, can also be found in all the cemeteries. Row after row of headstones are interspersed with small plants and shrubs that adorn the beautifully kept cemeteries. Mature trees, including the odd Judas Tree (*cercis siliquastrum*), grow majestically, providing valuable shade on a hot sunny day.

Suvla is within the Gallipoli (*Gelibolu*) Historical National Park, which also encompasses the battlefields of Anzac and Helles. On the northern outskirts of Eceabat (Maidos in 1915) is the National Park Main Information Centre, which was opened in 2005. This building has many modern facilities, including a library, cinema, conference centre, internet resources, souvenir shop, exhibitions and refreshments. From the main information centre it is approximately nine kilometres to Gaba Tepe (*Kabetape*). Located here are the Gaba Tepe Information Centre and Museum, and well worth a visit. The museum contains an interesting collection of battlefield artefacts, photographs and maps of the campaign. From the grounds are views of Anzac and the Sari Bair ridge, this battlefield being covered in the book

Anzac – The Landing (2008). If you have not visited this area already a slight detour is worthwhile, not necessarily to visit the Anzac battlefield in detail but to sample the superb views of the Suvla battlefield from the heights of Chunuk Bair (*Conkbayiri*).

Leave the Museum and follow the road signs in a northerly direction towards Anzac Cove. On a clear day looking out into the Aegean you can see the Turkish island of Gökçeada (Imbros or Imroz), which was used as Sir Ian Hamilton's headquarters from June 1915. The island, then Greek, was captured from the Turks during the Balkans Wars of 1912-13. In February 1915, the Greek government offered Imbros[1] to the British as a base for their assault on Gallipoli. In 1923 the island was ceded to Turkey under the terms of the Treaty of Lausanne, which brought a final post-war settlement to the area. During the campaign Imbros acted as a rest and recreation area for the troops on Gallipoli, where it housed a multitude of tented camps, casualty clearing stations, field bakeries, airfields and supply depots. Nestled behind this island to the northwest is the Greek island of Samothrace. It was on Samothrace that the statue of Nike, the Greek Goddess of Victory, was discovered and which today can be seen in the Louvre Museum in Paris.

Driving past Anzac Cove, and then the Anzac Commemorative Site and the Sphinx, continue along North Beach, passing Canterbury CWGC Cemetery and the CWGC base and cottage. Carry on, passing No2 Outpost CWGC Cemetery, the New Zealand No2 Outpost CWGC Cemetery and finally the Embarkation Pier CWGC Cemetery. All of this area is important to the August Offensive at Anzac, but this is a subject of another book.

1. The Landings

Allow a full day to complete this walking and driving tour of the beaches. The tour will cover Suvla Harbour as well as the main landing beaches used by Kitchener's New Army on 6/7 August 1915, and the subsequent captures of Lala Baba, Hill 10 and Ghazi Baba.

Continue slowly past the Embarkation Pier Cemetery and, after approximately 100 metres, on the left, is a narrow track. This track can be very rough and in the wet season do not attempt to drive it as further down you will need to cross the Azmak Dere, dry in summer but wet in winter and spring.

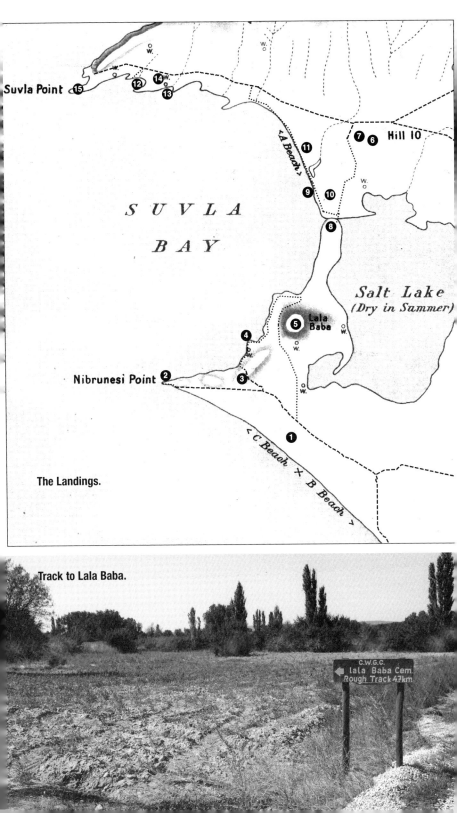

Suvla Point

⑮
⑫ ⑭ w.
⑬

< A Beach >

⑪

⑦ ⑥ Hill 10

S U V L A

B A Y

⑨ ⑩

⑧

Salt Lake
(Dry in Summer)

④

⑤ Lala
Baba
w.

Nibrunesi Point ②

③

w.

①

< C Beach X B Beach >

The Landings.

Track to Lala Baba.

C.W.G.C.
◄ Lala Baba Cem.
Rough Track 4?km.

Running parallel to the coast for approximately six kilometres, the track will eventually end at Nibrunesi Point.

A slightly better track to reach Lala Baba is further along the main road. This is reached by continuing on the road from Embarkation Pier Cemetery, passing 7th Field Ambulance CWGC Cemetery, Damakjelik Bair *(Damakgilbayir Yaziti)* Turkish memorial and at the Hill 60 *(Bomba Tepe)* junction take the left-hand turn (heading in a northerly direction) towards Suvla. About 250 metres on the left, near the site of Susak Kuyu, is another track, which should be sign-posted to Lala Baba CWGC cemetery. Following this track for 4.7 kilometres, you will pass Kazlar Chair to the south, marking the Anzac-Suvla boundary as it was in 1915. Again you will need to cross the Azmak Dere, but at least the track surface and ford (at the time of writing) is better and passable, with caution, without the need of a 4x4 drive vehicle. Depending on the time of year all tracks can be in poor condition so please take note, especially if it has been raining, which luckily is a rare occurrence in Gallipoli.

On the approach to Lala Baba you will soon notice concrete bunkers between the track and the beach; these are all post campaign. Soon you will come into view of the small rise called Lala Baba (49m), which is also known as Lale Baba (Tulip Hill) or Yorkshire Hill, after 6/Yorks, who captured it. The sign post to the CWGC cemetery is to the right. Continue on the track, without turning off, until you reach the beach; here you can stop and park. The open 1600 metre stretch of sandy beach formed **C AND B BEACHES (1)**, with Anzac and the Sari Bair ridge in the distance to the south. A last minute change in orders amended the original sequential naming of the beaches from A, B and C to A, C and B. B Beach was then 'moved' to the south of C as the original area within Suvla Bay was thought to shoal by the

The Landing Beaches - C and B Beach today.

Royal Navy. The moving of beaches only added to the chaos during the initial landings. At about 10.00 pm on 6 August the beetles grounded on B Beach, bringing ashore the first elements of 11th Division. The 7/South Staffords and 9/Sherwood Foresters (33 Brigade) landed with no casualties and then advanced to entrench a flanking position from the edge of the Salt Lake to the coast. To their left the 6/Yorks and 9/West Yorks (32 Brigade) landed and attacked Lala Baba. Both beaches were also used to land artillery, mules, horses and general supplies, as well as men, and remained in use until the evacuation. Once situated along this shore were numerous brigade field ambulances as well as the larger No.14 Casualty Clearing Station (CCS). These were all part of the casualty evacuation chain that brought the sick and wounded from the front line and treated them, either to return to duty or, in most cases, to enable them to be taken by hospital ship to a base hospital (situated on Lemnos, Malta and Egypt).

To the north is **NIBRUNESI POINT (2)**; today this is known as Small Rib Point *(Küçük Kemikli Burnu)*, so named as it is the lesser of the two promontories of Suvla Bay. It was here that the first British troops came ashore during the night of 6 August, as it was also witness to the last British troops leaving during the evacuation on 20 December 1915. 6 August was not the first time that British troops had ventured into this area. Five days before the 25 April landings on Gallipoli the Royal Navy landed a small party at Nibrunesi Point to destroy a telephone wire. Later, on 28 April, after an air reconnaissance reported Turkish activity in the area, the Royal Navy shelled Lala Baba as an artillery battery had been sighted in the area. At dawn on 2 May a party of fifty five New Zealanders under the command of Captain Charles Cribb, Canterbury Battalion, landed at the point. The small force thoroughly searched the area for guns but found no sign of any. Several startled Turks were killed or wounded and, at about midday the party returned to Anzac with no casualties and a prize of fifteen Turkish prisoners.

Lala Baba CWGC Cemetery (3), which is situated on a spur from the hill called Little Lala Baba and, along with Nibrunesi Point, was cleared of the Turkish piquets by Major William Shannon, 6/Yorks, during the night of 6 August. The cemetery contains 200 graves, of which fifty three are unknown and sixteen are special memorials. During the war many little cemeteries like this grew in size over the course of the

Lala Baba CWGC Cemetery.

campaign, their graves marked by an assortment of markers made from wood and tin packing cases, inscribed by purple field service pencil or engraved with the help of a soldier's clasp knife. Today the originals have long since gone, replaced with stone-faced pedestal grave markers carefully engraved by the stonemasons of the Commonwealth War Graves Commission.

The senior officer buried here is Brigadier General Paul Kenna VC, 21/Lancers. Born in August 1862, he was educated at Stonyhurst College and then Sandhurst. Commissioned initially into the West India Regiment, he then transferred into the 21st Lancers, where he served in Egypt during the 1898 Nile Expedition. He was awarded the VC for rescuing another officer whose horse had been killed during the charge at Omdurman. During the Boer War he commanded a cavalry column, and gained his DSO; after South Africa he took part in the action at Jidballi with the Somaliland Field Force. A personal friend of Winston Churchill, he was appointed to command 3 Mounted Brigade in 1911, being made a brigadier general in August 1914. Whilst inspecting the lines at Chocolate Hill on 29 August he was mortally wounded, dying of his wounds the following day. He is buried in II.A.1.

Another notable burial is that of Lieutenant

Brig-General P. A. Kenna VC.

D Beach by Lala Baba.

One of the Lala Baba beaches today.

Hon. Kenneth R. Dundas, Anson Battalion, Royal Naval Division. Born in Tenerife in 1882, he was the fourth son of the 6th Viscount Melville and was formerly a district commissioner of British East Africa (Keyna today) before the war. He was killed by an aerial bomb on 7 August. He is buried in III.B.9.

To the northeast of Nibrunesi Point is a small cove where the Royal Australian Naval Bridging Train built a stone pier for use in the evacuation, named South Pier, the remains of which can be seen today. This small beach, reached by crossing the fields between the cemetery and coastline, is occasionally referred to as **D BEACH (4)**, although it played no part in the initial landing during 6/7 August. Because the beaches from D Beach around the seaward side of Lala Baba were sheltered from enemy observation they became the headquarters of many formations and units including the 53rd (Welsh) Division and 2nd Mounted Division. Please take care when walking along the cliffs and beaches as they can be dangerous and also avoid walking through fields with crops; remember that most of this land is private property and must be respected as such.

LALA BABA (5), which dominates the surrounding area, was captured by 6/Yorks just before midnight on 6 August. This would be the first attack made by a Kitchener's New Army battalion in the First World War. The hillock was garrisoned by a company of *2/31 Regiment*; Kitchener's men put them to flight. It is possible to walk around most of Lala Baba by using the various tracks, the very same that were prominent on British Army maps of the time, and still used today by the local farmers. Trenches and dugouts can still be found on and around the hill, another remnant of the campaign. It was also here that Major General Hammersley positioned his headquarters for 11th Division during the first weeks of August. If you head in a northerly direction over Lala Baba it is worth mentioning that you cannot reach the original Cut any more, due to a modern canal that now divides this isthmus. There are actually three 'Cuts' today, the original 1915 position is now filled with sand, the other two are post campaign and are open to the sea. To reach the historic 'Cut' you need to approach it from the Hill 10 Cemetery track.

Leave Lala Baba by car, and retrace your route back to the main Suvla road. Continue in a northerly direction past the Green Hill CWGC Cemetery, following the signs to Hill 10 CWGC Cemetery.

The road runs behind the old British front line, with the Salt Lake to the west and the area known as Sulajik to the right. Remain on this road (in 1915 it was named Sulajik Road) as it enters the plains of Küçük Anafarta Ova and then gently curves round towards the coast, following the signs to Hill 10 Cemetery. You will soon cross the Azmak Dere (a different stream to the one further south, but sharing the same name), and from there it is a kilometre to the cemetery. HILL 10 (6) (*Softatepe* – Fanatic Hill), which stands at ten metres, is barely discernable against the landscape, as its gorse covered slopes rise gently behind the cemetery. The hill was another of the fortified positions organised by Major Willmer to help defend against any landing. One Gendarmerie company defended the hill from narrow slit trenches that overlooked the beach, supported by a field gun. There was no barbed wire, although on the beach mines, connected to trip wires, were laid. It was an initial objective of the landing, a task assigned to Brigadier

Hill 10 CWGC Cemetery.

General Sitwell's 34 Brigade, which captured the position on the morning of 7 August.

HILL 10 CWGC CEMETERY (7), with the exception of three graves, was made after the war when isolated battlefield graves and small cemeteries (88th Dressing Station, 89th Dressing Stations, Kangaroo Beach, B Beach, 26th Casualty Clearing Station and Park Lane) were consolidated together. Today there are 699 men buried or commemorated in the cemetery, 150 of the burials are unidentified. Amongst the graves is that of Lieutenant Colonel Harry Welstead (V.D.1), the commanding officer of 9/Lancashire Fusiliers. He was shot and wounded whilst wading ashore and soon after found dead on the beach with a bullet in the back of his neck (date of death on his headstone should read 7 August). He is buried close to his fellow battalion officers who were killed capturing Hill 10; these include Lieutenant Leslie Osborne (I.C.15), whose headstone bears an epitaph to his brother, Second Lieutenant William Osborne (Helles

CWGC at work.

209

Lieutenant Leslie Osborne, killed capturing Hill 10.

Mem. Panels 58-72), who was wounded the same day, died of wounds and was buried at sea. The Osbornes were born in China. Interestingly, Leslie was in Germany at the time war was declared, arrested as a spy but soon released and expelled from the country. Another pair of brothers is Second Lieutenant Duncan Hook (I.C.18) and his older brother, Lieutenant Robin Hook (I.C.17), again killed whilst capturing the Hill. The Hooks were working as civil engineers in Canada when war was declared, immediately offering their services to King and Country, were commissioned into the Lancashire Fusiliers on the same day and, sadly, killed on the same day. Second Lieutenant Roland Raw (I.C.19) and Lieutenant Horace Brierley (I.C.16) are also buried here. Raw, although ill before the landing, and instructed to remain behind at Imbros, but insisted in accompanying the battalion at any cost. He paid the ultimate price, as did so many of his fellow officers and men. Another battalion commanding officer's grave is that of Lieutenant Colonel Horace Johnston (V.D.3), DSO, 8/West Ridings, who was killed alongside his adjutant on 9 August, during 32 Brigade's failed attempt to capture the Tekke Tepe heights.

A B-P Scout in Gallipoli - Lieutenant E. Y. Priestman.

Second Lieutenant Edmund Yerbury Priestman (I.H.14), 6/Yorks & Lancs, is also buried here. His letters were published in *With a B.-P. Scout in Gallipoli: A Record of the Belton Bulldogs (1916)*. Priestman was a pre-war scoutmaster and during the attack on Hetman Chair on 21 August he had the opportunity to be able to do real, serious scouting work, with people's lives depending on it. Priestman was killed on 18/19 November during a night patrol to capture a position near Jephson's Post. In a Sheffield newspaper in February 1916 an article was printed about his death:

Our trenches ran along the coast, near

Jeffson's Post [Jephson's]*, and orders had been received for us to work along the furthermost sap to enable us to gain a portion of higher ground on the left of our sap. In order to do this it was necessary to leave our trenches at night, run forward with sandbags to the place marked, and dig in as rapidly as possible. On this particular night, Lieutenant Priestman and about thirty NCOs and men were detailed to make good this position. Leaving the trenches about 1am, they gained the position without incident, and commenced to entrench as quietly as possible. Shortly afterwards the Turks rushed the position. Lieutenant Priestman did not retire, but opened a rapid fire, which kept the enemy at bay for a while but, coming on again with a combined rush, they decimated the whole of the gallant little band. Lieutenant Priestman fell, fighting till the last, and Regimental Sergeant Warr was also killed whilst taking up a message to him. We attacked the position again in larger force next night, and succeeded in holding it. The bodies of Lieutenant Priestman and several men were discovered, all the wounded having been removed by the enemy. The captured position was named 'Priestman's Post' by Headquarters, to commemorate the gallantry of this young officer, who was respected by all who knew him.*

Also buried in the cemetery is Regimental Sergeant Major Frederick Warr (I.I.11), however no record of what happened to the wounded is recorded and they appear on no surviving Prisoner of War lists.

Also killed near Jephson's Post was an Australian sniper from 8/Australian Light Horse; Lance Corporal Herbert Peters (I.I.18), who was killed on 30 August. From Victoria, he was a prominent member of the Stratford Rifle Club, joining the Australian Light Horse when war was declared. Later attached to 161 (Essex) Brigade, Peters was manning a position with another scout, from which they had been sniping at the Turks. They were at dinner at the time when Peters was killed by a shrapnel bullet. Originally buried at Park Lane Cemetery, he was reinterred at Hill 10 Cemetery after the armistice. Also from Victoria, Australia, is the grave of Chief Petty Officer Edward Perkins (Sp.Mem.47), Royal Australian Naval Bridging Train, who was killed on 6 September when his dugout received a direct hit by a shell; the

In the foreground, the sand filled 'Cut' as it is today.

only one of the unit's four casualties to be buried in Gallipoli; the other deaths occurred at sea or on Lemnos Island.

Leave the cemetery and continue on the narrow track that leads around the cemetery and Hill 10. This track will take you to **THE CUT (8)**, and also A Beach, where 34 Brigade came ashore. Depending on the condition of the track it may be wiser to leave your vehicle at the cemetery and continue on foot; the distance to the Cut is approximately one kilometre. The opening to the sea, which connects the Aegean Sea with the Salt Lake (Tuz Gölü), was made after the campaign, when this area was used as a fish factory, since closed. Today a few local fishermen use the area to moor their boats. Using the small bridge by the remains of the factory you can cross the waterway to find the original 1915 period Cut, which is approximately fifty metres to the south of the opening used by the fishing boats. The original Cut is now full of sand and closed to the sea.

Leave the Cut and crossing back across the bridge, follow the track onto A Beach. Approximately 150 metres along the beach is the remains of a beached **LIGHTER (9)**, one of the few that still survive today and original to the Gallipoli campaign. Behind this part of the beach are many small sand dunes, the larger **'HILL 10' SAND DUNE (10)** being the one mistakenly 'captured' by the 9/Lancashire Fusiliers, who believed it to be Hill 10. Trenches can be found on the top of this dune today, along with a view of the 'real' Hill 10 further inland. Continue to walk along the beach, which was code named **A BEACH (11)** for the landings. There were several beaches of this name during the planning and execution of the Suvla landings and this caused much confusion. Prior to the landing this beach was code named A Beach but when, due to navigation error, the navy landed 34 Brigade to the south of the Cut, this beach became known as Old A Beach, and A Beach was then 'moved' close to Lala Baba. After the landing a pier was built and No.53 CCS, along with unit field ambulances, were positioned here amongst the sand dunes. You have a choice to either return to the cemetery the way you came, or continue to walk along the length of A Beach and then walk along the road, and then return to your vehicle at Hill 10.

Leave Hill 10 Cemetery and continue on the Sulajik road for a further two kilometres. You will notice A Beach on the left of the road. Where the ground gets rockier are the small coves and inlets known during the war as Kangaroo Beach, Little West Beach and West Beach. Stop and park on the side of the road near the fishermen's cottages. It was near here that elements of the 10th (Irish) Division landed, although not without difficulty from the shoal rocks and sandbars that are still visible in the water today. After the landing the Royal Engineers built up this area, which soon became the main Suvla port, and because of that was under constant Turkish shell fire. During the campaign two steamers, *Pina* and *Fieramosca*, were sunk to form a breakwater and piers were made from rock leading out into the sea. Today little remains, although by the cottages at West Beach Harbour is the wreck of another large **LIGHTER (12)**, its

Wrecked Lighter on A Beach

metal ribs seen clearly as it rests just below the surface of the water. This lighter was probably sunk in the November 1915 storms that wreaked havoc along the Gallipoli coastline, destroying piers, washing away stores and sinking shipping.

Walk on to **KANGAROO BEACH (13)**, which was where the Royal Australian Naval Bridging Train (RANBT) was based. This unit was attached to IX Corps during the Gallipoli operations, and by

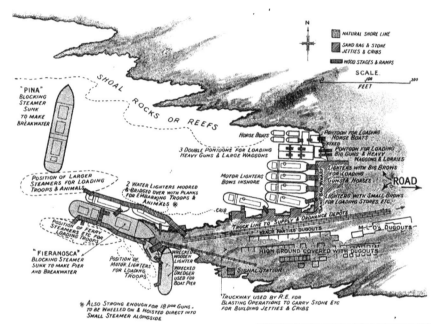

NATURAL SHORE LINE
SAND BAG & STONE JETTIES & CRIBS
WOOD STAGES & RAMPS

SCALE.
FEET

"PINA" BLOCKING STEAMER SUNK TO MAKE BREAKWATER

SHOAL ROCKS OR REEFS

HORSE BOATS

PONTOON FOR LOADING HORSE BOATS
FIXED PONTOON FOR LOADING BIG GUNS & HEAVY WAGGONS & LORRIES

3 DOUBLE PONTOONS FOR LOADING HEAVY GUNS & LARGE WAGGONS

LIGHTERS WITH BIG BROWS FOR LOADING GUNS & HORSES

MOTOR LIGHTERS BOWS INSHORE

POSITION OF LARGER STEAMERS FOR LOADING TROOPS & ANIMALS

2 WATER LIGHTERS MOORED & BRIDGED OVER WITH PLANKS FOR EMBARKING TROOPS & ANIMALS ※

ROAD

LIGHTERS WITH SMALL BROWS FOR LOADING STORES ETC

CRIB

TRUCK LINE TO SUPPLY & ORDNANCE DEPOTS

POSITION OF FERRY STEAMERS ETC FOR LOADING TROOPS

BEACH PARTIES DUGOUTS

M·L·O's DUGOUTS

"FIERANOSCA" BLOCKING STEAMER SUNK TO MAKE PIER AND BREAKWATER

POSITION OF MOTOR LIGHTERS FOR LOADING TROOPS

WRECKED WOODEN LIGHTER

HIGH GROUND COVERED WITH DUGOUTS

WRECKED DREDGER USED FOR BOAT PIER

SIGNAL STATION

※ ALSO STRONG ENOUGH FOR 18 POR GUNS. TO BE WHEELED ON & HOISTED DIRECT INTO SMALL STEAMER ALONGSIDE

TRUCKWAY USED BY R.E. FOR BLASTING OPERATIONS TO CARRY STONE ETC FOR BUILDING JETTIES & CRIBS

Suvla Harbour in late 1915.

Suvla Harbour area today.

the armistice in 1918 had become the most highly decorated Royal Australian Navy unit of the war. As early as 9 August the unit had constructed a one hundred and twenty metre pier, which was put into immediate use for evacuating the wounded. Surrounding this were a scattering of field ambulances, medical store depots and No. 26 CCS. One field ambulance member was Private John Hargrave, who wrote of the area:

> It was one muddle and confusion of water-tanks, pier-planks, pontoons, huge piles of bully-beef, biscuit and jam boxes. Here we came each evening with the water-cart to get our supply of water, and here the water-carts of every unit came down each evening and stood in a row and waited their turn. The water was pumped from the water-tank boats to the tank on shore. The water-tank boats brought it from Alexandria. It was filthy water, full of dirt, and very brackish to taste. Also it was warm. During the two months at Suvla Bay I never tasted a drop of cold water — it was always sickly lukewarm, sun-stewed.

> All day long high explosives used to sing and burst— sometimes killing and wounding men, sometimes blowing up the bully-beef and biscuits, sometimes falling with a hiss and a column of white spray into the sea. It was here that the field-telegraph of the Royal Engineers became a tangled spider's web of wires and cross wires. They added wires and branch wires every day, and stuck them up on thin poles. Here you could see the Engineers in shirt and

Sunken Lighter at West Beach.

RANBT working at Suvla Bay.

shorts trying to find a disconnection, or carrying a huge reel of wire. Wooden shanties sprang up where dug-outs had been a day or so before. Piers began to crawl out into the bay, adding a leg and trestle and pontoon every hour. Near Kangaroo Beach was the camp of the Indians, and here you could see the dusky ones praying on prayer mats and cooking rice and 'chupatties' [sic] (sort of oatcake-pancakes).

Suvla Point with the Island of Imbros on the horizon.

Here they were laying a light rail from the beach with trucks for carrying shells and parts of big guns. Here was the field post-office with sacks and sacks of letters and parcels. Some of the parcels were burst and unaddressed; a pair of socks or a mouldy home-made cake squashed in a cardboard box – sometimes nothing but the brown paper, card box and string, an empty shell – the contents having disappeared. What happened to all the parcels which never got to the Dardanelles no one knows, but those which did arrive were rifled and lost and stolen. Parcels containing cigarettes had a way of not getting delivered, and cakes and sweets often fell out mysteriously on the way from England.[2]

Apart from the lighter, all remnants of this busy harbour are gone. Return to the road and walk back to your car to continue on to Suvla Point.

During 7 August it was also the task of 34 Brigade to capture an enemy post at **GHAZI BABA (14)** (Veteran Father Hill), a slight area of rocky high ground on the seaward side of the road, by Kangaroo Beach. Even though they were landed on the wrong beach and had a three kilometre night march, the 11/Manchesters cleared Ghazi Baba of its small picket of Gendarmerie and advanced onto the Kiretch Tepe Sirt (Limestone Ridge), clearing the Karakol Dagh (Police Station Mountain) in its wake. At **SUVLA POINT (15)** (Büyük Kemikli – Big Rib Point) is a Turkish monolith with inscription that reads,

The enemy forces which landed at Ariburnu [Anzac] on the morning of 25 April 1915, and at Port Anafarta [Suvla Bay]

during the night of 6-7 August realised, after bloody battles lasting many months, that they could not overcome the Turkish defence and therefore evacuated these fronts on 20 December.

By the point is the picturesque bay called Suvla Cove, above which was the site of a naval signal station and IX Corps headquarters later in the campaign.

End of the landings tour.

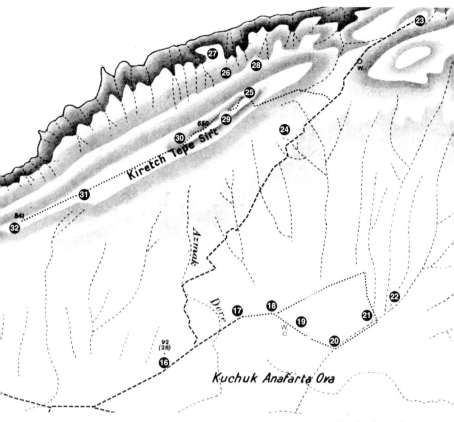

The Northern Sector.

2. The Northern Sector

This tour, again filling a whole day, will allow time to visit Azmak CWGC Cemetery and walk the ground over Küçük Anafarta Ova where 163 Brigade advanced on 12 August. There will also be time to visit the Kiretch Tepe ridge, visiting the Manchesters' furthest advance and exploring the areas prominent in the Irish division's fighting during August 1915.

On the approach to Hill 10 and Suvla Point is a road that heads east, signposted to Azmak CWGC Cemetery and Kireçtepe Jandarma Sehitligi. From this signpost, follow the track for about 600 metres; here it passes south of Hill 28, also known as **POINT 28 (16)**. It was this position that 9/West Yorks and 5/Dorsets reached by midday on 7 August and from here that 163 Brigade, including 1/5 Norfolks, began their infamous advance on 12 August. Continue along the track, which soon forks. To the left the track will take you up onto the southern side of the Kiretch Tepe ridge and the Gendarmarie memorial, but for now continue on to Azmak CWGC Cemetery.

The cemetery is situated to the east of the Azmak Dere and is approximately 500 metres behind the eventual British front line, on this northern part of Küçük Anafarta Ova. To the east is the Tekke Tepe ridge, with two dominant peaks, to the left is Kavak Tepe (Poplar Hill) at 274 m and to the right, above Küçükanafarta, is Tekke Tepe (Convent Hill) at 272 m. It was on Tekke Tepe that signallers from 6/East Yorks reached on 8 August and signalled that the hill was unoccupied. Delays in launching the main brigade attack that same day allowed the Turkish reserves to get there first, and in their hands it remained, helping to seal the fate of Stopford's beleaguered troops below.

AZMAK CWGC CEMETERY (17) was made after the Armistice by concentrating many isolated battlefield graves and sixteen smaller cemeteries from the area (Dublin Cemetery, Sulajik Cemetery, 5th Norfolk Cemetery, Borderers' Ravine Cemetery, Oxford Circus Cemetery, Worcester Cemetery, Kidney Hill Cemetery, Irish Cemetery, Azmak No 1, 2, 3 and 4 Cemeteries, Jephson's Post Cemetery, Essex Ravine Cemetery, Hill 28 Cemetery and Lone Tree Gully Cemetery). Today Azmak Cemetery contains 1,074 burials, 684 of which are unidentified. Among the unidentified are 114 officers and men of the 1/5 Norfolks who died on 12 August 1915.

Chaplain Leonard Egerton-Smith, who was attached to the Graves Registration Unit (GRU) in 1919, wrote of finding the missing Norfolks:

For a long time all search for these men was fruitless. And quite by accident their bodies were discovered. A private attached to the GRU was purchasing local supplies from a farm situated far over in what was the enemy terrain and found a Norfolk badge. Further search revealed the remainder. Only two were possible of identification, Corporal Carter and Private Barnaby. I rode out to see their bodies brought in.[3]

Private John Millar, Herefords, was kia 15 August, only 18 years old (Azmak Cemetery).

Private Walter Carter (I.C.7) and Corporal John Barnaby (I.C.6) are now buried side by side in Azmak Cemetery. The date died is stated as 28 August, which is incorrect as this is the date the service records state that they were posted *missing, presumed killed*; both men were actually killed on 12 August.

Also buried here are Lieutenant Colonel Edward Henry Chapman (Sp.Mem.5), commanding officer of 6/Yorks, killed during the storming of Lala Baba on 7 August, and Captain Arthur Preston (Sp.Mem.50), 6/RDF, who was killed in the bayonet charge at The Pimple on 15 August. Another grave is that of Captain John Gowan (I.H.1), 1/4 Essex, who was killed by a sniper on 16 August. Snipers, being a constant menace in Gallipoli generally, took a high toll of officers and men alike. Gowan was a treasurer and accountant to Ilford Urban District Council before the war, was a very keen pre-war Territorial officer and was the Battalion's musketry officer. Another Essex officer is Captain Harold Tyler (Sp.Mem.54), shot on the

Captain J. C. Gowan, 1/4 Essex, died 16 August.

lower southern slopes of the Kiretch Tepe ridge. His body lay in the open for nearly two days until an unarmed officer and six men with a stretcher volunteered to go out to retrieve it. Under observation by the Turks, they held their fire to allow Tyler to be recovered. He was buried originally in the Lone Tree Gully cemetery before being reinterred here after the war. Corporal Ewart Clifton (I.F.17), 6/Lincolns, one of the men who volunteered to help Captain Percy Hansen VC rescue the wounded in Scimitar Hill's burning scrub, is buried here. He was killed in October 1915.

Leave the cemetery on foot; the rough farm tracks used in this walk are not possible to drive in a car. This walk is approximately three kilometres and will take you over the ground where 1/5 Norfolks advanced on that fateful day of 12 August 1915. After following the track for approximately 300 metres you will cross a shallow, dry (depending on season) stream bed or ditch **(18)**. This area marks the approximate, southern most, position where the 1/5 Suffolks and 1/8 Hants advance finally came to a halt and began to establish a line by the sunken ditch, a distance of just over a kilometre from the jumping off point behind Hill 28. Elements of these battalions

Ruined farm buildings on the Kuchuk Anarfarta Ova.

did advance further north, but were beaten back by Turkish machine gun and rifle fire from the vicinity of Kidney Hill. This track, from here to the next stream bed, became the British front line later in the campaign. On 12 August, however, there were no trenches to talk of in this area; it was open farmland as you see it today; a No Man's Land denied to both sides. The 1/5 Norfolks, separated from the rest of 163 Brigade and veering off to the right, were able to continue their advance as Turkish resistance in their direction was initially not as severe. Continue on another 300 metres to the next dry stream bed **(19)**; it was close to here that the Norfolks began to suffer from casualties and, realising that the rest of the brigade was not on their left flank, two companies briefly waited for them to catch up. But this was to no avail as the rest of the brigade had already been fought to a standstill. Pressing on, the Norfolks continued their advance. After another 300 metres is another, much deeper, stream bed, in an area that is dotted all over with old stone buildings **(20)**. From roughly this position the Norfolks, a party now of fourteen officers and about 250 men, continued forward but, unsupported, they found themselves cut-off. If the fields are passable it is possible to follow the line of the advance, a further 600 metres, along the northern side of this stream bed. It was along this line that the survivors of the party, Lieutenant Colonel Sir Horace Proctor-Beauchamp being one of them, ran forward to find shelter within the farm buildings **(21)**, sometimes erroneously described in accounts as a small village, ahead. It was within these that, the survivors made their last stand; very few survived to tell the tale. Interestingly, most of these buildings are clearly marked on the 1915 British maps, so are believed to be period constructions from the time of the campaign. If the fields are not passable due to crops, either back track to the first stream crossing, where you will find a rough farm track, that will lead you another kilometre in a easterly direction, from there, turn south and walk for approximately 350 metres; this will take you directly behind the Norfolks area. Alternatively continue along the track you are now on, but note this will add approximately another four kilometres to the walk. Leaving the ruined buildings, continue across the fields, and follow the farm track in a northerly direction for about 350 metres, where it will then fork; turn left, or westwards and follow it for another kilometre; this will return you close to the first stream crossed at the beginning of the walk. Away from this track are further stream beds, one of which is quite deep **(22)**. This is believed to be the location that the Turks counter attacked from, and also possibly the area where Pierrepont Edwards stated the bodies of the 'missing' Norfolks were located after the war.

Return to Azmak Cemetery and car. Leave the cemetery and follow the track towards the Kireçtepe Jandarma memorial. This route will take you to the Turkish Gendarme Cemetery and Memorial, and the heights Kiretch Tepe ridge *(Kireçtepe)*: the Pimple, Jephson's Post and the Karakol Dagh, all synonymous with the 10th (Irish) Division. The five kilometre track, at the time of writing, is in poor condition, so drive along with caution. From the junction it is approximately a two and a half kilometres drive until you are due south of Jephson's Post (marked by a stone cairn) which was the final British front line, and after another kilometre you are then by Kidney Hill, with a further stone cairn on the crest above. The Turkish front line went over Kidney Hill to a position approximately midway between the cairns, and a rock formation named the Pimple.

Continue on the track until you reach the **Gendarmerie Memorial and Cemetery (23)**, which stands between Hill 156 and 161. The green memorial, made from Turkish shells, is believed to have been erected in late 1915 but has since been

Mustafa Kemal visiting the Gendarme Memorial in late 1915.
The memorial today.

Gendarme Monolith.

An original Ottoman grave in the Gendarme Cemetery.

rebuilt several times. It is not known how many burials the cemetery contains but we do know that many are of the local Gendarmerie battalions and men from the *5th Division*, serving in *127, 19, 17* and *39 Regiments* and *11* and *12 Artillery Regiments*. By the cemetery is a Turkish Monolith Memorial with the inscription:

Between 6 – 8 August 1915, three companies from the Gelibolu and Bursa Gendarmerie Battalions, after heroic fighting, stopped the English forces, equivalent of two brigades, at Karakol Dagi and Kireçtepe, and defended the northern flank of Anafartalar Group.

Return to the main road; or if you choose to walk the Kiretch Tepe ridge, stop and park on the track beneath Kidney Hill.

Walking the Kiretch Tepe ridge, which is marked on some campaign maps as Kazlar Dagh, can be very rewarding, although the dangers of it need to be noted. From a distance the whale-backed ridgeline with its gentle green slopes can be misleading. Firstly there are no real tracks, other than the odd goat trail, to follow, so the walking is over very rough ground, rocky in places and covered in loose shale. Other areas are interspersed by thick, almost impassable, thorny scrub, some twelve feet high, and deep ravines and gullies; all adding to the difficulties. Never walk here alone and come equipped with a stick, plenty of water and a mobile phone, also ensuring that you have informed your hotel where you are walking, just in case!

You can tackle the approach in several ways, either walk from the western Suvla Point end and from there ascend onto the ridgeline or alternatively approach the ridge from the Gendarmerie Memorial. There are very few tracks to follow and so it is literally a question of finding your own way through the rough. To walk the whole ridge in one go is quite a feat so some people chose to do parts of the ridge. Remember that if you leave your transport at one end of the ridge you will need to return to it, so account for this time in your walk. A third option is to walk the Hogsback (approximately a kilometre in length), which will be described here. To do this, park below Kidney Hill (under the eastern most cairn), and then walk to the top as if approaching the area from the Turkish reserve positions.

To the east of Kidney Hill is a very rough farm track and a field in the immediate area. Walk along this track in a north westerly direction, it will take you behind Kidney Hill and then around the field. There is a further track which you will then need to follow; this leads up onto the northern slopes of **KIDNEY HILL (24)**. The only part of this hill that was captured was its south western spur, when on 15 August 1915 a mixed group of men from the 1/5 Bedfords, 1/10 and 1/11 Londons briefly held this ground before they were forced to withdraw. The easternmost cairn should be clearly visible on the ridge line to the north. This is your aiming point. From here the walking is very rough, so take care. Turkish rock walled trenches can be found all over this slope, and in places can be followed towards the top.

After approximately thirty minutes you will soon come to the first of three stone cairns. This cairn marks the **KIRETCH TEPE SUMMIT (25)**, which was near Major Willmer's headquarters during the attack of 15/16 August. To the northerly, seaward side, now thick with holly oak scrub, were the extreme northern British defence lines, known as **GREEN KNOLL (26)** and **THE BOOT (27)** and to their east is the Turkish **NORTHERN REDOUBT (28)** also known as Hill 103. Today these are very difficult to reach, so an excursion is not recommended. Leave the cairn and walk carefully along the ridge towards the area of the Turkish front line, on some maps this is called the **BENCH MARK (29)**, approximately 500 metres away. This position marks the centre

Modern day view looking from the Turkish lines towards Jephson's Post.

of the Hogsback, sometimes referred to as the Razorback, because of its sharp, spine-like crest line. Before you get there one infamous position to find close to this area is the rocky outcrop known as the Pimple, and is positioned roughly between the Bench Mark and the easterly cairn. On the northern slopes of the Pimple are the remains of a shallow rocky Turkish trench, the very same one which was hotly contested over by bomb and bayonet when briefly captured by the Irish on 15/16 August 1915. Once itself marked by a cairn, this has long since collapsed and is difficult to find within the thick scrub that covers this area. To the north is the Gulf of Saros, from which the Royal Navy provided flanking fire to the troops in this sector, one destroyer gaining the nickname, the Munsters 'Guardian Angel'.

Continue on approximately 500 metres towards the third and most westerly cairn. About fifty metres east of this cairn you will pass **Jephson's Post (30)**. The post was captured by 6/RMF on 9 August in an attack led by Major John Jephson. Jephson was mortally wounded in the same area on 15 August, evacuated on a hospital ship and died two weeks later; he is now buried in

East Mudros Military Cemetery in Greece. Describing Jephson's Post, Major Thomas Gibbons, 1/5 Essex, wrote:

... the rock was nearly bare and all it had been possible to do was to scrape out the fissures into something like trenches and fill up the gaps with sandbags. All movement by day had to be made on hands and knees in most parts of the redoubt.

Today the ground is hardly changed, with original trenches with rock parapets and sangars still found in and around this area, a remarkable legacy of war almost a century ago.

From here you can either choose to return the way you have just come, or continue on to the Karakol Dagh, a distance of nearly two kilometres. After leaving the last cairn you will descend slightly as you walk down from the Hogsback, which is 200 metres in height. After just over a kilometre, you will arrive at the **KARAKOL GAP (31)**, which drops down to 150 metres in height. The British called the gap Oxford Circus, through which communications tracks and trenches led to and from the front line. Other trench and junction names in the area were based after famous London street names, which included Park Lane, Hyde Park Corner, Cannon Street, Oxford Street, Bond Street, Shaftesbury Avenue, Sloane Street, Haymarket, Hampstead Heath, Clapham Junction and Piccadilly Circus.

Continue from the gap for about 300 metres, this will take you onto the **KARAKOL DAGH (32)**, which stands at 165 metres. It was here that Major Willmer organised one of his defence areas, using the *Gelibolu Gendarmerie* under the command of Captain Kadri Bey. He posted a company of Gendarmerie there, their aim to delay any landing and subsequent advance. Supporting the detachment at the Karakol Dagh were a further two companies in the Pimple area. The Karakol was captured by 11/Manchesters during the early morning of 7 August, who made a magnificent advance to almost as far as Jephson's Post. Today you can still find the remains of the old August trench lines and dugouts in an area that was packed with stores dumps, artillery batteries and reserve positions.

From here, retrace your steps and return to your vehicle.

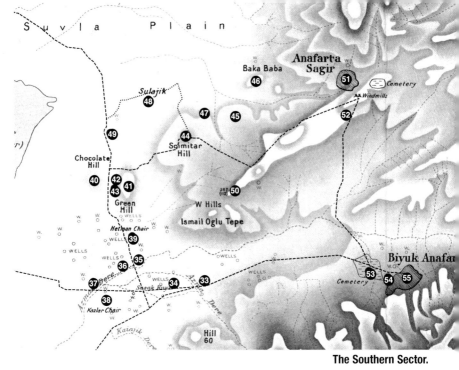

The Southern Sector.

3. The Southern Sector

This combined drive and walking tour will fill a whole day, allowing time to walk over the Azmak Dere and Hetman Chair regions of the battlefield. With stops at the 'Chocolate Hills' and then at Scimitar Hill with its Turkish Memorial, there will be time for those wishing to walk over the ground that featured in the

An old well near Lala Baba.

attacks on Scimitar Hill during 8, 9, 10 and 21 August 1915. The tour will end in the village of Büyükanafarta.

This tour will begin at **DERVISH ALI KUYU (33)**, which is located where the track joins the main Anzac – Büyükanafarta road, the failed second objective of 34 Brigade attack on 21 August. What you see today is similar to how it was in 1915; open ground, cultivated with many irrigation ditches, hedges and an abundance of wells (the Turkish word *kuyu* meaning well). The wells in this area became tactically important and the fighting intense in the battle to dominate these water rich fields. In and around this area were many important wells, including **Susak Kuyu (34)**, where in late August IX Corps at Suvla and the Anzac Corps were eventually joined. Continue along the Suvla road to the north, crossing the Azmak Dere, where there is a small building on the left-hand side of the road. Stop and park by the side of the road. This marks the approximate position of **AIRE KAVAK (35)**, where there was an important Turkish trench that went in a northerly direction to Hetman Chair, almost mirroring the route of the road today. In this area elements of 34 Brigade did manage to capture a small section of this trench on 21 August, but during the night it had to be relinquished. Azmak Dere itself is a stream that is dry in summer and autumn months, but wet in winter and spring. On the north western side of the road is a rough farm track that runs alongside the Azmak Dere. Follow this track, walking over No Man's Land as it was in 1915, for approximately 200 metres. It was in this part of the stream, which marks the British front line, that a mixed group of East Yorks, Lancashire Fusiliers, Manchesters and South Staffs erected a sandbag barricade in a failed effort to hold on to the gains captured on 21 August. Later in the campaign the British advanced their line slowly back to this position, naming this point **HIGHLAND BARRICADE (36)**. Continue along the track for

Azmak Dere, near
Highland Barricade,
as it is today.

approximately another 450 metres, where you will come to a stone ford across the stream. This location was known as **PERTH STATION (37)** on British trench maps of the area, and marks the British reserve line. Cross the stream and follow the track (the one that leads from Lala Baba to the main Suvla road) for approximately another 650 metres until you return to the main Suvla road. As you are walking along note the fields to the south; this agricultural area is known as **KAZLAR CHAIR (38)**, marking the boundary with Anzac. It was here that Major General Cox's 29th Indian Brigade, with its Ghurkas, held the line alongside IX Corps. Turn left at the junction with the main Suvla road and, in a northerly direction, walk back to your vehicle. Continue along the road, and after approximately 350 metres, is the site of **HETMAN CHAIR (39)**, the approach to the W Hills. Incidentally the word Chair comes from the Turkish Cayir, which means field or meadow. It was here that Hammersley's 11th Division's attack collapsed against such an effective Turkish defence, in the failed attempt to capture the W Hills (Ismail Oglu Tepe) on 21 August. Even though in summer months the area becomes hot and arid, drinkable water can be found one to five metres beneath the surface, as the many water pumps and wells bear witness today.

Continue along the road until you come onto the Chocolate Hills (Yilghin Burnu). The 53 metre hill to the left of the road is **CHOCOLATE HILL (40)**, named after the dry and burnt scrub that covered it in 1915; the 50 metre hill to the right of the road is called **GREEN HILL (41)**, because it remained mainly green. Today it is the site of the CWGC cemetery of that name. The naming of the Gallipoli features can be as confusing today as it was for the men in 1915. Not only did Chocolate Hill burn but also parts of Green Hill and Scimitar Hill, and at one stage all three were known as Burnt Hill. To add to the confusion both Green Hill and Scimitar Hill were also known as Green Knoll, not forgetting that Chocolate Hill and Green Hill were also known collectively as the Chocolate Hills or Yilghin Burnu.

Chocolate Hill was one of the three defensive strongpoint's that Major Wilhelm Willmer had established prior to the August landing, garrisoned by two companies of *1/31 Regiment*, supported by two mountain guns. The Chocolate Hills therefore became one of the primary objectives for the first day of the landing, but were not captured until sunset on 7 August. Both

Green Hill CWGC Cemetery.

Chocolate and Green Hill remained in British hands until the evacuation.

GREEN HILL CWGC CEMETERY (42) was made after the Armistice when several smaller war time cemeteries (named York, 40 Brigade, No.1 and 2, Green Hill No.1 and 2, Chocolate Hill, Inniskilling, Salt Lake and Scimitar Hill) and other isolated graves were concentrated into the picturesque cemetery we see today. There are now 2,971 servicemen buried or commemorated in this cemetery, but only 499 have named graves. Among those identified is Dublin born Brigadier General The 5th Earl of Longford, KP MVO, commander of 2 Mounted Brigade. A friend of Winston Churchill, he was killed, aged 50, during the attack on Scimitar Hill. Longford was born in October 1864 and educated at Winchester and Christ Church, Oxford. He succeeded his father as Earl in 1887. Commissioned initially into the Life Guards, he served in the Boer War where he was wounded and captured when a captain with the 45th Imperial Yeomanry. He was given command of 2 Mounted Brigade in 1912 and promoted to Brigadier General in August 1914. He is buried in Sp.Mem.E.3.

Also buried here is Lieutenant Colonel Henry Glanville Moore (II.B.13), commanding officer 6/East Yorks, and Major Francis Brunner (Sp.Mem.A.8), 67th Field Company, Royal Engineers. Both these officers were with an advanced group, totaling about seven officers and 140 men, who were overwhelmed by the sudden Turkish counter attack on 9 August. An account of this action was written by the battalion adjutant, Lieutenant John Still, who was captured along with Moore and Brunner. He survived and later wrote, *A Prisoner in Turkey* (1920), in which he described his experiences of captivity. The book also contains an account of how Moore met his end:

We reached the point where the ravine ended, and in the scrub ahead of us we saw a number of men who fired upon us. For a moment we thought they were our own, firing in ignorance. Then we saw that they were Turks. We had run into the back of an enemy battalion which held the lower slopes against our supports. They had crossed the range at a point lower than that we had attacked, and had cut in behind our climbing force. We could do nothing but surrender. When we held up our hands some dozen or more of the enemy charged towards us with fixed bayonets. And we began to experience that strange mixture of nature, so characteristic of the Turks, from which we and our fellows were to suffer much in the years to come. The man who took possession of me searched my pockets and annexed everything of military use except my revolver, which had fallen out of my hand a minute before, when I had been knocked down by a bullet that glanced off a rock on to my leg. He took out my purse and saw that it contained five sovereigns in gold (more than I have ever seen since) and a good deal in silver. Then he gave it back to me, and apparently told me to keep it. The pay of a Turkish private is, or was, ten piastres a month, nominally about one shilling and eight pence. My captor was a good Turk. Later on, when I came to know how rare good Turks were, I was filled with marvel. Of those taken with me, one was not molested; one was fired at from five yards' distance, missed, and quietly captured; one was beaten and fired at. Thank God the man who fired at him hit the man who was beating him and broke his wrist. The fourth, my Colonel, was bayoneted. Then, for the moment their fury ceased. I was permitted to tend the Colonel. He did not seem to suffer pain at all, only to be intensely thirsty. He drank the whole of the contents of my water-bottle as well as his own. They even allowed me to carry him on my back; and on my back the Colonel died. May he rest in peace! He was a brave man, a good friend to me.

232

Also buried here is a poet, Nowell Oxland (I.C.7), then a lieutenant in the 6/Borders, who was killed on 9 August. Oxland, an Old Dunelmian, was close friends with William Noel Hodgson, who was killed on the Somme. Oxland, son of a clergyman, entered Durham School as a King's Scholar in September 1903, where he excelled in sports, particularly rowing. In 1909 he left to attend Worcester College, Oxford where he was reading history when the war broke out. While at Oxford he played rugby for Rosslyn Park, Richmond, Middlesex and

Lieutenant Nowell Oxland.

Cumberland. Gazetted into the 6/Borders in 1914, he went to the Dardanelles in June 1915, and was killed only two days after he landed. He showed promise of becoming a poet and prose writer of distinction. Some verses of his, entitled *Outward Bound*, appeared in *The Times* in

August 1915 and much of his work was collected and published as *Poems and Stories* in 1917.

Another notable burial is Lieutenant William Niven (Sp.Mem.F.10), 1/1 Berks Yeomanry, father of British actor David Niven. Niven was killed during the 21 August attack on Scimitar Hill. Niven's body was never found at the time and like many telegrams with the word 'Missing' must have left some optimistic hope that he may have been a prisoner of war. This faded when an eye-witness, Private William Deacon, reported that he and Lieutenant Niven had actually reached the Turkish trenches in the dark and it was then that Niven was killed. It was some seventeen months later that his wife received official confirmation of his death. In February 1919 she managed to track down another Berkshire yeoman, Private Archibald Calder, who had been captured by the Turks during the same attack. Calder had also witnessed Niven's death and confirmed that he had been shot in the head and killed instantly.

In his autobiography *The Moon's a Balloon* (1971), David Niven wrote of his memories of hearing about his father's death:

Lieutenant William Niven with his son David.

David Niven, film star. 1910 – 1983.

My sister and I were swapping cigarette cards on an old tree trunk in the paddock when a red-eyed maid came and told us our mother wanted to see us and that we were not to stay too long... after a rather incoherent interview with my mother, who displayed a telegram and tried to explain what 'missing' meant, we returned to the swapping of cigarette cards and resumed our perusal of endless trains lumbering along a distant embarkment loaded with guns and cheering young men.

Another grave is that of Major John Blackburne (I.C.2), Second in Command, 9/Sherwood Foresters. Educated at Charterhouse and then RMC Sandhurst, he was gazetted in 1892 into 1/Sherwood Foresters. He went on to serve during the Boer War with 45th Company Imperial Yeomanry. At the outbreak of war he was second in command of 9/Sherwood Foresters, being killed on 21 August 1915, aged 42. Mentioned in Despatches for gallant and distinguished service in the field, Brigadier General Robert Maxwell wrote:

I saw a great deal of your husband as I had to be constantly up and down the trenches, and it was during this time I fully grasped his value as a soldier. He had no Adjutant or Quartermaster, and only two youngsters with him, and had to do the work of ten, and was always so full of good spirits and encouragement to his men and an example to all, and, above all, never complaining. God knows how I felt for them all; no words of mine can express the courage and determination of all ranks, and the debt I owe them is inestimable. We left those lines in the night of the 20th, and went down to the beach and got ready for the big battle next day. We were in Divisional Reserve, with orders to push through at all costs, the attack to start at 3 p.m.

The Brigade consisted then of about 1,600 men, and I had to divide the officers who were left so that each battalion had only four or five officers. The Sherwoods were the

234

Looking down on Green Hill.

leading battalion. The last I saw of your husband was on the top of Lala Baba, as I gave him and his Commanding Officer final directions, and pointed out the line of attack and wished them good luck. Your husband was in front with the leading company, and I watched them all down the hill and into the plain, and followed myself with Colonel Bosanquet and the rear company. On the low ground I lost sight of the leading lines, and after about a mile I had to stop and send a report, and give instructions to the other battalion who were coming up to the rear. I never saw either of them again.

Major General Frederick Hammersley also wrote:

Major Blackburne was perfectly splendid in every way, and everyone was simply devoted to him. While Major Blackburne was in command for some time when the Colonel was wounded, he did splendidly. I couldn't say enough to his praise. He was a terrible loss to the regiment and the country, as he was such a fine soldier and so splendid in every way, and all ranks regretted his loss, and a brother officer: It seems that on the 21st August, about 3 p.m., a party of men were held up by the enemy's fire south of Chocolate Hill. Major Blackburne went to rally these and get them forward. He then shouted, 'Are there any Sherwoods here?' and fifteen men got up; these he led

235

forward and he was shot while jumping a bush. His body was afterwards recovered and buried by another unit. His loss was felt by all the battalion, and we were left without a leader who had worked wonders in organizing those men left after the advance of Aug. 9th.

Blackburne was a well-known cricketer, and played for the Charterhouse XI, the Army whilst in Ireland and also for Devonshire. He is also commemorated on the Lord's Members Cricket Great War Memorial. Tragically, his brother, Lieutenant Colonel Harold Blackburne DSO, 5/Dragoon Guards, along with his son, daughter and their children's governess, were lost when RMS *Leinster* was torpedoed in the Irish Sea on 10 October 1918. Only Harold's wife survived.

There were three soldiers 'shot at dawn' during the Gallipoli campaign, one of whom is buried here: Private Harry Salter (I.G.26), 6/East Lancs, from Bridgwater in Somerset. He was shot for desertion on 11 December; seven days before his battalion were evacuated from Gallipoli for good. Private Edward Roe, who was in the same battalion as Salter, wrote:

11 December: Execution of Private Salter at 7.15 am. This youth, barely nineteen years of age, was shot by twelve of his comrades for taking 'French leave' from his Regiment on two occasions and attaching himself to the Anzacs. Not by any stretch of imagination could my comrades and I catalogue it as desertion, as 'twas impossible to desert from the Peninsula even had he so desired. Our position in comparison to the position that the Anzacs held was a heaven compared to Hell. He therefore did not seek safety; he absconded because his life was made hell by the CSM (Company Sergeant Major) of my company (D). In barrack room parlance he was 'sat upon'. I was one of the firing party; he was marched from a dugout about eighty yards away, to a kind of disused quarry where the final scene was enacted. A clergyman preceded the doomed youth and his escort, reading prayers for the dying (the mockery of it all). The doomed youth was tied up to a stake, his grave already dug. His last request was, 'Don't blindfold me'. What followed I'll leave to the reader's imagination, in other words, I'll pull the pall of oblivion over the ghastly scene – 'If I can ever forget it'. I only wish that the distinguished person who signed the death warrant, without taking into consideration extenuating circumstances, would leave his comfortable island residence and visit the men under his command who were 'going through it'. Well, we'd have a bit more faith in our leaders and confidence in ourselves.[4]

In August 2006 Salter was one of 306 executed men in the Great War who were posthumously pardoned. The location of the quarry is believed to be on the south western side of Green Hill, not far from the side of the road.

At the time of writing there are plans to erect a **GREEN HILL IRISH MEMORIAL (43)** by the cemetery. A temporary memorial was actually unveiled in March 2010 by Mary McAleese, President of Ireland, but information at this time as to its permanent position is not known. The memorial is to all the Irish who died at Gallipoli, in particular the 10th (Irish) Division. This will have a plaque that shows the regimental badges of the Royal Irish Regiment, Royal

Mary McAleese unveiling the Green Hill Irish Memorial.

Inniskilling Fusiliers, Royal Irish Rifles, Royal Irish Fusiliers, Connaught Ranges, the Leinster Regiment, Royal Munster Fusiliers and the Royal Dublin Fusiliers.

From Green Hill Cemetery, take the road that goes in an easterly direction towards Küçükanafarta. After approximately one kilometre you will come to **SCIMITAR HILL (44)** (Hill 70, Lincoln Hill or Burnt Hill), which is positioned towards the lower tip of the Anafarta Spur. The hill was so called due to its long curved shape that resembled a Turkish sword. The Turks referred to it as Kusufçuktepe, meaning Dragonfly Hill. This key

Scimitar Hill Turkish Memorial.

position was captured three times by the British on 8, 9 and 21 August, but it was also retaken three times by the Turks. Capturing this hill was difficult; retaining it proved impossible. It was here that one of the biggest and fiercest battles that ever took place at Gallipoli was fought and lost. The two Victoria Crosses awarded during the Suvla campaign, to Captain Percy Hansen on 9 August and then Private Frederick Potts on 21 August, were both for life saving on Scimitar Hill. Today three Turkish stone monoliths now stand on its crest, with translated inscriptions:

Panel 1 – *In order to envelop the Turkish forces at the Ariburnu front* [Anzac], *the enemy had landed on 7 August 1915 at Anafarta Harbour* [Suvla Bay], *and advanced as far as Ismailoglu* [W Hills] *and Kusufçuktepe* [Scimitar Hill] *against the weak Turkish observation units.*

Panel 2 – *At the end of the first battle of Anafarta, 9th – 12th August 1915, Turkish forces under the command of Colonel Mustafa Kemal, commander of the Anafarta group, defeated the enemy forces and drove them back to the line of Kireçtepe and Mestantepe* [Chocolate Hills].

238

Panel 3 – At the end of the second battle of Anafarta, 21/22 August 1915, which was fought by larger forces from both sides, the assaulting enemy forces were defeated along the Sivritepe [Jephson's Post] and Mestantepe lines. The losses of this battle were 8,155 Turkish and 19,850 enemy casualties.

About 75 metres east of the hill is a narrow farm track. Follow this track on foot around Scimitar Hill, and down its northern slopes for about 450 metres, where it will bend at a right angle to the right. To the east (right) are the hills of **ABRIKJA (45)** and **BAKA BABA (46)**, both in Turkish hands during the campaign. The closest the British got was when the 6/East Yorks and 9/West Yorks were in the area early on 8 August, but then were withdrawn later in the day for the attack on Tekke Tepe. Scouts actually got onto Baka Baba, where they found a recently evacuated trench and could observe the Turks pulling back to the village. Closer to the track, also on the right is a small hill that was known to the British as 105 D8, and, to the Turks as **TOMBA TEPE (47)**. It was from here that the Turks, with a machine gun, enfiladed the British attacks on Scimitar Hill. The hill, and much of the surrounding area, is still honeycombed with trenches and dugouts, many recently re-exposed after a scrub fire in 2008. Continue on 200 metres where the track joins another path. To the north is the area known as **SULAJIK (48)**,

Tomba Tepe after the fire in 2008.

today, as it was in 1915, consisting of a few old farm buildings. Please note that this area is still private property, so remain on the track. Turn left and follow the path for about a kilometre until it returns to the main Suvla road. Follow the road up the slope towards Chocolate and Green Hill. You will pass a small farmstead on the eastern side of the road, which marks the approximate position of **ALI BEY CHESHME (49)**, an important watering point within the British lines. Continue up the hill and then walk along the road back to Scimitar Hill.

Leave Scimitar Hill and drive over its crest towards Küçükanafarta (Little Anafarta or Anafarta Sagir), about two kilometres distant. The road will follow the crest of the spur; to the southern end is **HILL 112 (50)**, the summit of the W Hills. This was the failed objective of both 29th Division and the Mounted Division attack on 21 August. **KÜÇÜKANAFARTA (51)** has a history that goes back to the 1356. The village was destroyed during the war and later rebuilt; today the means of living are livestock and agriculture (wheat, sunflower and tomatoes). From the British positions in 1915 they could easily make out the village but not quite as one can see it today, its landmarks then were its slender white minaret and a cluster of four windmills. All the latter were destroyed during the war and only the minaret was rebuilt. At the T-Junction turn right towards Büyükanafarta (Big Anafarta). About 200 metres along this road you will come to the position of an original **TURKISH GUN BATTERY (52)**. Two 210mm German manufactured Krupp guns, dated 1875 and 1876, remain that were used during the campaign to fire on the British at Suvla and Anzac. One gun is almost intact and sits on its original carriage within the gun pit; the other is in worse condition, possibly the result of a direct hit from British counter fire.

Continue along the road for another three kilometres until you near the village of Büyükanafarta. Just before the village, on either side of the road, is an old **OTTOMAN CEMETERY (53)**, containing many graves from the period. Two recently restored graves are those of two *7th Division* officers who were killed in the August battles; Lieutenant Colonel (Yarbay) Halit Bey, *20 Regiment*, who was killed at Hill 60 and Yarbay Ziya Bey, *21 Regiment*, who was killed near Asmali Dere. This area became key as it marked that spot where the Suvla and Anzac forces were joined. Two further graves identified as relating to the local operations are those of Lieutenant Hasan Tahsin, *7th Division*

Anafarta Turkish Gun Battery.

Artillery Regiment, and the regimental *mufti*, who were both killed on 21 August. The *mufti* did similar work to the British chaplains, serving with the troops in the trenches, morally encouraged the soldiers in action, said prayers for the dying and wounded and whenever possible wrote home to the next of kin of the slain or wounded.

Continue on a few yards to the **BÜYÜKANAFARTA TURKISH CEMETERY AND MEMORIAL (54)**, which was constructed in 2005 and lists the names of 749 Turkish soldiers commemorated in the cemetery, either buried here or in other smaller battlefield cemeteries in the area. The fallen were from the *3rd Division (31 and 32*

Büyükanafarta Turkish Cemetery and Memorial.

Büyükanafarta 1915.

Büyükanafarta 2010.

Regiments), 7th Division (19, 20 and 21 Regiments) and also units of 33, 45 and 17 Regiments and the Bursa Gendarmerie.

Leave the cemetery and enter the village of **BÜYÜKANAFARTA (55)**. The village, like its smaller sister, was evacuated by civilians after the landings. Heavily shelled and bombed during the war, it had to be rebuilt after hostilities. Mustafa Kemal stayed here on the occasions he visited the front. Today it has a population of around 400 people, whose main living is from livestock and agriculture. There is a small café in the square where a good Turkish coffee or tea can be had, behind which is a small shop that sells cold drinks and ice creams. Public toilets are also nearby, the only toilets within reach of Suvla, so take note! Whilst in the village it is recommended that you visit the small, but very good Gallipoli Campaign Museum, situated between the café and cemetery. This museum contains many exhibits found locally on the Suvla battlefield, making a nice end to the tour.

1 Greece also offered the islands of Límnos (Lemnos) and Bozcaada (Tenedos).
2 Hargrave, J, At Suvla Bay: Notes and Sketches. (London: Constable, 1916).
3 National Archives WO32/5640.
4 Roe, E., Diary of an Old Contemptible, (Barnsley: Pen & Sword, 2004).

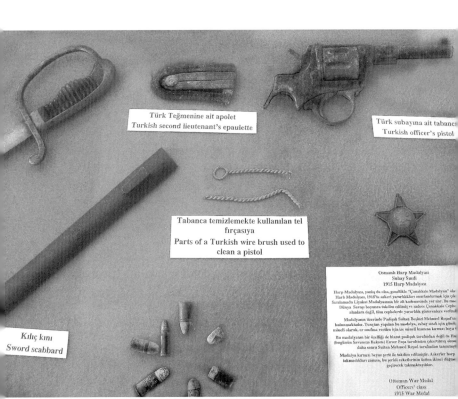

Türk Teğmenine ait apolet
Turkish second lieutenant's epaulette

Türk subayına ait tabanca
Turkish officer's pistol

Tabanca temizlemekte kullanılan tel
fırçasıya
Parts of a Turkish wire brush used to
clean a pistol

Kılıç kını
Sword scabbard

Osmanlı Harp Madalyası
Subay Sınıfı
1915 Harp Madalyası

Harp Madalyası, yanlış da olsa, genellikle "Çanakkale Madalyası" ola...
Harb Madalyası, 1915'te askeri yararlılıkları onurlandırmak için çık...
Sıralamada Liyakat Madalyasının bir alt kademesinde yer alır; bu ma...
Dünya Savaşı boyunca tokdisi edilmiş ve sadece Çanakkale Cephe...
alınlara değil, tüm cephelerde yararlılık gösterenlere verilmiş...

Madalyanın üzerinde Padişah Sultan Beşinci Mehmed Reşad'ın...
bulunmaktadır. Tunçtan yapılan bu madalya, subay sınıfı için gümü...
mineli olarak, er sınıfına verilen için ise mineli kısmına kırmızı boya e...

Bu madalyanın bir özelliği de bizzat padişah tarafından değil de Ha...
(bugünün Savunma Bakanı) Enver Paşa tarafından çıkartılmış olma...
daha sonra Sultan Mehmed Reşad tarafından tanınmış...

Madalya kırmızı beyaz şerit ile takdim edilmiştir. Askerler harp...
takındıkları zaman, bu şeridi ceketlerinin üstten ikinci düğme...
geçirerek takmaktaydılar.

Ottoman War Medal
Officers' class
1915 War Medal

Found on the battlefield - Museum Exhibits.

SUVLA ORDER OF BATTLE – AUGUST 1915

IX CORPS
Lieutenant General Hon. Sir F. W. Stopford

10TH (IRISH) DIVISION
Major General Sir B. T. Mahon

29 Brigade (Attached Anzac Corps)

30 Brigade: Brigadier General L. L. Nicol
6/Royal Munster Fusiliers
7/Royal Munster Fusiliers
6/Royal Dublin Fusiliers
7/Royal Dublin Fusiliers

31 Brigade: Brigadier General F. F. Hill
5/Royal Inniskilling Fusiliers
6/Royal Inniskilling Fusiliers
5/Royal Irish Fusiliers
6/Royal Irish Fusiliers
    Pioneers: 5/Royal Irish Regiment

11TH (NORTHERN) DIVISION
Major General F. Hammersley

32 Brigade: Brigadier General H. Haggard
9/West Yorkshire Regiment
6/Yorkshire Regiment
8/West Riding Regiment
6/Yorks & Lancs Regiment

33 Brigade: Brigadier General R. P. Maxwell
6/Lincolnshire Regiment
6/The Border Regiment
7/South Staffordshire Regiment
9/Notts & Derby (Sherwood Foresters) Regiment

34 Brigade: Brigadier General W. H. Sitwell
8/Northumberland Fusiliers
9/Lancashire Fusiliers
5/Dorsetshire Regiment
11/Manchester Regiment
    Pioneers: 6/East Yorkshire Regiment

53RD (WELSH) DIVISION TF
Major General Hon. J. E. Lindley

158 (North Wales) Brigade: Brigadier General F. C. Lloyd
- 1/5 Royal Welsh Fusiliers (Flintshire)
- 1/6 Royal Welsh Fusiliers (Carnarvonshire & Anglesey)
- 1/7 Royal Welsh Fusiliers (Merioneth & Montgomery)
- 1/1 Herefordshire Regiment

159 (Cheshire) Brigade: Brigadier General E. A. Cowan
- 1/4 Cheshire Regiment
- 1/7 Cheshire Regiment
- 1/4 Welsh Regiment
- 1/5 Welsh Regiment

160 (Welsh Border) Brigade: Brigadier General J. J. F. Hume
- 2/4 Queen's (Royal West Surrey) Regiment
- 1/4 Royal Sussex Regiment
- 2/4 The Queen's Own (Royal West Kent Regiment)
- 2/10 The Duke of Cambridge's Own (Middlesex Regiment)

54TH (EAST ANGLIAN) DIVISION TF
Major General F. S. Inglefield

161 (Essex) Brigade: Brigadier General F. F. W. Daniell
- 1/4 Essex Regiment
- 1/5 Essex Regiment
- 1/6 Essex Regiment
- 1/7 Essex Regiment

162 (East Midland) Brigade: Brigadier General C de Winton
- 1/5 Bedfordshire Regiment
- 1/4 Northamptonshire Regiment
- 1/10 (County Of London) Battalion (Hackney)
- 1/11 (County Of London) Battalion (Finsbury Rifles)

163 (Norfolk & Suffolk) Brigade: Brigadier General C. M. Brunker
- 1/4 Norfolk Regiment
- 1/5 Norfolk Regiment
- 1/5 Suffolk Regiment
- 1/8 Hampshire (Isle of Wight Rifles) Regiment

2ND MOUNTED DIVISION
Major General W. E. Peyton

1 (1st South Midland) Brigade: Brigadier E. A. Wiggin
    1/1 Warwickshire Yeomanry
    1/1 Worcestershire Yeomanry (Queen's Own Worcestershire Hussars)
    1/1 Gloucestershire Yeomanry (Royal Gloucestershire Hussars)

2 (2nd South Midland) Brigade: Brigadier General the Earl of Longford
    1/1 Buckinghamshire Yeomanry (Royal Bucks Hussars)
    1/1 Berkshire Yeomanry (Hungerford)
    1/1 Dorset Yeomanry (Queen's Own)

3 (Notts & Derby) Brigade: Brigadier General P. A. Kenna VC
    1/1 Nottingham Yeomanry (Sherwood Rangers)
    1/1 Derbyshire Yeomanry
    1/1 Nottingham Yeomanry (South Nottingham Hussars)

4 (London) Brigade: Brigadier General A. H. M. Taylor
    1/1 County of London Yeomanry (Middlesex, Duke of Cambridge's Hussars)
    1/3 County of London Yeomanry (Sharpshooters)
    1/1 City of London Yeomanry (Rough Riders)

5 Brigade: Brigadier General J. D. T. Tyndale-Biscoe
    1/1 Hertfordshire Yeomanry
    1/2 County of London Yeomanry (Westminster Dragoons)

29TH DIVISION (*attached from* VIII CORPS)
Major General W. R. Marshall

86 Brigade: Brigadier General C. J. Perceval
    2/Royal Fusiliers
    1/Lancashire Fusiliers
    1/Royal Munster Fusiliers
    1/Royal Dublin Fusiliers

87 Brigade: Lieutenant Colonel C. H. T. Lucas
    2/South Wales Borderers
    1/Kings Own Scottish Borderers
    1/Royal Inniskilling Fusiliers
    1/Border Regiment

88 Brigade: Brigadier General D. E. Cayley
    4/Worcestershire Regiment
    2/Hampshire Regiment
    1/Essex Regiment
    5/Royal Scots

OTTOMAN FIFTH ARMY

General Otto Liman Von Sanders

First Battle of Anafartalar – 9 August 1915
Anafarta Group: Colonel Mustafa Kemal

Willmer Group: Major W. Willmer
    2/31 Regiment: Captain M. Sevki
    1/32 Regiment: Major Kazim
    Gelibolu Gendarmarie: Captain Kadri
    Bursa Gendarmarie: Major Tahsin
    4 Cavalry Regiment: Lieutenant Colonel Hamdi

12th Turkish Division: Colonel Selahattin Adil
    34 Regiment: Lieutenant Colonel Mehmet Ali
    35 Regiment: Lieutenant Colonel Ali Abbas
    36 Regiment: Lieutenant Colonel Münip

Second Battle of Anafartalar – 21 August 1915
Anafarta Group: Colonel Mustafa Kemal

5th Turkish Division: Colonel W. Willmer
    1 Regiment: Lieutenant Colonel Talat
    19 Regiment: Lieutenant Colonel Irfan
    127 Regiment: Lieutenant Colonel Hasan Lüftü
    1/17 Regiment: Lieutenant Colonel Hakki
    1/39 Regiments: Lieutenant Colonel H. Nurettin

9th Turkish Division: Lieutenant Colonel Sabri
    25 Regiment: Major Mehmet Ali
    64 Regiment: Lieutenant Colonel Servet
    126 Regiment: Lieutenant Colonel Mustafa Sevki

BIBLIOGRAPHY

AND RECOMMENDED FURTHER READING

Bartlett, Ashmead, *Despatches from the Dardanelles*, (London: George Newnes, 1915).

Chambers S. J., *Anzac The Landing,* (Barnsley: Pen & Sword, 2008).

Denham, H. M., *Dardanelles: A Midshipman's Diary*, (London: Murray, 1981).

Erickson, E. J., Gallipoli: *The Ottoman Campaign*, (Barnsley: Pen & Sword, 2010).

Gallishaw, J., *Trenching At Gallipoli*, (New York: The Century Co., 1916).

Gillam, J. G., *Gallipoli Diary*, (London: Allen & Inwin, 1918).

Göncü, G., Aldogan, S., *Gallipoli Battlefield Guide*, (Istanbul: MB Books, 2008).

Hanna, H., *The Pals At Suvla Bay.*, (Dublin: Ponsonby Ltd, 1917).

Hargrave, J, *The Suvla Bay Landing*, (London: Macdonald 1964).

Hamilton, Sir. I., *Gallipoli Diary*, (London: Edward Arnold, 1920).

Hamilton, Sir. I., *Ian Hamilton's Final Despatches*, (London: George Newnes, 1916).

Hatton, S. F., *Yarn of a Yeoman*, (London: Hutchinson, 1930).

Herbert, A., *Mons, Anzac and Kut*, (London: Hutchinson, 1919).

Holts, T & V., *Major & Mrs Holt's Battlefield Guide: Gallipoli*, (Barnsley: P&S, 2000).

James, R., Rhodes, *Gallipoli*, (London: Pan Books Ltd, 1984).

The Earl of Granard, 5 Royal Irish Regiment in his Lala Baba dugout.

Jones, Rev D., *The Diary Of A Padre At Suvla Bay*, (London: The Faith Press, 1917).

Mackenzie, *Gallipoli Memories*, (London: Cassell and Company Ltd, 1929).

McCrery, N., *All The King's Men*, (London: Simon & Schuster 1992).

Mortlock, M. J., *The Landings at Suvla Bay*, (North Carolina: McFarland & Co, 2006).

North, J., *Gallipoli: The Fading Vision*, (London: 1936).

Oglander, Aspinall-, *Military Operations Gallipoli*, (London: Heinemann , 1929-32).

Orr, P., *Field of Bones: An Irish Division on Gallipoli*, (Dublin: Lilliput, 2006).

Pemberton, T. J., *Gallipoli To-Day*, (London: 1926).

Priestman, E. Y., *With A B-P Scout In Gallipoli*, (New York: Routledge & Sons, 1917).

Prior, R., *Gallipoli: The End of The Myth*, (London: Yales, 2009).

Rayner, R., *The Sandringhams at Suvla Bay* (WFA, Reading 2000)

Roe, E., *Diary of an Old Contemptible*, (Barnsley: Pen & Sword, 2004).

Snelling, S., *VCs of the First World War – Gallipoli*, (Stroud: Sutton Publishing, 1995).

Steel, N and Hart P., *Defeat at Gallipoli*, (London: Macmillan, 1994).

Still, J., *A Prisoner in Turkey*, (London: John Lane, 1920).

Taylor, P., Cupper P., *Gallipoli: A Battlefield Guide*, (Kangaroo Press, 1989).

Teichman, O., *The Diary Of A Yeomanry M.O.*, (London: Fisher Unwin, 1921).

Travers, T., *Gallipoli 1915*, (Stroud: Tempus, 2001).

Walker, R., *To What End Did They Die: Officers Died at Gallipoli*, (Worcester, 1985).

Wedgwood-Benn, W., *In the Side Shows*, (London: Hodder & Stoughton, 1919).

Wilkinson, N., *The Dardanelles*, (London: Longmans, Green & Co. 1916).

Index